Palgrave Studies in the History of Finance

Series Editors
D'Maris Coffman
Bartlett Faculty of Built Environment
University College London
London, UK

Tony K. Moore
ICMA Centre, Henley Business School
University of Reading
Reading, UK

Martin Allen
Department of Coins and Medals, Fitzwilliam Museum
University of Cambridge
Cambridge, UK

Sophus Reinert
Harvard Business School
Cambridge, MA, USA

The study of the history of financial institutions, markets, instruments and concepts is vital if we are to understand the role played by finance today. At the same time, the methodologies developed by finance academics can provide a new perspective for historical studies. Palgrave Studies in the History of Finance is a multi-disciplinary effort to emphasise the role played by finance in the past, and what lessons historical experiences have for us. It presents original research, in both authored monographs and edited collections, from historians, finance academics and economists, as well as financial practitioners.

More information about this series at
http://www.palgrave.com/gp/series/14583

Carol Beardmore

Financing the Landed Estate

Power, Politics and People on the Marquis of Anglesey's Estate, 1812–1854

palgrave
macmillan

Carol Beardmore
University of Leicester
Leicester, UK

Palgrave Studies in the History of Finance
ISBN 978-3-030-14551-4 ISBN 978-3-030-14552-1 (eBook)
https://doi.org/10.1007/978-3-030-14552-1

Cover illustration: Archivart / Alamy Stock Photo

This Palgrave Macmillan imprint is published by the registered company Springer Nature Switzerland AG
The registered company address is: Gewerbestrasse 11, 6330 Cham, Switzerland

To Geoff with much love and thanks

Acknowledgements

This volume comes out of the research for my Ph.D., and its completion owes a great deal to many people. Firstly, to Professor D'Maris Coffman who believed that my thesis was worthy of converting into this volume and reminded me of this fact more than once. To the Dorset History Centre who over many years have patiently helped me to navigate through the Anglesey Archive and answered all of my questions with interest and complete professionalism. To Liz Mills at the Pilkington Library, University of Loughborough your forebearance over books has been much appreciated. I owe a significant debt to Irene Jones without whom this study would never have taken place. While holidaying on Anglesey in 1990, she found the archivist of Bangor University sitting on six sacks of paper relating to the Marquis of Anglesey's Dorset and Somerset estate and set about having them transferred to the Dorset History Centre. She stated, 'The biggest thrill was handling scraps of paper: bills handwritten by Stalbridge glaziers, thatchers, masons, quarrymen, carpenters and builders for work done nearly two hundred years ago'. A sentiment many other historians and I understand and one with which I wholeheartedly concur. Much thanks must go to Dr. Elizabeth Hurren, for her amazing teaching, support and advice across many years. Her ability to nurture students gave me confidence in myself at a time when I badly needed it. I still have the early essay on which she wrote, 'perhaps we have the making of a historian here'. Indeed, Elizabeth, perhaps we do. A huge debt of gratitude must go to Professor Steven King who has read and commented on many drafts of this volume, he probably knows William Castleman as well if not better than I do. While he has sought to guide and advise over structure and content, his extraordinary skills as a writer and academic mean he has never overwritten or removed my voice from this book. It is a much better volume for his input. I must add though that all the remaining mistakes are mine alone. For Sue my sister who will never read this book but will enjoy showing off the copy sitting on her shelf, long live the difference. To Rhona Workman and Liddy Parker, your friendship and evenings spent over a gin and tonic have helped to keep me sane during this process. Your friendship and patience over many cancelled meetings are much appreciated. Liddy, I am still waiting for the jam. The greatest thanks must go to my friend Dr. Geoff Monks, who started me off on my journey as a mature student. His unerring support, kindness, patience and friendship are unparalleled, and my world is a much better place for it. There are many others who have provided tea and biscuits and who are too many to mention but to whom much thanks are also due.

Carol Beardmore

Contents

List of Tables

CHAPTER 1

Introduction

Overview

The history of the landed estate remains under-researched and much neglected until a recent renewal of interest in the role of the land agent.[1] While various studies have explored themes such as agricultural rent, the Agricultural Revolution, the impact of absentee landownership, improvements, repairs, under-draining and landowner and tenant relationships, they have rarely been explored within the context of a single volume. Each individual estate was a complicated and complex melding of social, economic and political relationships which were underpinned by a financial thread. At the core of the landed estate was the need for sustainability, and this was particularly difficult in the fragile economic climate of the post-Napoleonic period. Some, for example, the Portlands in Nottinghamshire and the Leveson-Gowers in the West Midlands, turned to mining and other industrial investments to promote profitability. Other rural estates with no means of boosting income in this manner were left to juggle their financial commitments alongside high rental arrears and considerable reductions in rent to promote tenant retention and viability. Yet, few historians have considered how the daily management of a large agriculture estate was underpinned by a range of fiscal decisions beyond the bonds paid by land agents and other officials. This might consist of but was not limited to supporting those tenants who could be relied on for voting loyalty, the retention of good tenants through the accrual of eye-wateringly

C. Beardmore, *Financing the Landed Estate*, Palgrave Studies in the History of Finance, https://doi.org/10.1007/978-3-030-14552-1_1

high rental arrears, partnerships in draining and improvement or even monies spent on schools and charities to exert a modicum of control over the labouring poor. Understanding the finances of an estate opens a new window onto rural society and the way in which it functioned. This we can only really do through the multiplication of detailed studies and their associated agents. Through a single meticulous estate study, it is possible to explore how landowners and tenants worked together to ensure both personal and economic stability, and this can then be used to create a different view of working communities that rarely appears in the historiography.

The Marquis of Anglesey inherited his Dorset and Somerset estate in 1812, which included land and property in a number of villages spread across the Blackmore Vale. Why Anglesey inherited this part of his estates remains a mystery, and a summary of the way the family came to own these properties will be explored below in greater detail. Mr. Cox and Admiral Aylmer were at the time of his inheritance employed in managing the estate, but by 1814 William Castleman had taken over as land agent and was in full control. It is the correspondence between these Anglesey and Castleman, combined with the estate voucher and rental/disbursement accounts which form the basis of this research. Anglesey was an absentee landowner who like many others in the same position continued to take an active interest in the day-to-day organisation, supervision and financial administration of his asset. In Castleman (and then his sons) he found capable reliable men whom he could trust. Consequently, this is a well-documented estate with a considerable archive of surviving correspondence and estate documentation which amounts to some 3000 letters, more than 10,000 estate vouchers and biannual rental/disbursement accounts.[2] These papers create an unbroken run across four decades and make it possible to forge a greater understanding of the financial history of the landed estate as well as the way in which the rural community was organised, managed and changed in the turbulent economic period at the end of the Napoleonic Wars. The historical prism created by the surviving archive allows the researcher to explore estate life multi-dimensionally: that is, socially, economically and politically. Pecuniary decisions form an integral part of the diurnal management, which extend beyond the compiling of accounts and the collection of rents. Choosing the right person to run an estate really mattered; it required a man who understood the local community, had good entrepreneurial and financial skills, understood the local community and could be relied on to manage with the minimum of supervision. Much of the shape of this Dorset and Somerset estate was, therefore, the work of William Castleman, the land agent. He used his skills to manage all the estate's social, economic and political relationships.

Contemporary writers were not enamoured by land agents and advised landowners not to leave too long a gap between their visits and where possible to visit annually during the summer. It was suggested that these measures would prevent unnecessary losses or attempts to defraud the estate of stock or money. Edward Laurence emphasised 'that nothing has tended more to the Abuse and Ruin of brave Estates than the Lord's Neglect'.[3] More recent research has suggested that absenteeism was not in fact anywhere near as disastrous as writers such as Laurence advocated nor was it likely to encourage poor farming practices or duplicitous practices by tenants or land agents.[4] Discovering whether a landowner was resident or not is often hard to establish as many estate records especially correspondence, rental accounts and vouchers conceal both absence and its impact.[5] Modern historians have mixed views on the impact of absenteeism and in many respects much depended on the individual owner and who was left to manage the estate. For example, Sir Marmaduke Constable of Everingham absented himself for long periods, leaving England in May 1730 and spending all but one of the next 16 years travelling on the continent; this was an exceptional case, but not by any means unusual.[6] More widely because a landowner was not physically present, it did not necessarily follow that an estate was neglected.[7] For larger landowners holding land in more than two or three counties often meant visiting was simply too time-consuming and unrealistic. It becomes more difficult in this instance to ascertain the absence, as Anglesey was a keen sailor and when possible regularly visited Cowes, which is not at a great distance from the estate. There is no doubt that he trusted the Castleman family, and the correspondence particularly between the pair reveals an avid demand for information, an in-depth knowledge of the area, its problems and his estate in the south more generally.

Land was a significant asset and there was little reason to neglect an estate unless there was an economic reason to do so, for it formed the basic financial underpinning of aristocratic and gentry families. Incomes were derived from rental revenues and the exploitation of natural resources such as timber, stone and increasingly coal. An estate might be left unsettled so that it could be sold, financial crisis could mean cutting back on the monies expended and land might be left untended in order to purchase more land closer to the main estate. Rumours abounded, for example, in 1824 when it was suggested the Duke of Devonshire had disposed of his Wetherby holdings in order to buy additional land in Derbyshire.[8] Estates were thus valuable investments, a fact which is often overlooked when considering absentee landowners. There is no doubt absenteeism at times caused discontentment and nowhere is this more obvious than in the anonymous letters that were written to landowners decrying the competencies of resident land agents.[9] It was impossible, however, to leave an estate unattended for even short periods of time, and no matter how unpopular in those circumstances, it was essential to employ someone who could be trusted with the day-to-day management. Protecting revenue for most landowners was essential if they were to continue their extravagant life-styles. Absenteeism was not therefore necessarily disadvantageous to the interests of the countryside, and landowners wherever possible sought ways to ensure their property was put into the hands of capable and honest men. John Beckett argues a managed estate under the correct land agent may actually have been the most efficient. The documentary evidence where it has survived suggests that non-residents showed a healthy respect for their property and sufficient financial gains could still be made through competent and well-organised management.[10] It is the daily correspondence, rental accounts, estate vouchers and other estate documents which detail the social, economic, political, financial and business history of the landed estate.

Historiography

Of all areas of agricultural history or that surrounding the country house, the financial history of the landed estate remains relatively unknown. Agricultural history reached its zenith in the 1970s and 1980s, and while new studies are beginning to appear, it has never recovered its previous prominence. In recent years there has been a renewed interest in the country house and its consumption, and this is slowly beginning to encompass the greater and outer estate itself.[11] Elizabeth Hurren contends that the sheer volume of surviving archives in both public and private archives has deterred even the most intrepid of researchers.[12] There is no doubt that by and large these immense archives are in the main uncatalogued and often wieldy to navigate. Overall much of the historiography of the landed estates relies on the work of Gordon Mingay, F. M. L. Thompson and David Spring and was written more than 30 years ago.[13] Commonly these works are generalist in nature and sacrificed depth for breadth and contain little primary source material. More recently Richard Hoyle's edited volume *Farmer in England 1650–1980* explores the farmer within the panorama of agrarian society.[14] While Rab Houston's latest work investigated socio-economic relationships within the Celtic regions of Britain and only fleetingly explores England.[15]

More recently Vanessa Doe has examined the life and achievements of Richard Westbrook Baker who was steward of the Exton Estate in Rutland. Her volume intertwines the biographical narrative of Westbrook Baker's life with his work at Exton and the surrounding community.[16] It is not a financial history. Other source books such as *A Lancashire Gentleman* exist; this one, for example, contains the correspondence of Richard Hodgkinson who was steward to the landed gentry in the north of England. Rather than providing a meticulous case study, this is in effect an edited volume of his letters and does not take an analytical approach to the management of the landed estate or the form and function of the role of the land agent. Neither does it provide a detailed study of the estates for whom he worked.[17] In other words there is a wide gap in the historiography regarding the business and financial history of the landed estate. A new set of sources enables us to focus on the economic aspects of the landed estate; these reveal that it mattered both who owned and managed the estate. Fiscal health was a balancing act between landowner and agent, and this relationship could make or break an estate. The land agent was part of a triumvirate relationship. On one side he had to ensure that his employer's pecuniary needs were met while ensuring that the tenant farmers were able to farm efficiently. This latter group were after all the spine of the estate and with whom fiscal stability rested. Consequently, the form, function and development of the landscape reveal a community which was fashioned and moulded by the landowner and agent and founded on the prevailing financial conditions of the economy.

The idea that rural England was not a single entity is a theory explored by Barry Reay who suggests that it is was instead a vista made up of many places, each area a 'landscape within a landscape'.[18] By placing a small community under the microscope, it is possible to evaluate the complexities of social, economic and political processes and how they played out individually, locally, regionally and nationally. By his own admission, the focus in Reay's *Microhistories: Demography, Society and Culture in Rural England, 1800–1930* is the labouring classes of agrarian society and thus limited in its outlook. Often the rural landscape and the landed estate within its panorama have been blurred by romantic illusions. It is not unusual for artists and authors to recreate agrarian society as a simple collection of picturesque thatched cottages inhabited by contented individuals and surrounded by fat, happy and playing children.[19] Once this idyll is stripped of its quixotic ideals, what is left remains an unpretentious grouping of houses and other residential units alongside their concomitant farms, workshops, public houses and other businesses which seem shapeless and characterless.[20] In neither view is there any sense of the workings of the estate or the struggle to survive post-1815 when depression hit farmers and agricultural labourers alike. As will be seen in Chaps. 2 and 3, this period was far from tranquil as a string of economic depressions which affected prices resulted in tenant distress, and rural unrest; moreover, under- and unemployment were ever-present problems. The agricultural labour has frequently been seen as the instigator of protest and unrest. Carl Griffin in particular sees many of their actions whether it be tree maiming, arguing over customary rights, stealing underwood, incendiarism or the destruction of agricultural machinery as equal elements of protest.[21] Many of these outbursts were based on crippling poverty and a desire to return to the status quo of full employment. Estate relationships as will be seen in Chap. 4 were fragile, and it is only through a wider contextual study that the intricate balance of relationships within the agrarian community can be fully developed. Certainly, in the aftermath of the Swing Riots of 1830, it is possible to deduce a conscious decision to bolster rapport with the labourers through financial considerations. This will be taken up further in Chap. 4.

Estate records allow a thorough examination of how local tensions were played out in practice and highlight the importance of employing an agent who understood these peculiarities and could micromanage tenants, labourers and other members of the rural economy. This volume argues that all the different types of rural relationships depended on some form of fiscal input and the estate needed to weigh both the cost and the impact of this investment. As will be seen in Chap. 6, there were times when the estate withheld monies as they did not deem the expenditure equated to value for money. In the difficult economic conditions of the first half of the nineteenth century, deciding where best to capitalise expenditure could be challenging and required the firm but flexible hand of someone who grasped both local attitudes and the state of the economy.

The Macro-economy

Landed estates despite creating their own local economy were not isolated from wider national trends; they did not in other words exist in a vacuum. Farming in England by 1700 was vastly different to anything on the continent where agriculture faced problems caused by longstanding indebtedness, poor or exhausted soil, low grain yields and a fragmentation of holdings which meant they were unable to make a profit. In England a farming system based on large farms would ensure that the country did not suffer another subsistence crisis. The question was not, therefore, an absence of grain but whether the price was 'just'. Agriculture was not, thus, immune to market pressures.[22] This exposure to the market was evident both during and immediately after the Napoleonic Wars when farmers and landowners' prosperity had been built on trade blockades and bad harvests. In this atmosphere farmers and landowners had been encouraged to try out new methods of cultivation such as enclosure, crop rotation and selective breeding. Large numbers had taken out mortgages to finance these changes; this policy left many heavily in debt as they had foolishly believed that high wartime prices would continue indeterminately.[23] Well before the Battle of Waterloo, there were indications that the high price of grain was under threat. The bumper harvest of 1813 saw the price of wheat tumble, and by the end of the year, it had reached 75s 10d a quarter. This was less than half that of August 1812 when wheat fetched 155s for the same amount. Further falls followed in 1814 and 1815.[24] It had become clear to many observers that English agriculture had 'turned the corner' towards overproduction and farmers had, it seemed, outrun the capacity of a large and expanding domestic market to absorb all that they could produce.[25] Furthermore the prospect of peace brought with it the threat of cheaper grain from the Continent. Consequently, those involved in agriculture began to seek ways of building a home market which was protected through state legislation.[26]

Against this background petitions were sent to Parliament from occupiers and owners across the country asking for the introduction of a new Corn Law.[27] Landowners, the predominant group in government, sought to protect their own interests, while those from towns, cities and manufacturing districts registered their protest. The rhetoric of the anti-Corn Law movement did not become personal until after the late 1820s although there were still glimpses in the petitions of how the narrative of protest might develop. Robert Torrens summed up the sentiments against such an act when he argued 'To increase the rent roll of proprietors, by compelling all other members of the community to pay more for their corn than they otherwise need to do, would be as gross a violation of natural justice, as it is possible for the mind to conceive. It would be tantamount to a tax upon bread'.[28] The protest had little effect and in 1815 a Corn Law was passed which effectively prohibited the import of Corn until the price of the domestic product had risen above 80s a quarter. Despite the prevailing idea that this statute would protect prices, it was unsuccessful, not least because merchants and dealers hoarded corn to keep prices artificially high. The impact of the introduction of this law and the ensuing high cost of bread, which was a staple food, meant that less was spent on other agricultural produce, and this in effect created an agrarian recession.[29] Depression stalked the estate for much of the period between 1814 and 1836, and this will be taken up again in Chap. 3 through an exploration of rental arrears and abatements in relation to tenant distress. The Corn Laws were a reaction to the threat of lower prices by the landed interest who dominated both the upper and lower houses in Parliament. Although they had sought to protect their interests, it is now apparent that the Act in fact created a deeper, wider and longer lasting depression than anyone had anticipated.

This was not the only problem which the economy faced. Some 300,000 servicemen were demobbed at the end of the Napoleonic Wars. These men needed to find employment in a rural economy which had changed shape to cope with their absence from the workforce. This had included the introduction of threshing machines and other technology, and consequently reduced the number of men needed to effectively farm the land. The return of demobilised men saw an increased determination by parish officials to only relieve those entitled under the settlement laws. As farmers faced increasingly low prices and struggled to pay their rents, they sought to force local authorities to meet ever greater percentages of their labour costs.[30] The Speenhamland scales had been created by magistrates in Berkshire to attempt to relieve residents in the aftermath of the poor harvests in the late eighteenth century. In southern counties such as Dorset and Berkshire, the precedent set forced poor law authorities to examine the problems created by low wages and under- and unemployment, rising food prices and housing. Mick Read and Roger Wells argue that Speenhamland constituted a practical charter for the intervention of the parish into the lives of working families.[31] For the landed estate, the conundrum was between setting a realistic poor rate which would cover the cost of relief and destroying the loyalty of the tenants who were the mainstay of political support on election day. The balancing of managing rental arrears, political support and the setting of the poor rate are themes that run throughout the Anglesey/Castleman archive up to and beyond the Great Reform Act of 1832.

The post-war period was difficult for many farmers particularly those who had taken out leases with high rental agreements. However, the discussion around leases within the economy of the landed estate was far more complicated than many historians have considered. As will be seen in this volume, leases and the rental of land never fitted within one single system or idea. At the beginning of the nineteenth century, there was considerable discussion among agricultural commentators on the efficacies of the long lease. James Caird, for example, argued that 'the investment of a tenant's capital in land seldom contemplates an immediate return'.[32] While John Lawrence wrote that to let out an estate/farm on a lease 'is beyond all question, of equal benefit to the lord, as to his tenants'.[33] Notwithstanding the advice in the post-Napoleonic War period, there was a wane in the fervour for issuing and taking up leases. This was not to say that landlords had lost interest in keeping tenants for their political domination but rather the huge fluctuations in rents and prices affected the way that they and potential tenants wanted to rent land. Both landowners and tenants were aware of the inherent dangers in being tied to fixed rents and farm practices for extended periods of time. The static nature of rents linked with leases meant that landowners could not increase these sums during times of plenty, but tenants would still request abatements during economic downturns.[34] Matters were not clear-cut and each form brought both financial benefits and problems. The complexities of leasing land in this period will be taken up in much greater detail in Chap. 2 as the financial health of the estate depended on its farms being rented profitably. Economic conditions shaped the type of lease offered and ensuring that the right type was issued fell in this case to the Castlemans. Effective working partnerships allowed an estate to function and success here spilled over into other interactions which allowed landowners and tenants to survive in a fragile and ever-changing economic climate.

Estate and Social Relations

Tenant farmers are at the heart of any estate and yet have attracted relatively little research and remain one of the least understood groups within the rural community. The problem is exacerbated because they have singularly left few records and consequently must be viewed through a different lens. The Anti-Corn Law League unflatteringly called the farmer 'a rustic dullard, an ignoramous, a servile retainer who unthinkingly followed the landowners lead in politics and county affair'.[35] Richard Hoyle, however, argues that tenant farmers were instead a formidable group who exhibited 'great diversity of character, means and attainments'.[36] Estate archives such as those used here contain enormous amounts regarding the financial history of agriculture, revealing the amounts spent on drainage, improvements, repairs and rent abatements and even maintaining tenant political loyalty. It is also possible to ascertain how different tenants dealt with adversity not just when agriculture prices fell but through weather events, the change of rights of way and increases in the poor rate which were perceived as excessive. Those who leased farms encompassed all strata of society: rich, poor, good and bad, some were members of families who had worked the same land for generations, while others took up farming as conditions improved after 1836. In the wake of the depression after the Napoleonic Wars, it became increasingly common to ask tenants to prove they owned sufficient capital to stock a farm and provide an income until the first harvest was gathered in or beasts were fattened and sold. Historians have argued that landowners needed their tenants much more than their tenants needed them.[37] Good tenants were in other words an asset to be valued. It was not unusual to allow arrears to accrue in leaner periods to extraordinary levels. There was an implicit understanding between the parties that debts would be paid off when the economic situation improved. Questions must be asked as to why tenants who ended up owing incredibly large sums of money were not evicted sooner. The answers are more complex than simply considering that eviction would mean the debt was never paid or that farms might be re-let at a much lower rate. Tenants who could be relied on at election time were important to the security of a small political borough such as Milborne Port in Somerset. It might be argued that loyalty was repaid through the financial loan of the rent when needed. There was a clearly defined reluctance to remove those who exhibited electoral steadfastness. Fortunately, many of the largest landowners held land in different counties and problems varied accordingly. Thus, while one area experienced poor prices, another might well remain buoyant. Any form of financial problem meant some reduction in income, but it was not necessarily disastrous. By choosing to act in a fiscally benevolent manner during periods of economic fragility, a landowner could encourage political deference. Although this appears a somewhat mercenary attitude, it was in fact a well-understood two-way process. The landowner/tenant relationship bestowed on tenants' political status and voting rights which in theory gave them a 'say' in the decision-making process at local, county and national levels. Chapter 5 will explore the complicated political relationship whereby deference and loyalty were closely interwoven concepts and not easy to delineate into separate ideas. The culture surrounding elections and the franchise should be viewed as a community collective appertaining to its welfare as a whole rather than an individualistic reaction to a specific candidate. It did, however, ensure a 'conditional acceptance' of local leadership. Should this not represent the interests of an agrarian society, they had the opportunity through the ballot to exert pressure and bring about change. It further underpinned the fabric of an entire socio-economic situation.[38] Politics stood as a unifying force in the landowner/tenant relationship whereby loyalty was both visible and demonstrable on both sides.

Finding ways to work with the agricultural labourers who were the other noteworthy population living and working on an estate was more difficult as there were few socio-economic means of control. In the long-lasting depression which followed the Napoleonic Wars in southern England, this group faced grinding poverty in hand with under- and unemployment. During the first half of the nineteenth century, Dorset had the unenviable reputation of paying the lowest agricultural wages of any county in England.[39] In 1824 Arthur Lyon Bowley calculated average wages in the county as being 6s 11d per week, reaching a peak in 1833 of some 8s 4d, but by 1850 had slipped back to 7s 6d. By this time though Suffolk, Wiltshire, Gloucestershire and Salop all had lower weekly wages suggesting that the situation in the county had improved somewhat.[40] Dorset Magistrate David Parry-Okeden commented in 1830 that a 'Labourer should receive from his Employer such wages as shall enable him to lay by a provision for age, sickness and infirmity'; however, when unable to earn sufficient money because of such ills, he should 'be supported by the persons who employed him in youth, health and vigour'.[41] Okedon's ideas in principle dealt with those classed as the 'deserving poor', but for those who did not fall into these categories, the post-war period proved extremely difficult. Financially the Dorset and Somerset estate of the Marquis of Anglesey sought to mitigate the highest levels of poverty through a range of one-off payments made to the poor and will be examined in greater detail in Chap. 6. It is possible through overseer, vestry records, estate vouchers and the diurnal correspondence to gain not just a sense of the amounts paid but that these remunerations might be withheld as a form of social control. Importantly historians have frequently neglected the ways in which large estate and parishes worked together in the economy of makeshifts. There is no doubt that financial recession amongst the tenants had a wide impact on all aspects of the rural community. Throughout their agency the Castlemans grappled with how on the one hand to keep the poor rate as low as feasibly possible for political expediency but on the other high enough to ensure the poor were kept from outright rebellion. Dissent was a shadow that during the period covered by this volume was never far away. Most visibly the Swing Riots of 1830 were a culmination of a range of problems. In the past historians such as the Hammonds, Eric Hobsbawm and George Rudé have argued that these riots were the result of low wages, under- and unemployment, enclosure and the introduction of threshing machines. There is a danger here that dissent will be seen in the smallest of actions when in reality many actions were simply the poor seeking to survive. The question must be asked, therefore, where the crossover point occurs between simple subsistence measures and outright dissent. Indeed, is it even possible to discern the difference? These ideas will be taken up again in Chap. 4 when Swing will be explored as part of a much longer and more diverse cycle of rural protest and machine breaking in general. Both before and after Swing, the estate sought ways to find leverage to moderate the behaviour of this lower socio-economic group.

F. M. L. Thompson's 'Social Control in Victorian Britain' although concentrating on urban areas contains much that relates to social control within the landed estate.[42] Socialisation he argues concerns specific individuals particularly children. It is the process by which people learn the rules, practices and expected behaviour of a given group. This is clear enough when an individual group or class constructs its own means of communicating and instilling its own 'mores' through the family, school and peer groups. The situation is much more blurred when another class attempts to impose its own notions of suitable behaviour, habits, morals and attitudes upon another class usually through schools and education. Schools provided from above for the instruction of a lower class raise questions of who guides and controls the behaviour of the recipient. Popular education, Peter McCann argues, was more about political socialisation rather than an attempt to transmit literacy, skills and knowledge. As will be seen in Chap. 6, this is still too simplistic and education was used as a visible extension of an estate's power and reflected its desire to modify the behaviour of the more rebellious elements of the estate.[43] For the estate the financial outlay in support of local schools was money well spent. Furthermore, it was a sound investment in creating and shaping future labourers and employees of the estate.

Using the archive left by the Marquis of Anglesey and William Castleman, it is possible to interpret almost every decision made as having a financial connotation. Yes, agriculture formed the basis of this and indeed every landed estate for at least the majority of the nineteenth century. Eric Jones has recently argued that landowners were adept at passing on the burdens and risks of farming onto their tenants, who in turn passed the costs on to their labourers laying them off during periods of economic hardship.[44] While there is some truth in this argument, ignoring the labourers became much harder after the Swing Riots of 1830. In essence this volume will create a multilayered and three-dimensional study of a landed estate and investigate its financial history alongside its social and political narrative. At the centre of this estate was the Marquis of Anglesey and the Castleman family in particular William Castleman.

The Marquis of Anglesey and Castleman Family: The Dorset and Somerset Estate

It remains a mystery as to why the Paget family inherited their Dorset and Somerset estate. It was left to them through Peter Walter. He had in the eighteenth century managed to accumulate a large fortune during his nefarious career as steward to several of the local aristocracy, including the Duke of Newcastle.[45] Little is known about Walter's early life, but he is thought to have been born at Wyke Champflower, near Bruton in Somerset, the son of Peter Walter, who died in the same village in 1696, leaving his wife and son Peter a mere two shillings and sixpence. In 1699 Viscount Richard Shannon mortgaged Stalbridge to Peter Walter whose address was then given as St Margaret's, Westminster.[46] He was to amass a substantial estate worth £300,000 which passed on his death to his grand-son, yet another Peter Walter, his son having already pre-deceased him.[47] The will of this member of the Walter family revealed his grandfather's wish that in the absence of a male heir, the estate was to pass to Nicholas Bayley and his sons, who later changed their name to Paget from their mother's line of descent.[48] There are four seemingly unconnected factors which link the Walter and Paget families together. Firstly, Peter Walter senior acted as steward to the 1st Earl of Uxbridge who died in 1743. Secondly, a conundrum exists as to why Peter Walter who made the will was called Paget Walter. Thirdly, Uxbridge is supposed to have continued to pay Walter's daughter Mrs. Bullock a sizeable annuity throughout her life even though this was not stipulated in her father's will.[49] Finally both Edward Walter and Lord Paget were Lords of the Manor at Kingsbury Regis, one of the villages which formed the Dorset and Somerset estate.[50] Indeed none of the above provides an answer to the question but instead add to the mystery.[51]

The estate in 1812 was considerable and encompassed land in a number of villages including Bradford Abbas, Clifton Maybank, Sixpenny Handley, Gussage St. Michael, Kington Magna and Nyland, Manston, Marnhull, Stalbridge, Stour Provost and Todber, Stourpaine, Thornford and Wyle in Dorset and Charlton Horethorne, Cheriton, Henstridge, Templecombe, Coombe Abbas, Horsington, Kingsbury Regis, Milborne Port and Wyke, Maiden Bradley, Yarnfield, Stotford and Norton Ferris in Somerset. The majority of these villages lie in close proximity to the Vale of Blackmore. Sixpenny Handley (hereon in referred to as Hanley) was one of the exceptions lying to the east on the edge of Cranborne Chase. The estate's property had always been fluid and those areas of the estate which were most unprofitable had been consequently sold in 1789. There was a further important sale in 1825 when Clifton Maybank was offloaded, Milborne Port went in 1837, Charlton Horethorne and Templecombe in 1848, Thornford in 1849, Sixpenny Handley in 1850, Stour Provost and Todber in 1851 and then Stalbridge and the remainder of the estate in 1854.

The estate came to Henry William Paget 2nd Earl of Uxbridge in 1812; he is today remembered for his military exploits, particularly the Battle of Waterloo where he lost a leg to grapeshot. As a result of this injury, his descendants have nicknamed him 'One-Leg'.[52] In order to compensate for the loss of this limb, Uxbridge was offered an annual annuity of £1200 which he refused. On 4 July 1815 in recognition of his military endeavours, he was created the 1st Marquis of Anglesey.[53] Despite his achievements both in war and peace, relatively little has been written about him; the comments made in the margins of the letters he returned to his land agent provide an insight into his ideas of estate management and personal beliefs. These notes underpin both his interest in the estate and the way that it functioned and detail the level of trust in the financial decisions made daily by his land agent.

Outside of the military, Anglesey was a colourful character and scandalised both contemporaries and society by his relationship with Charlotte (Char) Wellesley. She was the daughter of the Earl of Cadogan and the wife of Henry Wellesley, the youngest brother of the Duke of Wellington.

The relationship commenced in 1808 but cooled while Anglesey was away fighting in Spain; however, it appears to have quickly resumed on his return and finally ended in their elopement.[54] In an attempt to contain the situation, Anglesey's relations pleaded with him to return to his wife but he refused. Char's outraged brother seeking retribution challenged Anglesey to a duel, but he declined. Instead he posted a note which appeared in a wide range of newspapers stating 'She [Char] has lost the world upon my account ... I feel, therefore that my life is hers, not my own ... It distresses me beyond all description to refuse you that satisfaction which I am most ready to admit you have a right to demand'.[55] On 12 May an action filed by Char's husband Henry Wellesley was heard in the Sherriff's Court when damages against Anglesey of £20,000 with costs were levied. Whilst Anglesey was away, Cadogan issued a second challenge which was accepted and played out on Wimbledon Common on 30 May 1809. Afterwards friends of the two men put out a statement which suggests that neither man had intended to hit the other, but justice had been done.[56] Ultimately Caroline or as she was known Car (his wife) begun divorce proceedings as she was by now all but engaged when 'free' to be married to the Duke of Argyll. Under English Law a husband could divorce his wife for adultery, but only in Scotland could a wife seek the same remedy and so both parties moved north. It was inconsequential whether the act had been committed there or elsewhere so long as both parties resided in the country for 40 days.[57] The decree was made absolute in October 1810. Anglesey and his second wife would go on to have ten children the first of which had been born in March 1810 some seven months before his divorce was finalised. The entire business had cost around £55,000.[58]

More than a year before his father's death on 13 March 1812, Anglesey had taken over the responsibility of running his multifarious affairs and discovered they were in a very precarious situation. The old Lord Uxbridge had been living above his means for a considerable period of time. There is no suggestion that this was the result of 'heedless' extravagance, although it no doubt played a part. The main cause was undoubtedly a lack of attention to business matters.[59] An investigation revealed that the profits from the copper mines in Anglesey had been grossly over-estimated. This was problematic because all his father's expenditure on elections, various domestic establishments (both building and improvements) and generous allowances to poorer relatives were based on these calculations. In order to try and bring a sense of order managers had to be appointed to take over the daily organisation of at least the remoter areas of his inheritance.

The Dorset and Somerset parts of Anglesey's overall acreage were perhaps the most remote of his estate, and he consequently appointed Admiral Aylmer on a salary of £1500 to work with the other half and pay Admiral Bentinck as supervisory agent.[60] It was said that Aylmer had absolute possession of Anglesey who believed he was the only thing standing between him and bankruptcy.[61] Anglesey's concerns surrounding his financial position are emblematically illustrated when he commented, 'This sort of thing goes to trifles, which, I am sure till now, I hardly considered as expenses. Who, for instance, w[ould]d conceive that a few almonds and raisins dealt out daily to two persons (who by the by never touch them) sh[oul]d amount to a serious charge?'. When his father died, Anglesey inherited not just his title becoming 2nd Earl of Uxbridge but also his debts. Despite the entire Welsh, Staffordshire, Dorset and Somerset lands which had an annual turnover between 1819 and 1835 averaging £76,000 per annum, he continued to overspend at the rate of £1600 a year.[62] Anglesey's financial situation was perilous, and the cost of his divorce only exacerbated the problem. Prestigious but costly appointments which included two spells as Lord Lieutenant of Ireland,[63] the Lord Lieutenants of Anglesey and Staffordshire, Constable of Caernarfon Castle, ranger of Snowdon Forest and Captain of Cowes Castle put further pressures on his already strained finances.[64] Consequently, throughout his tenure large parts of the estate were continuously mortgaged, and a sense of his indebtedness will be examined in greater detail in Chap. 2. This financial backdrop is important in understanding the difficulties faced by the Dorset and Somerset estate. The situation was one which needed a skilled land agent who would negotiate the economic problems of both agrarian society and the Marquis of Anglesey himself.

On inheriting this estate in 1812, Anglesey was confronted with the problem of an incompetent and possibly fraudulent agent. Cox who was then in charge of the Dorset and Somerset estate was said to have left Anglesey's employment with debts of some £6000 to £7000 and consequently faced a Chancery Suit which had been filed against him. More evidence came from Chitty of Shaftesbury who wrote to William Castleman stating that Cox had greatly deceived him and 'every other branch of his family'. Furthermore, he alleged that Cox's encumbrances amounted to around £100,000.[65] This errant agent was to create greater confusion due to his poor record-keeping which made it difficult to produce a satisfactory statement of the monies outstanding.[66] Admiral Aylmer as mentioned above remained in overall charge of the estate during this period but did not become further implicated in the Cox scandal and continued to keep the estate books until taken over by William Castleman in 1814.

The first time William Castleman appeared in the estate archive was 1804 in the case of *Place v Burt* when he was paid £31 10s 0d for his work. He had connections with the estate long before he became its agent; his father, of the same name, had taken a lease at Stalbridge in 1766 when his infant son William was named as one of the lives. Castleman the elder was a minor estate official at the Stalbridge Weston Court in 1781 and on his death was buried at Hinton St Mary. As yet nothing has come to light within the records to suggest how his son may have come to be employed by Anglesey. Newspaper adverts of the period reveal that Castleman under the auspices of his Wimborne practice was already selling property. For example, in August 1804 an advertisement appeared in the *Salisbury and Winchester Journal* offering for sale the freehold estate of the late George Wagg. This was 'a capital Mansion House, with convenient stabling for 14 horses, a double coach-house, dove-house, large garden, fish ponds and pleasure ground'.[67] Besides this substantial property, two other farms were offered as separate lots with the point of contact being registered as William Castleman. He also appears in local newspapers as Clerk to the Trustees of the Poole Turnpike and was agent for the Hanham and Bankes estates and coroner for the Cogdean Hundred. In 1823 he built a substantial family property in Wimborne, Dorset: Allendale House, which was designed by Sir Jeffry Wyatville and remains a symbol of his reputation and standing within the locality.[68] There can be little doubt that Castleman was a prominent lawyer and respected estate manager within the area, already a man of status and position before he worked for Anglesey. Once employed he worked loyally for the estate from 1814 until his death in 1844. The strength of the partnership between Anglesey and agent was demonstrated on Castleman's death when Anglesey commented that he was an 'amiable and zealous man of business'. While Thomas Beer, the agent-in-chief, remarked 'I have never received more satisfactory information in matters of detail or accounts from any of Lord Anglesey's agents'.[69] After his death he was followed by his sons, firstly by Henry but his time with the estate was cut short by ill health and then Edward who continued until the property was sold off in 1854.

Chapter 2 will reassess the role and scope of the work of the land agent in the management and financial administration of the landed estate and argue that having the right man at the helm was imperative. This was especially important in the fragile economic period of the 1810s and 1820s. It will explore the traditional functions of tenanting farms and leasing property without which no estate could survive. An essential part of the land agent's role was the compilation of accounts, and although those used by the estate are primitive charge and discharge accounts, they tell alongside the estate vouchers the financial history of the estate. Without William Castleman's skills in finding large sums of monies in the form of mortgages, the estate would have had an uncertain future. In effect this chapter will detail how financial decisions were an essential component of managing both land and people and argue that allowing high rental arrears was part of the overall working partnerships which are the subject of the next chapter.

Chapter 3 takes up the construction of working relationships which essentially relied on the wealth of the landowner. It opens with a survey of tenant distress through poor agriculture prices and disease in livestock and argues that it was in the estate's interest to allow rent abatements and other incentives to encourage the tenants to remain on their farms. While farming risks might be shared, a tenant expected well maintained buildings and help with repairs when exogenous factors caused extensive and unexpected damage. When Anglesey inherited this estate, it was in a dilapidated condition, and so this chapter examines how Castleman set about putting it back to serviceable state and then kept it so by an ongoing schedule of repairs. Capital investment came in the form of drainage and the introduction of mechanisation in the form of threshing machines. This volume will argue that working relationships were a partnership which relied on the landowner fiscally supporting his tenants.

Chapter 4 turns to social relationships which often relied on a series of expected customary rights. While the financial underpinning of this aspect of estate life is less obvious here, it remains the single most important factor in maintaining the balance of relationships. It begins by examining the tensions created by the estate's decisions to veer away from traditional expectations. It also investigates other forms of unrest which are not governed by under- or unemployment and low wages, such as timber stealing. This chapter, through the Swing Riots, explores what happened when one side of the relationship broke down. It concludes by arguing that the provision of community benefits such as new roads, investment in weighing machines or negotiating with wayward tenants whose activities impacted on the community were an essential part of estate life. Ensuring that the community worked together cost the estate less in financial expenditure but much more in terms of Castleman's time.

Chapter 5 investigates the political landscape of Milborne Port. Landowners bestowed on their tenants the franchise and gave them the chance to participate in the political decision-making process. There are three core aspects to this chapter, it commences by exploring the political landscape of Milborne Port through the contested election. It will then move to the election process which is most often constructed as a political process. This volume argues that it was in reality far more a financial procedure because without the wherewithal to fend off challengers, to expend monies on canvassing both before and during the election, Anglesey would never have managed to retain his patronage. Finally managing the election process was the responsibility of William Castleman: not only did he have to ensure that voters cast their vote for the right candidate, but he was also required to pay the bills and to compile the election accounts.

Chapter 6 explores the ways in which the estate sought to exert at least a modicum of social control over its tenants. This type of activity is most often seen in the form of philanthropy or education. The financial consideration here is different, in that monies were frequently spent on visual entities, and so this chapter explores church expansion and monies paid to local clergymen for the relief of the poor in terms of food, clothes and coal. Perhaps the area where the estate was most active was in supporting schools, including day, Sunday and vocational establishments. It moves the story of rural education away from the battle over which religious domination had the right of control to one of financial decisions as to which school would have the most impact on local behaviour. Unlike in other areas, the fiscal expenditure had to be value for money, and schemes were often rejected because it was felt they might be ineffective. Charitable payments might also be withdrawn as a punishment for poor behaviour.

Previous studies have concentrated on the agricultural history, industrial development and consumption of the country house within a single estate. Using a new and well-documented set of sources, it is possible to take the study of the landed estate into a new direction which argues that financial decisions were essential if it was to simply survive in the turbulent pecuniary climate of the first half of the nineteenth century. In this sense an exceptional land agent was needed to navigate the complexities of managing an estate which heavily relied on the most volatile of industries—agriculture. Every decision made had a cost to the estate and it was often a balancing act to ascertain what or who should be helped and supported and what should be left to collapse. These decisions could be controversial, in its simplest form estate profitability ensured the landowner maintained his extravagant life-style while the tenants farmed responsibly and improved rather than decreased the value of the land.

Notes

1. See, for example, C. Beardmore, S. King and G. Monks, (eds) (2016) *The Land Agent in Britain: Past, Present and Future* (Newcastle: Cambridge Scholars); C. A. Beardmore, (April, 2016) 'The Rural Estate through the Eyes of the Land Agent: A Community in Microcosm c1812–1854', *Family and Community History*, 19:1, pp. 17–33; C. A. Beardmore (2015) 'Landowner, Tenant and Agent on the Marquis of Anglesey's Dorset and Somerset Estate, 1814–1844', *Rural History* 26:2, pp. 181–199; G. Monks (2018) 'William Gould, Land Agent and the Rural Community in Nottinghamshire and Derbyshire', *Family and Community History*, 19:2, pp. 67–81 and L. A. Rees, C. Reilly and A. Tindley (eds) (2018) *The Land Agent 1700–1920* (Edinburgh: Edinburgh University Press).
2. Irene Jones who wrote *The Stalbridge Inheritance* while on holiday in Anglesey in 1990 found the archivist of Bangor University sitting on six sacks of paper relating to Anglesey's Dorset and Somerset estate. She immediately set about having them transferred to the Dorset History Centre.
3. E. Laurence (1743) *The Duty and Office of a Land Steward* (London: J. and P. Knapton, T. Longman, H. Linto and J. and H. Pemberton), p. 37.
4. See J. V. Beckett (1983) 'Absentee Landownership in the Later Seventeenth and Early Eighteenth Centuries: The Case of Cumbria' *Northern History*, 19:1, pp. 87–107.
5. P. Roebuck (1973) 'Absentee Landownership in the Late Seventeenth and early Eighteenth Centuries: A Neglected Factor in English Agrarian History', *The Agricultural History Review*, 21:1, p. 1.
6. Ibid., p. 2.
7. Ibid., p. 88.
8. Beckett 'Absentee Landownership in the Later Seventeenth and Early Eighteenth Centuries', p. 89.
9. There are four surviving anonymous letters written to the Marquis of Anglesey regarding William Castleman. As to how many might have originally been sent, it is impossible to know.
10. Beckett (1983) 'Absentee Landownership in the Later Seventeenth and Early Eighteenth Centuries', p. 106.
11. For recent studies on the country house, see, for example, J. Stobart (2016) *The Country House: Material Culture and Consumption*, (Swindon: Historic England); J. Stobart (2017) *Travel and the British Country House: Cultures, Critiques and Consumption in the Long Eighteenth Century* (Manchester, Michigan: Manchester University Press); J. Stobart and M. Rothery (2016) *Consumption and the Country House* (Oxford: Oxford University Press); B. McDonagh (2018) *Elite Women and the Agricultural*

Landscape, 1700–1830 (Abingdon: Routledge) and E. L. Jones (2018) *Landed Estates and Rural Inequality in English History: From the Mid-Seventeenth Century to the Present* (London: Springer).
12. E. T. Hurren (2016) 'The Making of the Modern Land Agent in Victorian Times', C. Beardmore, S. King and G. Monks, *The Land Agent in Britain: Past, Present and Future* (Newcastle: Cambridge Scholars), 169.
13. See, for example, G. E. Mingay, (ed.) (1981) *The Victorian Countryside Vols I and II* (London: Routledge and Kegan Paul, Ltd.); G. E. Mingay, (1977) *Rural Life in Victorian England* (London: Heinemann); F. M. L. Thompson (1971) *English Landed Society in the Nineteenth Century* (London: Routledge & Kegan Paul) and D. Spring (1963) *The English Landed Estate in the Nineteenth Century* Baltimore: John Hopkins Press).
14. R. W. Hoyle, (ed.) (2013) *The Farmer in England 1650–1980* (Farnham: Ashgate).
15. R. A. Houston (2014) *Peasant Petitions: Social Relations and Economic Life on Landed Estates, 1600–1850* (Basingstoke: Palgrave Macmillan).
16. V. Doe (2018) *Improving Agriculture in Nineteenth Century Rutland: The Life and Achievements of Richard Westbrook (1797–1861), Steward of the Exton Estate* (Oakham: Rutland Local History Society).
17. F. Wood & K. Wood (1992) *A Lancashire Gentlemen: The Letters and Journals of Richard Hodgkinson 1763–1847* (Stroud: Alan Sutton Publishing Ltd).
18. B. Reay (1996) *Microhistories: Demography, Society and Culture in Rural England, 1800–1930* (Cambridge: Cambridge University Press), pp. 257–258.
19. C. A. Beardmore, (April, 2016) 'The Rural Estate through the Eyes of the Land Agent: A Community in Microcosm c1812–1854', *Family and Community History,* 19:1, p. 17.
20. D. R. Mills (1973) *English Rural Communities: The Impact of a Specialised Economy* (London: Macmillan).
21. See C. Griffin (2014) *Protest, Politics and Work in Rural England, 1700–1850* (Basingstoke: Palgrave Macmillan).
22. L. Patriquin (2007) *Agrarian Capitalism and Poor Relief in England, 1500–1860: Rethinking the Origins of the Welfare State* (Basingstoke: Palgrave Macmillan), p. 62.
23. R. Tames (1972) *Economy and Society in Nineteenth Century Britain* (Abingdon: Routledge), p. 61.
24. P. Horn (1880) *The Rural World 1780–1850: Social Change in the English Countryside* (London: Hutchinson), p. 72.
25. Tames *Economy and Society in Nineteenth Century Britain*, p. 61.
26. Horn (1880) *The Rural World 1780–1850*, p. 72.
27. Ibid.

28. Quoted in D. Grove Barns (2006) *A History of English Corn Laws From 1660–1846* (Abingdon: Routledge), p. 147.
29. C. Cook (2005) *The Routledge Companion to Britain in the Nineteenth Century, 1815–1914* (London; New York: Routledge), p. 198.
30. See M. Reed and R. Wells (1990) *Class, Conflict and Protest in the English Countryside, 1700–1880* (London: Cass).
31. Ibid.
32. J. Caird (1852) *English Agriculture in 1850–1851* (London: Longman, Brown, Green and Longmans), p. 503.
33. J. Lawrence (1806) *The Modern Land Steward* (London: H. D. Symonds, T. Ostrell, W. J. and J. Richardson), p. 72.
34. J. D. Chambers and G. E. Mingay, (1966) *The Agricultural Revolution, 1750–1880* (London: B. T. Batsford Ltd.), p. 165.
35. Quoted in G. E. Mingay, *Rural Life in Victorian England*, p. 52.
36. R. W. Hoyle, (2013) 'Introduction: Recovering the Farmer' in R. W. Hoyle, (ed.), *The Farmer in England 1650–1980* (Farnham: Ashgate), p. 1.
37. Ibid.
38. F. O'Gorman, (May, 1992) 'Campaign Rituals and Ceremonies: The Social Meaning of Elections in England 1780–1860' *Past & Present*, 135, p. 107.
39. K. D. M. Snell (1985) *Annals of the Labouring Poor: Social Change and Agrarian England 1660–1900* (Cambridge: Cambridge University Press), p. 375.
40. A. L. Bowley (December, 1898) 'The Statistics of Wages in the United Kingdom During the Last Hundred Years. (part 1)', *Journal of the Royal Historical Society*, 61:4, p. 704.
41. D. O. P. Okedon (1830) *A Letter to the Members in Parliament for Dorsetshire on the Subject of Poor Relief and Labourers' Wages, 2nd edition* (Blandford: John Shipp), p. 5.
42. See F. M. L. Thompson (May, 1981) 'Social Control in Victorian England' *Economic History Review*, 32:2.
43. See P. McCann (1977) *Popular Education and Socialisation in the Nineteenth Century* (London: Routledge).
44. Jones, *Landed Estates and Rural Inequality in English History*, p. 114.
45. The Marquis of Anglesey (1961) *One Leg: The Life and Letters of Henry William Paget K.G. 1768–1854* (London: Jonathan Cape), p. 346.
46. I. Jones (1993) *The Stalbridge Inheritance 1780–1854* (Dorchester: Friary Press), p. vi.
47. The Marquis of Anglesey *One Leg*, p. 346.

48. Jones, *The Stalbridge* Inheritance, p. x. The family had changed their name by royal licence to Paget from Bayley when Henry Bayley became in 1770 the tenth Baron Paget.
49. http://www.oxforddnb.com.ezproxy3.lib.le.ac.uk/view/article/21110/21111?back=,21110,21110
50. S. G. Mackay (1986) *Milborne Port in Somerset* (Milborne Port: Remus Ltd), p. 55.
51. The Marquis of Anglesey, *One* Leg, p. 346.
52. Ibid., p. 19.
53. Throughout this volume Henry William Paget is referred to as the Marquis of Anglesey although technically this title was not bestowed until 1815.
54. http://www.oxforddnb.com.ezproxy3.lib.le.ac.uk/view/article/21112?docPos=3
55. *Bristol Mercury,* 20 May 1809, although the letter was dated 30 March 1809.
56. *The Morning Post,* 31 May 1809.
57. The Marquis of Anglesey, *One Leg*, p. 110.
58. The equivalent today of almost four million pounds.
59. The Marquis of Anglesey, *One Leg*, p. 114.
60. Admiral Aylmer appears in the archive until 1814.
61. The Marquis of Anglesey, *One Leg*, pp. 114–115.
62. http://www.oxforddnb.com.ezproxy3.lib.le.ac.uk/view/article/21112?docPos=3
63. The first term was cut short when he was recalled for his Catholic sympathies.
64. http://www.oxforddnb.com.ezproxy3.lib.le.ac.uk/view/article/21112?docPos=3
65. Quoted in Jones, *The Stalbridge Inheritance*, p. 30.
66. DHC, D/ANG/B5/17, 1 July 1814.
67. *Salisbury and Winchester Journal*, 13 August 1804.
68. Jeffry Wyatville was a successful architect who worked for 17 Earls and 4 sovereigns. Much of his work involved improvements, remodelling and extending existing properties including some of the great houses such as Longleat, Wiltshire, Wollaton Hall, Nottinghamshire, Chatsworth, Derbyshire, Woburn Abbey, Bedfordshire and Windsor Castle. No one has yet been able to fathom how Castleman was able to persuade an architecture of this stature to work for him on this more modest property.
69. Dorset History Centre background to the Anglesey estate.

CHAPTER 2

Estate Finances and Administration

Overview

The landed estate at the outset of the nineteenth century underpinned the aristocratic classes and bestowed on them both power and status. Thomas Gisborne argued that the landowners of these estates had certain duties which resulted partly from the power they enjoyed over their estates and the tenants who occupied them and partly from the influence which the possession of land gave them within the local neighbourhood.[1] These obligations could take many forms and might include choosing and encouraging industrious tenants, charging fair rents, improving drainage, offering leases whether long or short and supplying 'constant and growing employment' thus preventing the vices and disorders which arose from idleness. In order to increase the population, families should be encouraged to settle. The whole process could be boosted by the landowner increasing the quantity but reducing the price of provisions.[2] By 1838 these duties had increased substantially according to Lord Sidney Godolphin Osborne. Land, he argued, meant the landowner had duties within the village economy which went beyond those outlined by Gisborne and their role should extend to the participation in a range of poor law chores. This might incorporate aiding in the establishment, organisation and support of clothing funds, benefit societies and savings banks; the building of good quality cottages; the granting of allotments and the run-

C. Beardmore, *Financing the Landed Estate*, Palgrave Studies in the History of Finance, https://doi.org/10.1007/978-3-030-14552-1_2

ning of schools, to which should be added industrial schools, which will be returned to in Chap. 6.[3]

Whatever the changes which had taken place, all estates had to be managed and administered in order to be productive. This could be approached in two ways—the landowner as in Thomas Coke at Holkham Hall might choose to personally undertake the daily tasks needed to ensure the smooth running of the estate, or more commonly, a land agent or steward might be employed. As Sarah Webster argues, the definition of agent was not stable and was often used concurrently with steward.[4] Whichever term was employed, ideally good management allowed the landowner to live a 'life of leisure' released from any diurnal involvement with the everyday maintenance of his estate.[5] Absenteeism as seen in the Introduction was a growing cause for concern amongst contemporary writers and one which might affect the smooth running of the estate. Whether resident or absent, the successful administration of an estate was the result of the formation of a partnership between the landowner and his agent, both working jointly to protect and improve the land. Colin Shrimpton advocates that the closest of bonds were those where both landowner and agent were resident members of the community. He argues that when this occurred, both had a stake in the financial health and success of the estate.[6] This was not necessarily true; it was far more important to employ a man who was trustworthy and had the ability to read the local community and who could then disseminate the knowledge gathered into the compilation of regular and clearly written reports. In any case, agents, such as William Castleman who ran more than one estate, alongside a successful country legal practice, had reputations to keep. Thus, even when they were not resident, it was in their best interest to ensure any estate or land under their administration thrived. Land agents walk across the archives of just about every great estate, and yet we still have only a rudimentary understanding of the ways in which they ordered their regimes

Despite being published more than 50 years ago, much of our knowledge on estate administration still relies heavily on the work of David Spring whose *The English Landed Estate in the Nineteenth Century: Its Administration* remains one of the few volumes dedicated to this subject.[7] Other historians have of course explored different aspects of the work undertaken by land agents and their role in managing a wide variety of projects.[8] As yet, however, no one has developed the ideas laid out by Spring using a more modern case study approach or examined how the fiscal decisions made originated from the successful organisation of the full range of socio-economic and political processes which formed the landed estate. Consequently, this case study begins to take up the narrative of estate administration, but overall much more work is needed to understand how local, regional and national nuances impacted on the creation of a more uniform system. F. M. L. Thompson suggests the landed estate in the nineteenth century witnessed a managerial revolution similar to that of the legal and medical professions and the changing structure of manufacturing companies.[9] While in time this regulated some aspects such as the compilation of accounts through double-entry book-keeping, others remained completely individualistic, such as the land farmed, the personality of the tenants and the requirements and foibles of the landowner himself. Firstly, this chapter will start by exploring the role and scope of the land agent, looking at the type of men who took up this position and the extent of the work which they undertook. Secondly, it will examine how property was leased. In the friable economic climate after 1815, this could be challenging and had to be tackled according to the prevailing situation. While historians have suggested that there was a general movement to rack renting, in reality the ways in which land was rented was more fluid and altered according to the perceived economic situation. Inevitably the personality of the land agent impacted on the type of tenure offered. It is argued here that even when there was a discrepancy of opinion between the landowner and agent, the landowner did not necessarily come out on top. Thirdly, this chapter will investigate the difficulties surrounding the use of rental accounts for research purposes. Although the accounts used here are problematic, in that they do not record the acreages rented, they can still be used to explore the financial well-being of the estate. Finally, during the first half of the nineteenth century, the aristocracy continued to accumulate large levels of debt. To remain solvent, the use of mortgages rose in popularity. Anglesey inherited his father's liabilities; his own divorce had been expensive, and his son exacerbated the problem. The accounts provide a sense of the amount of interest paid annually and demonstrate how his land agent with a range of local networks and links to men with ready money to invest provided significant sums in the form of mortgages. Essentially the role of the land agent continued to expand, and they often played a pivotal role in keeping landed properties afloat, but this was alongside more typical activities. In order to understand the importance of these men, this chapter now turns to survey their position within the landed estate.

The Role and Scope of the Land Agent

Most land agents came from the middling ranks of society, younger sons of country squires, minor gentry, lawyers and the clergy.[10] By far and away, the largest contingent in the first half of the nineteenth century were country attorneys. This is hardly surprising as much of the work involved in administering an estate was an extension of their usual work. They were already practised in conveyancing land, understood the precedents and customary rights intrinsically embedded in rural communities and were familiar with the type of common legal disputes inherent in any given locality. Despite their prevalence in the agrarian landscape, contemporary writers derided these men for their lack of agricultural knowledge.[11] Edward Laurence, for example, suggested that county attorneys were only interested in 'Court keeping and collecting of rents'. They allowed the tenants to do what they wished with their farms and encouraged over-ploughing and the poor management of the land.[12] As will be seen below, this is far from the truth with husbandry clauses inserted into leases and substantial fines levied if these were broken. Notwithstanding the general sentiments of the time, the majority of those who took up the profession of land management had grown up on farms or small landed estates or had become competent landowners in their right with a keen interest in the practice of agriculture. As seen in the Introduction, William Castleman was the son of a tenant farmer and a substantial landowner in his own right. While the public reputation of the land agent was mixed, all the agricultural writers saw professionalism, high moral responsibility and an aptitude which bred respect amongst the tenantry as essential attributes.[13] The land agent occupied a powerful position within the estate framework. He represented the interests of his employer in overseeing the management of the estate. While some landowners would offer direct instructions, others were more laissez faire and would leave the agent to exercise his best judgement as and when necessary.[14] Ultimately, therefore a successful agent needed two skills—firstly, to be 'self-effacing' so that his employer might claim the credit for the successful management of the estate and, secondly, to be able to encourage a reciprocation of respect between the landlord and community.[15] From the mid-nineteenth century onwards, country attorneys were steadily replaced by the professional land surveyor. The process was slow because despite the criticisms levied, most lawyers had provided a good service and landowners were slow to replace those they knew and trusted.

There was plenty of advice available to a landowner when searching for a land agent. The notable agricultural writer William Marshall emphasised the importance of specific traits. Besides being an accomplished agriculturalist, he advocated an agent should:

> ...be a man of fair character – of upright principles and conciliatory manners: – to set an example of good conduct to the tenants and to become their common counsellor and peace maker.[16]

Recompensing a steward by paying 'a liberal salary' for his labours was one way to avoid fraud and ensure adequate attention was paid to the estate.[17] The amounts of money that could pass through an agent's hands were staggering—even on a small estate, this could amount to more than £10,000 per annum. Keeping accurate accounts was essential as they provided information relating to the level of rent arrears; the monies expended on capital investments; the amount of rent abatements allowed; sums spent in supporting schools, churches and the poor; the interest due on mortgages; the cost of house building; and the aggregate cost of elections. When an employer was absent, there was a myriad of ways to commit fraud; this is perhaps one reason why landowners were slow to replace their trusted local attorneys.

Estates varied in size as did the extent and role of the land agent. Administratively they fell into two broad classes. The first type was composed of numerous small estates, and if they were very small, then the landowner would manage with the help of a local bailiff who was often himself a tenant farmer. As bailiff, his powers would be limited and the extent of his influence contained within the big house and its grounds or farm. He would not normally have been responsible for the compilation of accounts or the collection of rents. In effect his role was supervisory rather than managerial. Where there was a conglomeration of small estates in close proximity to each other, an outside agent (usually, as already discussed, a solicitor or professional land agent) might be called in to oversee the whole on a part-time basis. The second type of estate was larger and usually employed a resident land agent to whom considerable authority was delegated. As these estates grew both in size and complexity or where several large properties formed a wider estate spread over several counties, they would also employ an agent-in-chief. In many cases this person was a barrister and often bore the title auditor as his main role was to examine and verify the accounts.[18] The delineation of the land agent was often blurred. Thomas Coke at Holkham Hall in Norfolk employed Francis Blaikie as a resident agent. William Castleman technically oversaw a number of different estates but in many respects was treated as and acted in the manner of a resident agent—his role surpassed the usual collection of rents and drawing up of leases. Anglesey employed two agents-in-chief across the timespan of this volume: firstly, John Sanderson and then Thomas Beer. Overall, they respected Castleman's opinions and only when asked did they provide advice on the day-to-day management.

Despite Castleman's standing and status in the area, like all men in prominent positions and many other land agents, he was not without his critics. An anonymous letter sent to the Marquis of Anglesey, while clustering together the stewards/agents past and present, effectively and emblematically illustrated the types of complaint which might be levied. The writer proclaimed:

> I think your Lordship would find great cause for complaint against some of your Lordship's Stewards … did I dare to presume to give my opinion to your Lordship it would be to place a man in that situation (but not a Lawyer) but one that is more on the spot and one who would be ready to hear anything that the Tenants has to say, and would be at hand to do anything that is wanting to be done that would strive in the utmost for your Lordships Interests without oppressing the Tenants.[19]

Not unsurprisingly given the tone of the letter, the author 'has a friend', a schoolmaster at Marnhull 'who is a good accountant', who would prove a good fit for the estate. In 1822 another anonymous letter complained that the distance at which,

> Mr Castleman resides from your Lordship's Property in Dorset and Somerset[20] the multiplicity of Business that he is engaged in as an Attorney and the several Stewardships he holds besides your Lordship it is impossible for him to strictly attend to your Lordship's property.[21]

In this instance, the charge was one of neglecting the buildings and farms to such an extent that the land agent was named as one of the key factors in their continued decay rather than making savings by undertaking repairs in a timely fashion. Like the previous writer, this one too had a solution, and the author advocated that he should be personally appointed stating: 'I would be happy to serve your Lordship for half what it now costs'.[22]

Despite these adverse reactions, Anglesey seems to have taken little notice of the insinuations made and Castleman remained firmly in place until his death in post in 1844. The depth of the trust and the strength of the relationship between the two men is evident throughout the estate correspondence with a myriad of comments from Anglesey such as 'I leave this to your discretion' or 'I leave the arrangement to you'. In 1820 Castleman's success resulted in an invitation to spend Christmas at Beaudesert, the Staffordshire home of Anglesey. In the end the request was turned down with a declaration of ill health. A further statement declared that estate duties entailed an unbreakable appointment at Milborne Port on 28 December to ward off any appeal against the recent change in the poor rate.[23] Acting in this manner assured Anglesey that his agent's priorities lay with the estate.

Finding an agent with the right type of financial acumen, knowledge and entrepreneurial spirit was important, but so too was honesty and the ability to work hard. Historians in the past have generalised over the extent and scope of the work undertaken by the land agent, often failing to look beyond rent collecting, leasing farms and compiling the accounts. In general, the historiography surrounding this group of men and the work they undertook is generalist, lacking both breadth and depth. Eric Jones argues that the generalisations of history are needed 'to sift the perpetual of recurrent from the transient or the exceptional'.[24] This thinking may have a basis where there is a considerable historiography, but a detailed and close history of the landed estate and its management remains in its infancy. We know far more about the individual lives of the owners of large landed estates than we do the management of the acres which paid for extravagant life-styles and the building and alteration of large country houses. Fortunately, there is a renewed interest in rural history and particularly in the work of the land agent and his place within the administration of the landed estates and the rural community.[25] This new history explores the extent and scope of the land agent beyond his more traditional roles, and nowhere is this more evident than when moving to non-agricultural forms of income.

Diversification of revenue streams was essential in the fragile economic climate which followed in the wake of the Napoleonic Wars when rental incomes and arrears fluctuated erratically. The Marquis of Anglesey's Dorset and Somerset estate had two main alternative forms of income—timber and stone. Even the underwood which grew in the spring and was gathered annually belonged to the landowner and had a price. Timber raised questions of customary rights over ownership. As seen in Chap. 4, it could easily become a source of tension, dissent and even riot as fuel-hungry tenants and the poor sought to take what they needed for their own purposes. The cost of transporting coal in the early nineteenth century meant that those in the south of England continued to rely on timber for cooking and warmth. The other main source of non-agrarian income came from stone. This had two benefits: firstly, the estate was able to draw on its own supply of good building stone keeping costs down; and, secondly, any surplus could be sold. In 1813, for example, the Stalbridge commissioners took 4787 loads of stone for the formation of new roads after the enclosure of Stalbridge Common.[26] The stone from Stalbridge was also used extensively in the housing race which took place at Milborne Port in 1819 and 1820 this helped to keep Anglesey's costs down compared to those of his opponent Lord Darlington.[27] Although useful, over the years these quarries proved problematic—they were prone to fraudulent activities and production was a stop–start affair.

The quarries had proven to be stubbornly unproductive and nonprofitable. The problem continued, and in 1817 it was suggested that the difficulty lay in the lack of sales beyond the estate boundaries, as most of the stone raised was sold only to Anglesey's tenants. This issue was not exclusive to these quarries but extended to all others in the county.[28] The estate contained three types of stone, wallston[e], paver and tile, and the amounts drawn are listed in the surviving quarry accounts for 1816. That said the accounts are extremely complicated, and different amounts were charged according to the type of tenant who was doing the purchasing (see Table 2.1).[29]

Even these prices are incomplete as lifehold tenants were to be supplied with the amount of stone they needed to be used on their premises and were to be charged the same as the tenants at rack rent. Furthermore, each type of stone had a different price and was recorded separately. It may well

Table 2.1 Prices per ton of stone from the estate's quarries

	Freeholders	*Anglesey's farms*
Tile	16s	7s 6d
Paver	6s 2d	3s 6d
Wallston[e]	1s 9d	1s 0d

have been this overexaggerated system of pricing that left the quarries open to regular fraudulent activities, and without careful supervision, it would have been easy to record paver and to charge for tile. In 1822 Castleman wrote to Anglesey: 'The person who held these Quarries have in spite of all the regulations I could suggest [has] been guilty of frauds'.[30] Finally in 1836, a solution to these long-term problems seemed to have been found. Elias Duffett was employed as manager of the quarries at Stalbridge and Harpits. His duties among other things included attending both quarries twice a day. At each he was expected to keep an account of the quantity and quality of stone raised, to know where the stone was sold and delivered, have a grasp of the prices charged and then to procure the money from the sale.

To assert at least some form of managerial influence over this troublesome section of the estate, Duffett was ordered to produce weekly accounts that detailed the amounts of stone sold, the names of the labourers and any others employed as well as a list of the wages each received. The labourers were paid weekly, and one from each quarry was to accompany the manager to 'verify and certify' the amount delivered. Weights were also clearly defined whereby a pot load of stone 'ought to be a ton weight'. The price was fixed to this measurement and care should be taken not to exceed this amount.[31] Ultimately profitability was essential and, it would not need more than a small extra amount to be added to each pot load to affect remunerations. The amounts of stone which might be sold to the tenants in a six-month period can be seen in Table 2.2.[32]

The quarries had an extra benefit and could be used as a means of employing surplus labour and keeping them off the parish. In 1835, for example, a 'bumper' harvest had caused the price of grain to tumble, and tenant farmers had once again begun to turn their agricultural labourers off the land. To ease the situation albeit slightly, Castleman ordered that a few paupers out of employ, but not exceeding five might be given employment on a 'pauper scale of wages' in the quarries. There were several caveats added to this agreement; for example, should anyone in this group

Table 2.2 Monies received into the stone account July 1816 to January 1817

Stone supplied for the use of farms	*Stone sold to life holders*	*Stone sold to freeholders*
£36 2s 9d	£13 17s 3d	£36 15 9s

neglect their work, they might be instantly discharged. The amount of stone raised should not exceed that which might be used within a year as too much stone on the market would, firstly, depress prices and, secondly, 'encumber' the land on which it was allowed to lie.[33] Alternatives to agriculture could thus provide both long- and short-term forms of employment whereby pauper labourers might be put to work. This would in turn ease financial pressures elsewhere particularly in terms of the poor rate and put idle hands and minds to work.

The financial health of the landed estate often lay in the ability of its managers to think not just about farming but to diversify and use the full extent of the estate's assets. This meant that the land agent often needed to develop an expanding knowledge of non-agricultural process which could stave off economic depression. Sometimes this meant getting to grips with all the processes surrounding the mining of coal and other minerals. In the south of England, this was less of an issue, but there is no doubt that William Castleman had to look at where he might exploit the resources the estate had within its boundaries. At the same time, there was a growing political awareness among the electorate, and this meant that land agents needed a wide and broad understanding of politics at both national and regional levels. This will be discussed in greater depth in Chap. 5. Despite the widening of rural interest and the need for new skills, old attributes such as finding and keeping tenants remained important and the leasing of property at the core of good estate management.

Leasing Property

In the fragile economy of the first half of the nineteenth century, landowners as seen above sought to maximise estate income. The most obvious way to do this was to ensure that empty properties were let quickly and good tenants offered incentives to stay.[34] In order for the system to work, it depended upon landowners with considerable wealth, who could provide the tenant farmers with both security and the freedom to make the most of their farms.[35] That said, husbandry clauses and covenants in leases which laid out certain specifics were not uncommon.[36] Landlords were expected to invest their capital into their estates and it was generally assumed that they would not be excessively greedy in clawing back monies from any profits even though these were relied on to provide an extravagant life-style and public persona. Even when landowners were not particularly wealthy or had financial problems as did the Marquis of Anglesey, these were meant to be hidden. An appearance of wealth was necessary even if it at times hid a crumbling empire.[37] Despite the seemingly symbiotic sharing of the risk of farming, historians such as Richard Hoyle have argued that the relationship between landowner and tenant farmers was asymmetric. Principally without enough tenants, a landowner had two choices: firstly, to take the empty farm in hand, either farming it himself or paying his land agent to do so on his behalf which would have been expensive or, secondly, leaving the land idle. While the latter method cost little, it did mean that if too many farms fell into this category, then estate income would fall dramatically. Spending considerable sums of money on maintaining estates meant that landowners sought skilled farmers as tenants who would keep the land in good heart and continue to improve their holdings. Likewise those seeking farms were anxious to find first-rate holdings and would not be prepared to spend their capital without the opportunity of making a profit on their initial investment.[38] In return for their commitment, tenants expected their landowner to act as banker whereby he lent sums of money in poor years not as cash payments but in the form of rent accruals, deferment of rent payments and even writing off certain debts or even agreed amounts of outstanding rent. The subject of rental arrears and the impact on both the estate and tenants will be discussed again in Chap. 3. Increasingly there was a requirement for tenants who had both skill and capital. Immediately after the Napoleonic Wars continuing until the mid-1830s, there were episodic periods of poor prices and economic recession. Thus, finding men who could weather these periods of economic downturn while continuing to meet their financial commitments was essential.[39] At the same time, there was a growing discussion around the way in which land was let and the length of the ideal lease.

The well-known agricultural writer Arthur Young, in his *General View of the Agriculture of the County of Norfolk*, advocated that improvements in this county in the latter half of the eighteenth and the early nineteenth centuries were the result of granting 21-year leases.[40] William Marshall too argues that the granting of leases for a reasonable period of years encouraged improvements, while rack renting had the opposite effect. Landowners who refused to issue longer tenancies were often condemned. Young, however, suggested that the impact of renting from year to year could be obviated if the landlord included a clause which guaranteed to reimburse the tenant for any enhancement of the land or buildings.[41] By 1800, while several types of lease were in use, few farm leases ran for more than 14 years.[42] Renting out land in the post-Napoleonic Wars period was not a simple affair, and as will be seen below, a mixture of rental agreements might exist within one estate. Thomas Coke at Holkham Hall was renowned for the granting of long leases within which were strict husbandry and crop rotation covenants although this was not the case everywhere. J. D. Chambers and Gordon Mingay advocate that the significance of leases has been overexaggerated. Even when farms were rented on a yearly basis, tenants rarely felt insecure. In general, larger farms were rented formally as the value of the property meant that both landowner and tenant wanted a more official and prescribed definition of their respective duties and rights.[43]

To some extent there was a pattern to the way in which land was rented. Long leases, thus, tended to wane in periods of rapidly changing prices because one party would benefit at the expense of the other. For example, in a period of rising prices, the landlord might find his farms rented well below market price, while in a time of falling prices, a tenant could find himself paying out sums well in excess of current land values. Leases did, however, mean that during periods of severe economic depression, landowners could keep tenants on their farms especially if the land owner offered rate abatements, allowed arrears to amass or even granted a reduction in sums outstanding.[44] Rack renting or tenants-at-will meant the farm or property was taken on a year-to-year basis with the rent assessed at the present market value. Those who rented property in this way did not have the security of tenure provided by a lease, and the incumbent could technically be evicted at any time, particularly if the circumstances of the holding or landlord changed.[45] This insecurity was not necessarily damaging to either party nor did it increase tenant turnover. David Stead suggests that there were three main reasons why mobility remained low amongst those who took up farming on these terms. Firstly, a sense of patronage endowed many landowners with an inbuilt idea of social responsibility. Anyone who wished to keep their reputation as a 'good landlord' would not attempt to interfere with established farming families on his estate. Secondly, if a farmer voted and maintained political support for a preferred electoral candidate, then his co-operation in preserving the *status quo* was invaluable. Finally, long-standing sitting tenants had a mass of local knowledge relating to the soil and had acquired a range of business contacts that would take an incoming tenant time to build from scratch. These men thus possessed considerable advantages which together acted as barriers to entry and might prove insurmountable to anyone seeking to take over a given property.[46]

There was a third form of rental which was in common use during the period covered by this book and these were copyhold or 'lifeleaseholds'. Christopher Clay argues that there was a regional split in tenurial patterns whereby in the east and midlands, land was either rack rented, or leases were granted for a short fixed period. To the west of the Pennines, extending south from the Peak District through the middle of the Thames Valley down to the Solent, the most frequently used method was lifeleaseholds. This type of tenure meant the tenant purchased their tenancy by payment of a lump sum or fine, but consequent rental payments were set at a small percentage of their true value. This type of lease essentially equated to 99 years determinable on the three lives named which were usually those of the tenant, his wife and his eldest son. In practice this bought a lifetime of security for the tenant and his family. New names were frequently added upon payment of an agreed sum of money, and only when the leaseholder had no apparent heirs to top up the lease would it cease and fall into hand.[47] Typically, properties let in this way were small; for example, Shadrach Hannon was granted a lifehold on a dwelling house, barn, stable and a paddock of one acre, three roods and seven poles at Charlton Horethorne for which a fine of £155 was paid for three lives; rent was five shillings.[48] Other entries are not so detailed but do give a sense of the names and ages of those who appeared on these leases. In 1823 Elias Duffett was charged £30 for adding one life, which allowed himself, his son aged 34, and his grandchildren, respectively, 2 and 3, to appear on the lease. Likewise James Dike named his sons Thomas Dike 32, William Dike 16 and Fred Dike 9 on his lifeleasehold. On this occasion for adding the three lives he was charged £45. This system could provide useful additional income especially when rental income was slow in being paid. The amounts collected in fines could be substantial; for example, in November 1825, Castleman sent 16 leases to the Marquis of Anglesey for execution, the fines for which amounted to some £850 10s 0d.[49] Renting properties with small acreages in this way brought in a lesser rental, but the monies paid up front were a serious financial consideration and underpinned the decision-making process.

Renting properties (even small ones) as lifeleaseholds had a cost. A sense of what was involved appears in a letter to Mr. Lowe, a London barrister who provided legal advice to the estate. Firstly, it had to be ascertained what the property would fetch on the open market so that the fine might be fixed and the rent set.[50] Secondly, the ages of the lives needed to be taken into consideration and an enquiry into their health undertaken. Should this reveal that either the proposed life was ill or old, then a decision had to be taken on whether to allow this person's inclusion or to increase significantly the fine charged. This is unsurprising since it was likely an extra cost would be incurred if the revaluation had to be carried out again within a short period. Once the investigation had been concluded, terms were submitted to the tenant so that, if necessary, a discussion could take place between the two parties. It was worth the effort on the part of the tenant because it could 'occasionally induce some abatement in the Fines originally fixed' if he could persuade the land agent and estate of the efficacy of such an abatement.[51] The very high fines which could be raised led Castleman to comment, 'compared to former removals will shew the advantage which have occurred to Lord Anglesey by the Plans I have adopted in this respect'.[52] There was of course an element of trust involved in the process, and he further stated:

> ... if I were inclined to abuse the trust confided to me I should of course adapt my report to answer my own purposes, and neither Lord Anglesey nor Mr Sanderson could detect the fraud on paper, or without an actual examination by someone over me.[53]

In other words, any discrepancies in the monies received and those sent to Anglesey could easily be hidden by an unscrupulous agent.

Farms at least on this estate were let for a number of years which according to William Stevenson was typical for this part of England.[54] Although he surmised that the usual term was seven years, there does not seem to have been any hard or fast rules. Amongst Castleman's papers are leases for eight, six and twelve years with break clauses at various intervals. A similar process to that applied to leaseholds was undertaken when reletting farms, where as part of the process each was 'carefully surveyed and valued' and compared with the field books.[55] Henry Taylor in 1816 invoiced the estate £2 5s 6d for surveying the dilapidations on estates at Stalbridge and Stalbridge Weston which had recently been vacated.[56] Tenant farmers understood their worth, and in the difficult economic climate of the post-war period, the challenge for both parties was to fix a farm rent which was of financial benefit to all. There was, however, within the framework of the landowner–tenant relationship, a game to be played. No landowner or land agent would give in easily to demands for lower rents, even though the tenant might retreat victorious at the end. It was not unusual David Hainsworth argues for tenants to deliberately create delays as their lease became due for renewal, in the hope of gaining an advantage at the negotiating table.[57] The idea was to ensure that the season had advanced too far for another tenant to take up the farm, as they would start well behind with the required annual work.[58] Tenants would then attempt to set their own terms. The evidence suggests that neither Anglesey nor Castleman was a greedy man. Anglesey simply wanted 'the worth of the land' and 'not more than it is worth'.[59] The land agent was of course expected to gain the best possible price, but the level of rent should be such that the tenant received 'a reasonable remuneration for his [risk] and skill and the interest of his Capital'.[60] This did not, however, stop the tenants questioning the sums paid and to act defiantly by threatening to quit their farms.

Little is known about the ways in which tenants used their own agency to negotiate new lease agreements. An symbolic example of this process, however, was illustrated by Withers who was more than prepared to take advantage of the weak position of the Dorset and Somerset estate in 1823 to improve his own financial position. Waiting until almost the end of his lease, he suggested that his rent should be permanently reduced from £588 12s 0d to £243 4s 0d per annum,[61] a discounted figure of more than 50 per cent. Although Castleman was a proficient estate manager, this was beyond his remit and so he took the case to Anglesey himself. Expecting an outburst, he cautioned that in light of the current economic climate, Withers might be justified in asking for such an enormous reduction. Importantly, his standing as a farmer was impeccable, and he had a reputation for reliably paying his rent in full and on time. Despite an acceptance of Withers skills, there could be no recommendation for accepting the sums offered without first attempting 'to realise a higher rent', even if it meant finding someone else.[62] Realistically the discount requested was simply too high and would set a dangerous precedent and cause a chain reaction of similar demands. In the end, it was determined that Withers would be offered a decrease in rent of 25 per cent, and if he refused to accept, then a new tenant would be sought, and the farm advertised accordingly. The threat of losing the farm was enough and Withers signed a new lease agreement.

A further consequence of Withers' presumptive move was to arouse a sense of injustice in the Marquis of Anglesey. In a fit of pique, he declared a 'great dislike to leases' and argued that this type of tenant provided no advantage to the landowner; instead they expected him to pay for a larger percentage of repairs, the rents were less, and there were always greater amounts of rent arrears.[63] Consequently, Anglesey demanded that no more leases were to be issued at the present time. Disillusionment with leases was not uncommon, and they eventually became synonymous with slovenly farming. It was assumed that those with long leases would only carry out enough work to pay the rent and no more. This was not an opinion shared by Castleman who rejected Anglesey's order stating that such refusal was 'at least with regards to the Dorset and Somerset Tenants erroneous'.[64] He argued that those who were looking at taking a lease at this point are 'generally anxious to secure long terms'. This type of move would limit the estate's options and make it impossible to find and keep a 'good and responsible farmer on a holding from year to year'.[65] Leases allowed the insertion of repair covenants which legally bound the tenant to undertake any works as detailed. This had led to the opposite of Anglesey's assumptions and saved the estate according to his agent considerable expense. In the case of rack renting, any outstanding improvements or failure to comply with husbandry clauses could only be enforced through resorting to the legal process. In this instance, Castleman's tenacity won the day and leases continued to be issued throughout Anglesey's ownership. The methods chosen to contract a tenant varied according to the individual, their capital, the prevailing land values and the size of the farm. It was not simply a case of drawing up a lease and setting a rent, land needed to be valued and the level of yearly payment set so that the estate made profit, but not so high that the tenant would run into difficulty. In periods of settled prices and land values, this was a relatively simple process but when these fluctuated wildly as they did in the first half of the nineteenth century, getting it right was far more complicated. The estate needed to be careful, for the downside of misreading the fiscal situation could be costly and profitability seriously affected. Of all the roles undertaken, finding the right tenant and ensuring the appropriate contract was drawn up was and remained the most important role of the land agent.

Financial and Rental Records

As the management of estates became increasingly delegated, landowners needed to be able to check on the activities of their land agents, while at the same time, the agent needed some means of recording the various transactions which came within their remit, so that they became more accountable. An estate which was mainly agricultural would only have a limited range of transactions in any given year. Rents would have to be collected, while outgoings for improvements and repairs, the occasional property purchases, taxes and other costs needed to be paid. At their most basic estate accounts are statements of receipts and payments made by the estate's official presenting the account. If the official had more than one area under their management, then accounts could combine transactions relating to different aspects of the estate.[66] Historians have criticised these accounts for a variety of reasons; F. M. L. Thompson comments on the accounts of the house steward in Wentworth Woodhouse who confused 'the consumption of oats by racehorses' with the 'wages to coal-miners'. In effect Thompson argues that the steward was thus able to hide his real financial situation from the landowner, but it balanced his own accounts.[67] Frequently when separate men were employed to do different roles, their accounts were filed separately and it would then be left to the owner or the agent-in-chief to draw these together and make some comment on the financial health of the estate.[68] Annoyingly many rental accounts record the amounts paid but fail to give the acreage of each farm as on this estate. It is therefore often impossible to know the rent per acre for individual plots or how it rose or fell over time. Even when acreage is known, there is little sense of whether it is meadow, pasture or arable land or even if the price varied from village to village. A perfect example of this is a general summary which the estate compiled as part of the sale documents in 1844 which gives simply the locality, the acreage owned by Anglesey, and the net rental received. The best that can be achieved is an average rental for each part of the estate in shillings per acre. See Table 2.3.[69]

Table 2.3 Average rental value in shillings per acre

Name of estate	*Acreage*	*Net rental*	*Values*	*Net rental per acre in shillings*
Stalbridge	3937	6676	229,081	34
Charlton Horethorne	1255	1920	59,224	31
Henstridge	446	655	21,905	30
Templecombe	266	456	14,370	34
Kington and Nyland	418	662	20,480	30
Todber	124	218	6854	15
Stour Provost	142	306	9227	43
Bradford Abbas	952	1740	60,869	37
Hanley	3034	2144	66,993	14
Gussage St Michael	1255	1114	33,453	17
	11,829	15,891	522,456	

Overall, it seems that the estate retained 11,385 acres at an approximate value of £522,504.[70] Michael Turner, John Beckett and Bethany Afton estimate that the average rental per acre in the mid-1830s was around 20s per acre, so these figures seem somewhat high. When compared, however, to the abstract of rental for 1844 and the half year's rents due, there is not a vast difference between the two suggesting that these are a reasonable reflection of estate income.[71] Accounting for the *c.*£12,000 per annum meant that maintaining accounts in a well-organised manner mattered. A responsible agent needed to be able to track how and where monies were spent and was answerable for any mistakes. Indeed, it was not unusual for an agent to be held personally answerable for any errors.

A steward or agent's accounts were regarded as his accounts even they were devoted entirely to his master's affairs. The income was a 'liability' in that any excess needed to be handed over to the landowner and all outgoings on behalf of the estate were seen as a 'credit' which represented sums for which he and in the event of his death his estate would be liable.[72] In some respects accounting practices were symbolic of the relationship and trust between the landowner and agent as discussed in the Introduction. Invariably all the income from the estate passed through the hands of the steward or agent. It could then be sent directly to his employer in London, deposited in his London bank or used to pay the myriad expenses which the estate incurred. Quite often expenditure on the estate itself was relatively small, but large expenses could be incurred during a housebuilding programme, the rebuilding and repairs of farmhouses, outbuilding or as at Milborne Port in a housing race with Lord Darlington (see Chap. 5).[73] As the agent was expected to meet all overheads from the estate income, this could create problems. Many landowners at some point must have suspected their agents of 'feathering their own nests' either by speculating with their employer's cash or overtly stealing money. There is no doubt that agents had within their remit large amounts of ready money and needed to store these safely.[74] Accounts were audited by the landowner or agent-in-chief, but it could still be several years or more before a problem came to light especially if the agent failed to produce adequate detail within his accounts. In this instance it might only be when an agent was removed that the full extent of any fraud was discovered.

Contemporary writers offered advice on how to keep estate accounts. John Loudon advised '*Clearness and brevity* constitute the excellence of accounts, and these excellencies are only to be obtained by simplicity of method'.[75] He stressed that the groundwork of estate accounts should be the rent roll and from this the receiving rentals should be taken, and when combined with the miscellaneous receipts and disbursement, an 'account current' should be made out annually. John Mordant recommended that no one should consider taking the office of steward without being well qualified in 'arithmetic, book-keeping, architecture, hydraulicks, mathematicks and mechanics &c'.[76] By far and away, the most comprehensive information on the successful keeping of accounts was written in 1806 by John Lawrence.[77] He argued that the first objects should be arrangement, perspicuity and security. He advised all 'memorandums of payment, receipt, bargain, agreement', and so on should be made instantly; no monies should be paid 'without a discharge' and 'no security, agreement, lease or valuable paper' should be issued or lent without a written agreement. Transactions should be entered under appropriate headings and nothing should be left for more than a week. As little as possible should be trusted to memory or accident. All papers should be dated and the most valuable stored securely and at the end of the year bundled together and kept apart from any others.[78] Lawrence did not propose any 'precise *general* plan' but instead suggested the best way forward was to keep a set of books that followed a customary and regular pattern, for example, the keeping of a journal, ledger, a memorandum ledger and a general inventory. Each had a separate but interlinked function; the journal formed the book of reference and within it every transaction must be listed; the ledger should contain details of all the debtors, tenants and creditors of any consequence. The memorandum ledger was to have an alphabet and act as an artificial memory. The general inventory although likewise paged should be a detailed account of the estate's property and contain the quantity of land, amount of rent, length of lease and the tenant's name.[79] Above all administration should be logically ordered. As rents were collected in cash, there was the potential for fraudulent activity; but written records helped the landowner to keep a check on the honesty, reliability and integrity of his agents.[80]

In essence the basic form of accounting had changed little from that used in the Middle Ages, and the charge and discharge account method remained commonplace during the first half of the nineteenth century.[81] This system entailed the preparation and compilation of periodic accounting statements which showed the monies collected and how these sums had been spent as well as the surplus which was remitted to the landowner. By the sixteenth century, these accounts were presented in a 'bilateral form' whereby the charge was on the left-hand side and the discharge on the right which was a consequence of the growing number of entries. Charge and discharge accounts entailed charging the steward or agent with receipts for the goods and services rendered and then discharging the charge through the receipts for cash, good and services rendered. Often this method was viewed as a good indicator of the skills of an agent in managing the property, especially as the arrears of rent often remained as a charge against him until paid.[82] William Baxter's explanation is perhaps one of the simplest to grasp as he likened this system to a sandwich whereby the opening and closing amounts formed the outer layers and the cash account the filling.[83] This was in essence a simplistic form of record-keeping and could be effected even in illiterate societies by the use of an 'exchequer'.[84] The final statement of account formed the apex and allowed both owner and agent to assess the monies available for repairs, improvements and possible leeway in rental abatements. In practice, however, estate accounts were often simply 'elaborate cash accounts' presented annually. William Castleman used a form of charge and discharge accounts and was not unusual in doing so.

There were two annual sets of accounts compiled and these matched the audits at Lady Day and Michaelmas, the former being an interim report and the latter a more complex record of the business of the estate. In practice the estate vouchers were synthesised into one simple sum, and entered into the accounts, often the work of one builder in a locality being linked together. The estate vouchers which are numerous contain the detail of, for example, the weight of nails used, the yardage of timber or the payments of a few shillings for providing information on Milborne Port or watching a tenant who might be in danger of absconding. There has been little or no research undertaken on the contents of estate vouchers most likely because of the sheer depth of detail they contain or their numerousness. For this estate alone, there are more than 10,000, and the time needed to cross-reference every single one would be enormous. They have been used in this volume to add an extra layer of understanding to monies spent and to compare against entries in the accounts themselves. The rental accounts as will be seen below are problematic in a different way.

The seminal work on agricultural rent remains the study by Michael Turner, John Beckett and Bethanie Afton. They argue that while the business of paying rent was a matter for landlord, agent and tenant, it in effect acted as a guide to the financial health of the estate, community and the nation.[85] During the nineteenth century, no tax return was required, and thus we know little about how rents were assessed, the methods of payment, the techniques for agreeing rent abatements or even why some tenants were evicted and others were not.[86] Ideas about how tenants negotiated their leases have already been discussed above in the case of Withers. There is nothing to suggest that other tenants did not take the same approach. Rental accounts are problematic especially if trying to establish trends. Turner, Beckett and Afton selected their archives carefully, initially isolating around 200 which merited further investigation to establish the quality of the source. About a third were rejected due to a lack of adequate long rental series which included survey material containing acreages. A further 15 per cent contained land let under archaic tenures, and 3 per cent contain rentals where it was impossible to separate agricultural and non-agricultural uses.[87] Another 7 per cent were discarded because it would have been simply too time-consuming to extract the data. There were numerous reasons as to why other accounts were rejected. The Dorset and Somerset accounts would have been excluded from the study for all the above reasons especially as there contain no acreage or size of the farms. While they give an indication of the arrears outstanding and the amount of rent due, they do not state how much is paid, although they contain the level of arrears outstanding on audit day, but if these are paid at a later stage, the sums are not recorded.

Trying to match land tax to rental income is difficult on this estate. In some cases, the tenant paid all of it, in others Anglesey shared the cost, or the tenant might pay the land tax on the tithe. In some of the accounts, the land tax paid is recorded and in others not. It might be possible to trace the land tax paid through the estate vouchers which in some years record that paid by the tenants. This too presents further problems as the estate vouchers are less abundant after 1846. While there are many drawbacks to using the accounts, they do serve one useful purpose, and that is to explore the health of the estate itself. Each contains an abstract of rental which details the amount of rent with any outstanding arrears due and the arrears remaining after the audit. For example, see Fig. 2.1.[88]

It is then possible to ascertain that the estate was in the process of recovery in the latter part of the 1820s as rental arrears begin to steadily decline. They rise again in 1829 as the coathe, which is examined in Chap. 4, began to affect the tenant farmers. Although rental arrears rise again in 1830, they do not reach the exceptional levels of 1821, and in fact by 1831, these are falling again. While the Swing Riots were to impact on the

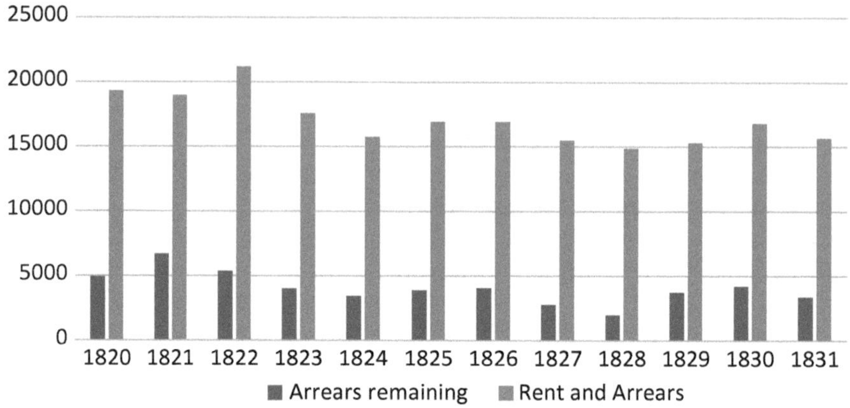

Fig. 2.1 Rents and arrears assessed and arrears remaining at Michaelmas 1820–1831

estate in 1830, from these figures, the fiscal well-being of the estate was if anything in better shape. For the family historian, the accounts list all the tenants within a given area and with the use of the census would provide useful cross-linkage into the effect of agricultural depression on the local community.

The rental accounts like those rejected by Turner, Beckett and Afton do not aid in assessing the amount of rent charged per acre for individual farms nor assist in exploring local trends in rental income. A single surviving document, however, illustrates how the estate set its terms for rack rentals for at least one tenant. At Gussage farm it was determined that the rent would be ascertained by taking the average price of wheat in the County of Dorset at each quarter day. This would then be used against the expected yield for the farm. For example, on a farm under a four-field system when 120 acres out of 750 were planted with wheat that yielded 15 bushels per acre at £13 per load this would produce a rental of £585.[89] The accounts are despite all their issues still an important indication of the financial health of the estate and can be used to explore the indebtedness of tenants which can be assessed against known downfalls in prices. For the land agent, the accounts were an indication of his success in collecting rents and a marker to the quality and efficiency of his management. In this instance, the vouchers contain all the minutiae which are then compiled into one record. The agent-in-chief checked both and was able to use the two as a way of checking the honesty, thoroughness and competence of the local agent. In this sense they played an important role in the fiscal maintenance of an absentee estate. No matter how robust an estate might seem, disaster could still loom around the corner especially when the landowner was himself heavily in debt. As seen in the Introduction, Anglesey inherited his father's perilous financial situation which was exacerbated by a range of factors. It is possible that without William Castleman's ability to raise substantial sums of money, the estate would have been sold off much earlier and in a poorer economic climate.

Mortgages

From the eighteenth century onwards, as a result of the introduction of strict settlement, the aristocracy were able to raise mortgages for specified family purposes. At the same time, there was a growth in the credit available for this sort of lending. Some of the cash came from institutions, some through private London banks who were prepared and indeed did make considerable mortgage advances or who might instead issue bonds to landowners. The majority, however, came from private lenders and significant sums through local country attorneys; often the individual lenders remain shadowy figures and are frequently unknown and thus missing from the archives.[90] Other factors which influenced and facilitated the rise in available credit stemmed from the lowering of interest rates, the early formation of insurance companies, the evolution of a provincial mortgage market and the professionalisation of land management.[91] Historians have suggested that most of this borrowing was used for the funding of short-term debts owed to tradesmen, gambling liabilities, the financing of personal extravagance and for the use of younger members of the family. The cost of maintaining an aristocratic life-style was expensive, and many including the Marquis of Anglesey found it difficult to remain debt free. Consequently, this was a common and accepted feature of life for the aristocracy during this period. As seen throughout this volume, income and expenditure in the early nineteenth century could fluctuate but rarely met together in the middle, and consequently borrowing money was often the only way to reconcile the situation. Not all landowners continued to accrue debts, and some such as the Duke of Portland at Welbeck Abbey in Nottinghamshire and Thomas Coke at Holkham in Norfolk were able to significantly reduce the amounts they owed. In general, the problem of indebtedness remained a problem for many landed families. It is impossible to know the true levels of the monies owed collectively by the aristocracy, as this was not something the landowners were eager to publish, and much of this information remains buried in private and public archives.

While landowners were able to borrow money more freely, F. M. L. Thompson advocates that little if any of the sums were used to improve the income-producing capacity of an estate.[92] In the beginning mortgages had been for six months only, the title of the property was transferred to the lender, but the borrower could claim back his property by paying the principal sum as long as the interest was paid when it became due.[93] Missing an interest payment could be risky as the lender could claim the land as their own. The development of the mortgage Martin Daunton argues helped to facilitate the switch from selling leases and copyholds to tenants for a large single sum in return for a nominal annual payment to rack renting.[94] As seen above, fines added substantial monies to an estate's yearly turnover and could assist in maintaining profitability when money was in short supply. The benefits of being able to raise credit separate to the estate had two main consequences: firstly, it provided a means of easing financial hardship caused by the temporary reduction in cash flow during the transitional period as an estate moved to rack rents. Secondly, landowners with a large portfolio of properties were able to gain the competitive edge in the land market, and this meant that they were able to continue to make further purchases without substantially reducing estate capital. From the early eighteenth century onwards, as land values began to rise, the largest landowners found they were able to borrow significant sums of money using their appreciating assets as security and the means to service their debts more easily.[95] Country attorneys often had clients with large sums of disposable monies ready to invest. Monies lent against a first charge on a substantial estate were seen by most as a safe investment. Although interest rates (which will be discussed in greater detail below) were not huge, they produced a steady return for those seeking a regular income.[96]

The Marquis of Anglesey as seen in the Introduction inherited alongside his estates the high levels of debt accumulated firstly by his father and secondly by the phenomenal cost of his divorce. Despite an income of *c.*£76,200 per annum from his estates in Anglesey, Staffordshire, Dorset and Somerset, it was not enough to cover his expenditure, and he continued to amass further debts. Fortunately, his land agent as a local solicitor and one of the owners of a small bank in Wimborne, Dorset, was perfectly placed to use his own assets and networks to bolster Anglesey's finances through the raising of mortgages and loans. As already stated, working out aristocratic indebtedness is difficult, and Anglesey is no exception and only a sense of the sums outstanding is possible. At the centre of the process at least in the south was William Castleman, not only in procuring monies but also in the monitoring and payment of interest. Whilst the essence of these debts is available in the correspondence and accounts, none of the legal documents have yet come to light. Those snippets of information which have survived reveal large levels of borrowing and a situation further complicated by his eldest son Lord Uxbridge who revealed before his second marriage in 1833 that he owed in excess of £100,000. Neither the agent-in-chief John Sanderson nor Mr. Lowe the London barrister who legally advised the estate on occasions had a full idea of the extent of the monies owed by their employer. This lack of understanding by those who were ultimately responsible for the financial health of the estate goes a long way to explaining why there is so little understanding of the extent of the problem of aristocratic indebtedness

The clearest indications of Uxbridge's financial problems are found in a letter early in 1833 from Mr. Lowe. He stated 'I had not until a day or two ago received communication in regard to them [Uxbridge's debts] by which I could ascertain with any degree of accuracy their amount'.[97] In fact the situation was far worse than anyone had estimated, and Lowe believed that the aggregate of monies owed would not be less than £100,000, which was far beyond what Anglesey himself had supposed. The Dorset and Somerset estate in which Anglesey had a life interest and with remainder to Lord Uxbridge in fee were the obvious place from which to find the ways and means to pay off the monies which each man owed. By using this estate, it was supposed that it would be possible for them to retain the bulk of the Staffordshire and Welsh lands. Lowe calculated that the total amount of existing liabilities and incumbrances by 'mortgage, bond or otherwise' affecting the two men was around £556,000.[98] Interest payable on this sum amounted to £23,352 per annum with an average interest rate of approximately 4 per cent. This level of annual expenditure was prohibitive and more than the entire income of the Dorset and Somerset estate. Unfortunately, these were not the only monies outgoing as further payments of £4000 were paid to Lord Uxbridge, £1000 to the Duchess of Argyll (Anglesey's first wife) and sundry others. Allowances to Anglesey's sons and unmarried daughters and the salaries of agents but excluding servant's wages or payments incidental to any of the domestic establishments amounted to at least a further £1264.[99] This meant that annually Anglesey had to find some £36,000.[100] Lowe was worried because Lord Uxbridge's debts now exceeded his entire annual income, and that if the situation continued, it would add to the already complicated condition of his father's affairs. For Anglesey the only way forward, it seemed, was to resort to further loans, but the state of the property Lowe argued would render this solution impracticable. The only sensible answer he argued was to sell off the Dorset and Somerset estate, and this would at least give Anglesey and Uxbridge a means of reducing their debts.[101] Further loans and mortgages were taken out by Anglesey and Uxbridge, and the details of these lie amongst the sale details compiled in 1846. Uxbridge had secured £25,000 from Drummonds Bank secured by an assignment of his rent charge of £3000 per annum on the Stalbridge estate during the joint lives of himself and his father.[102] A further £15,000 had been borrowed from Colonel Vernon Graham, £16,000 by Sir Edward Paget and £6000 by Sir Edward Paget and Reverend H. E. Paget. Perhaps the largest of all the loans was the mortgage to the Earl of Orkney for some £50,000 secured on the entire Dorset and Somerset estate.[103] To add to Lord Uxbridge's already miserable financial situation, tradesmen and others were clamouring to be paid and only remained quiet because Anglesey's representatives had reassured them they would be paid quickly. What is abundantly clear is the estate was used by both father and son as a means of ready cash. This southern outpost was perhaps the most expendable and therefore the easiest to risk if the financial crises which threatened overwhelmed them.

The debts of neither Anglesey nor Uxbridge were unusual; others including the Sneyds of Keele Hall, the Earls of Scarborough and the Lords of Hatherton all increased their encumbrances during the nineteenth century. The Bute's mortgages on their Welsh and English estates had surpassed more than £500,000 by the 1870s, and the Dukes of Devonshire's debts rose from £500,000 to more than two million between 1800 and the 1880s.[104] The rising level of debt within the Marquis of Anglesey's family ensured that William Castleman was constantly on the lookout for funds. He was not above lending his own money although he expected a decent rate of return. The Michaelmas accounts for 1821 record a mortgage to him of £8000 and in 1822 an interest payment for the half year of £200 or an interest rate of 5 per cent per annum. Irene Jones has estimated that altogether he lent £34,750 and the annual interest rose to £695.[105] Besides his agency work for Anglesey, Castleman also worked for the Bankes family, and in 1825 he arranged a loan from this source of some £10,000. The monies were to be used to purchase property from Lord Darlington who had mounted a political challenge on the borough of Milborne Port; this is taken up again in Chap. 5. At the time of the initial negotiations, the procurement price had not been settled and consequently the final purchase monies amounted to only £5902, considerably less than had been anticipated. Bankes, however, point blank refused to reduce the loan sum, sticking to the original agreement. Castleman as ever carefully recorded in his correspondence Mr. Bankes 'advanced on Lord Anglesey's and my note £4,500' and 'Lord Anglesey £3000 in further part of Mr Bankes's loan' as the securities were not at that time completed and in place. A small balance of £2500 remained. In order to pay Mr. Vizard's bill, Anglesey had advanced his land agent £1500 from Drummonds and this was repaid. Despite this loan and the myriad of others, Castleman was still needed to raise further sums of money, this time amongst his own clients, and he estimated that another £6000 could be readily available. Two temporary loans he had personally advanced in the summer of £1000 and £3000 had swallowed all his spare personal cash and he had no further funds available.[106]

Anglesey and his son's financial situation was further compromised in 1826 when Castleman asked for his temporary loans to be repaid, so he himself could complete his own purchase at Hartwell in Northamptonshire. By February of this year, he held mortgages for £12,250 and £4000 on the Henstridge properties. Having already purchased the tithes at Hartwell, land that had been created as part of a parliamentary act of enclosure in the village had come on to the market. The Commissioner who had made the original purchase on Castleman's behalf was now in negotiation for other tranches of land. He thus wrote to Anglesey stating that 'if affected will much improve my property there'. The first acquisition had been less than a £1000, but he now needed upwards of £3000 for the second purchase, and for this it was necessary to break into the mortgage. He intended to reduce the original £16,250 loan to £15,000 and would take a note from Anglesey for the remaining £1250. Although the money was needed urgently, he was aware of the difficulties this request might create and stated that if really necessary, he could try and raise the monies elsewhere.[107]

The struggle with cash flow remained high on the agenda. In March of 1826, the promised securities for the Bankes loan mentioned above had still not been completed. This was proving challenging especially as at the time Castleman was 'ignorant' of the overall debt owed by Anglesey and would have been even less aware of Lord Uxbridge's debts. Furthermore he was becoming increasingly desperate for the repayment of the sums owing to him so he could complete the purchase at Hartwell. The delay had been beneficial, however, as the amounts needed to procure Hartwell had crystallised to £5000, and this it was suggested could be found out of the imminent sale of Clifton.[108] Over the course of the following year, further significant mortgages were obtained on behalf of his employer. By the beginning of April 1827, new agreements and securities had been completed on one £10,000 loan, and another for £4000 was expected to be finalised within a short period of time. There was a suggestion that another £15,000 might be raised from other clients although Anglesey might have to consider a slightly higher interest rate of four and a half per cent. Given the not inconsiderable expenses incurred when setting up these private loans, Castleman suggested if the monies could be obtained through Drummonds even if the interest was 5 per cent, this would be preferable. The most obvious option was to sell further parcels of estate land; however, the price of land was so low it was in fact a buyer's market and not worth the effort or expense of drawing up the sale documents.[109] Due to the economic climate on this occasion, selling any property even as a 'quick fix' was unrealistic.

The land agent as part of his accounting duties was expected to arrange interest payments and to ensure that they were paid on time. In 1830 he wrote to John Sanderson the agent-in-chief asking whether he wanted cash notes sent to cover the interest payments. Even this process was laborious as it required splitting the sum owing into two or three different portions and then forwarding them to Drummonds. This was necessary to avoid exceeding Anglesey's privileges at the bank.[110] An emblematic example of the type of lists drawn up can be seen in the half year's interest illustrated in Table 2.4.[111]

Castleman played a crucial role in keeping Anglesey afloat, both personally and by making use of his own networks to arrange further financial loans. While it may have been possible to have borrowed elsewhere, having a land agent who had the contacts and experience to be able to undertake these tasks simplified the process. Without raising substantial mortgages, not only this estate but Anglesey's other holdings in Anglesey and Staffordshire would have come under intense pressure. No matter how hard the land agent worked to improve the profitability of the tenant farmers and the land, the debts of his employer were beyond his range of control. Even here where some of the documents relating to the monies owing have survived, it is still difficult to ascertain the full extent of the

Table 2.4 Statement of interest, autumn 1828

	Date due	*Amount*
Mr Bowle	1 September	£100
Vallis' trustees	17 September	£120
Admiral Rowles	10 October	£180
Mr Dean's executors	10 October	£200
Mr Churchill	10 October	£373
Mr Brown	10 October	£100
Mr Bankes	2 November	£175
Myself (William Castleman)	2 November	£27 10s 0d
Myself (William Castleman)	21 December	£622
		£1907 10s 0d

situation. Moves were taken in 1844 to begin the breakup and sale of the estate to liquidise the assets, but it was not until after the death of Anglesey in 1854 that this finally took place.

Conclusion

The financial administration of an estate was complex and diverse. While our understanding of the country house itself continues to expand, it is the outer estate with its intricate financial transactions which paid for building programmes and expanding consumption that continues to remain hidden. This meticulous case study reveals the way in which the financial decisions made here underpinned an entire community. An inefficient agent such as Cox who appears in the Introduction is indicative of the havoc that could be caused when accounts were neglected or completed sporadically. There is no doubt that the role and scope of the land agent expanded enormously from the latter part of the eighteenth century. As seen throughout this volume, the person who took up the reins of any estate needed to navigate a range of socio-economic and political relationships. All of which relied on financial input of some kind to function efficiently. None of which would have been possible without leasing farms to tenants. Contemporary agricultural writers argued that long leases were essential if farmers were to benefit from the capital they invested, yet in the volatile climate at the end of the Napoleonic Wars, both landowners and tenants were sceptical of the system. Farms were most likely to be rented for a number of years with break points at which either the landowner or tenant could terminate the agreement. There is no evidence to suggest at least here that renewals were refused especially when the farmer had a good reputation for paying his rent and maintaining the land in good heart. Indeed, as seen with Withers, it was possible to negotiate preferential terms; better to have a tenant who paid in full a lesser rent than one who accrued large debts. Smaller properties were rented for lives, and the amounts that were raised through fines are indicative of why they survived. While mortgages were raised to pay off larger debts, a poor economic climate meant rental income could be unreliable and therefore any alternative income was welcome.

The accounts of this estate although an unbroken run prove difficult to extract anything other than the most basic information. Neither are they reliable, in some timber sales are recorded but not regularly, likewise with the stone raised. Across the range the most consistent factor is the abstract of rental which gives an idea of the rents paid and the arrears outstanding at Lady Day and Michaelmas. Problematically they do not reveal extra payments made or late payments or the full extent of the monies spent on political activities. The real detail remains in the estate vouchers, and future research into these would yield another layer to our understanding of the financial history of the estate. These were sent with the accounts to the agent-in-chief to audit. That said, the accounts provide a sense of the fiscal health of the estate but not its landowner. He may well, as did Anglesey, teeter on the financial edge of bankruptcy and his personal liabilities dwarf the value of his landed estate. The extent of aristocratic indebtedness remains a hidden story. Fortunately, the correspondence concerning the amount owed by Anglesey and his son has survived and the sheer sums involved are eye-watering. While it is difficult to know how all of the loans he needed to maintain his life-style were arranged, William Castleman certainly made a significant contribution.

The administration of this estate fell to one man, who at its core sought to navigate the whole remit of managing tenants, land and farm rentals, charitable payments, mortgages and loans, valuing property and paying for repairs and improvements. Overall the financial management of the landed estate fell on a small number of people, and yet it was singularly the most important part of the managerial role. The estate was essentially a set of economic and financial processes of the sort that rural historians have in the past overlooked. The landed estate was more than its sum of its tenant farmers, and the historiography has tended to explore it in its component parts rather than as a single entity where each segment is closely interlinked. Land agents needed to be both entrepreneur and financial managers for on their shoulders rested the entire life-style of the aristocracy; poor decisions here would have brought about the collapse of the foundations on which the landed estate was based. It was a juggling act, but the information gained from compiling the accounts and collecting the rents allowed landowners to make decisions which affected the accrual of rents, how much was spare to invest back into the estate and indeed where and when to sell off property. The land agent's ability to judge the financial health of the land he managed was important because it was this that underpinned every other action within the rural community.

Notes

1. T. Gisborne (1794) *An Enquiry into the Duties of Men in the Higher and Middle Classes of Society in Great Britain* (London: B. and J. White), pp. 573–575.
2. Ibid., pp. 573–621.
3. See, S. G. Osborne (1838) *Hints To The Charitable Being Practical Observations On The Proper Regulation of Private Charity* (London: T. and W. Boone, J. Hatchard and Son, J. Nisbet and Son, Roake and Varty) and G. W. Perry (1846) *The Peasantry of England: An Appeal to the Nobility, Clergy and Gentry, On Behalf of the Working Classes* (London: C. Gilpin).
4. S. Webster (2007) 'Estate Improvement and the Professionalisation of Land Agents on the Egremont Estates in Sussex and Yorkshire, 1770–1835', *Rural History*, 18:1, p. 48.
5. F. M. L. Thompson (1971) *English Landed Society in the Nineteenth Century* (London: Routledge, Kegan & Paul), p. 151.
6. C. Shrimpton, (1977) *The Landed Society and the Farming Community of Essex in the Late Eighteenth and Early Nineteenth Centuries* (New York: Arno Press), p. 206.
7. D. Spring (1963) *The English Landed Estate in the Nineteenth Century: Its Administration* (Baltimore: John Hopkins Press), p. 128.
8. See for example, C. A. Beardmore, Steven King and Geoff Monks (2016) *The Land Agent in Britain: Past, Present and Future* (Newcastle: Cambridge Scholars) and L. A. Rees, Ciarán Reilly and A. Tindley *The Land Agent 1720–1900* (Edinburgh: Edinburgh University Press).
9. Thompson (1971) *English Landed Society in the Nineteenth Century*, p. 151.
10. E. Richards (1981) 'The Land Agent' in G. E. Mingay (ed.), *The Victorian Countryside* (London: Routledge & Kegan Paul), p. 443.

11. See for example, E. Laurence (1731) *The Duty and Office of a Land Steward* (London: Arno Press), p. 8 and G. A. Dean (1851) *The Land Steward* (London: Atchley & Co), p. 237.
12. Laurence, *The Duty and Office of a Land Steward*, p. 8.
13. Richards, 'The Land Agent', p. 443.
14. Rees, Reilly and Tindley, 'Introduction', p. 11.
15. Richards, 'The Land Agent', p. 440.
16. W. Marshall, *On the Management of Landed Estates: A General Work for the Use of Professional Men* (London: Longman, Hurst, Rees and Orme, 1806), p. 362.
17. J. Lawrence (1806) *The Modern Land Steward* (London: H. D. Symonds), p. 42.
18. Spring, *The English Landed Estate in the Nineteenth Century*, p. 4, and for an exploration of the relationship between land agent and agent-in-chief, see G. Monks (2018) 'William Gould, Land Agent and the Rural Community in Nottinghamshire and Derbyshire', *Family and Community History*, 19:2, pp. 67–81.
19. DHC, D/ANG/B5/22, Letter dated 1817 from an anonymous gentleman in Shaftesbury complaining about the various stewards and agents who have been running the estate.
20. Wimborne to Stalbridge is around 24 miles.
21. DHC, D/ANG/B5/31, This letter is undated but is amongst the 1822 letters. Castleman also acted as agent for the Hanham estate in Wimborne, the Bankes at Kingston Lacy and the firm of Chisletts and Rawlence also in Wimborne.
22. DHC, D/ANG/B5/31, This letter is undated but is amongst the 1822 letters.
23. DHC, D/ANG/B5/26, 22 December 1820.
24. E. L. Jones (2018) *Landed Estates and Rural Inequality in English Landed History: From the Mid-Seventeenth Century to the Present* (London: Palgrave Macmillan), p. 8.
25. See, for example, Beardmore, King and Monks *The Land Agent in Britain*; Geoff Monks (2016) 'The Duke of Portland and his Agent: The Education Act of 1870', *Family and Community History*, 19:2, pp. 95–105, Monks, 'William Gould, Land Agent and the Rural Community in Nottinghamshire and Derbyshire 1783–1788'; Rees, Reilly and Tindley, 'Introduction' in Rees, Reilly and Tindley *The Land Agent 1720–1900.*
26. See, I. Jones (1993) *The Stalbridge Inheritance 1780–1854* (Dorchester: Friary Press), pp. 100–105.
27. This narrative will be returned to in Chap. 5.
28. DHC, D/ANG/B5/25, 20 August 1820.

29. DHC, D/ANG/B4/37, Stone quarry accounts up to Michaelmas 1816.
30. DHC, D/ANG/B5/31, 18 April 1822.
31. DHC, D/ANG/B5/50, 27 March 1836.
32. DHC, D/ANG/B4/37, Stone quarry accounts up to Michaelmas 1816.
33. DHC, D/ANG/B5/50, 27 March 1836.
34. J. V. Beckett (1989) 'Landownership and Estate Management' in in J. Thirsk (ed.), *The Agrarian History of England and Wales VI 1750–1850* (Cambridge: Cambridge University Press), p. 564.
35. T. W. Beastall (1981) 'Landlords and Tenants' in G. E. Mingay, (e.d.) *The Victorian Countryside Vols I and II* (London: Routledge and Kegan Paul, Ltd.), p. 428.
36. The most well-known of this type of lease are at Holkham Hall in Norfolk.
37. Beastall 'Landlords and Tenants', p. 428.
38. L. P. Adams (1965) *Agricultural Depression and Farm Relief in England 1813–1852* (London: Frank Cass & Co. Ltd), p. 6.
39. R. W. Hoyle (2016) 'Introduction: Recovering the Farmer' in R. W. Hoyle, (ed.), *The Farmer in England 1650–1980* (Abingdon: Routledge), p. 2.
40. J. D. Chambers and G.E. Mingay (1982) *The Agricultural Revolution, 1750–1880* (London: B. T. Batsford Ltd.), p. 21.
41. Ibid.
42. L. P. Adams (1965) *Agricultural Depression and Farm Relief in England 1813–1852* (London: Frank Cass & Co. Ltd), p. 6.
43. Chambers and Mingay, *The Agricultural* Revolution, p. 44.
44. Ibid., p. 47.
45. Adams, *Agricultural Depression and Farm Relief*, p. 6.
46. D. Stead (2003) 'The Mobility of English Tenant Farmers, c. 1750–1850' *Agricultural History Review* 51:2, p. 174.
47. C. Clay (1981) 'Lifeleasehold in the Western Counties of England 1650–1750', *The Agricultural History Review*, 29:2, pp. 83–84.
48. DHC D/ANG/B5/58 although this leasehold was granted in 1819 it appears among the sale documents for the estate in 1844.
49. C. Beardmore (2015) 'Landowner, Tenant and Agent on the Marquis of Anglesey's Dorset and Somerset Estate, 1814–44' *Rural History* 26:2, p. 186.
50. See, W. Stevenson (1812) *General View of the Agriculture of Dorset* (London), p. 74.
51. DHC, D/ANG/B5/46 Letter to Mr. Lowe 1 February 1834.
52. Ibid.
53. Ibid.
54. W. Stevenson (1812) *General View of the Agriculture of Dorset* (London).
55. DHC, D/ANG/B5/46 Letter to Mr. Lowe 1 February 1834.

56. DHC, D/ANG/B4/4/37 Estate Vouchers for 1816.
57. D. R. Hainsworth (1992) *Stewards, Lords and People: The Estate Steward and His World in Later Stuart England* (Cambridge: Cambridge University Press), p. 59.
58. Ibid.
59. DHC, D/ANG/B5/16, 21 December 1814.
60. DHC, D/ANG/B5/46, 1 February 1834.
61. DHC, D/ANG/B5/32, 28 January 1823.
62. Ibid.
63. Comment by the Marquis of Anglesey on the letter from Castleman, 28 January 1823.
64. DHC, D/ANG/B5/32, 8 February 1823.
65. Ibid., 23 January 1823.
66. See, C. J. Napier (1991) 'Aristocratic Accounting: The Bute Estate in Glamorgan 1814–1880', *Accounting and Business Research*, 21:82, pp. 163–174.
67. Thompson, *English Landed Society in the Nineteenth* Century, p. 153.
68. Napier, 'Aristocratic Accounting', pp. 163–174.
69. DHC, D/ANG/B5/63 General Summary of the Estate in 1845, this is a smaller estate than the one inherited in 1812, it does not take into account any lands previously sold off.
70. Using https://www.bankofengland.co.uk/monetary-policy/inflation/inflation-calculator the estimated value of the estate in 1844 was £65,213,195.87 based on an inflation rate of 2.8 per cent per annum.
71. DHC, D/ANG/B4/1/82. Michaelmas Account 1844.
72. Hainsworth (1992) *Stewards, Lords and* People, pp. 33–34.
73. Ibid.
74. For example, William Castleman had a safe within his office at home with an elaborate concealed lock.
75. J. C. Loudon (1826) *An Encyclopaedia of Agriculture* (London: Longman Orme, Brown, Green and Longmans) p. 769.
76. J. Mordant (1761) *The Complete Steward or The Duty of a Steward to his Lord* (London: W. Sandby), p. 340.
77. Lawrence, *The Modern Land Steward*, pp. 120–123.
78. Ibid.
79. Ibid, pp. 124–126.
80. J. R. Edwards, 'Accounting on English Landed Estates During the Agricultural Revolution – A Textbook Perspective', *Accounting Historians Journal*, 38:2 (December, 2011), pp. 9–10.
81. See C. W. Noke (1981) 'Accounting for Bailiffship in Thirteenth Century England', *Accounting and Business Research* 12:2, pp. 137–151.

82. See, Rees, Reilly and Tindley, 'Introduction' and Oldroyd, *Estates, Enterprise and Investment at the Dawn of the Industrial Revolution*, p. 18.
83. W. T. Baxter, 'The Account Charge and Discharge', *The Accounting Historians Journal*, 7:1 (Spring, 1980), p. 70.
84. This was an unsophisticated system whereby lines were drawn on a table to act as columns for units, tens, scores etc.
85. M. E. Turner, J. V. Beckett and B. Afton (1997) *Agricultural Rent in England, 1690–1914* (Cambridge: Cambridge University Press).
86. Ibid., p. 6.
87. Ibid., pp. 85–87.
88. DHC, D/ANG/B4/1/34; D/ANG/B4/1/36; D/ANG/B4/1/38; D/ANG/B4/1/40; D/ANG/B4/1/42; D/ANG/B4/1/44; D/ANG/B4/1/46; D/ANG/B4/1/48; D/ANG/B4/1/50; D/ANG/B4/1/52; D/ANG/B4/1/54; D/ANG/B4/1/56.
89. DHC, D/ANG/B5/67.
90. F. M. L. Thompson, (1969) 'Landownership and Economic Growth in England in the Eighteenth Century' in E. L. Jones and S. J. Woolf, (eds) *Agrarian Change and Economic Development: The Historical Problem* (Abingdon: Routledge), p. 54.
91. See, D. Cannadine (1994) *Aspects of Aristocracy: Grandeur and Decline in Modern Britain* (New Haven & London: Yale University Press).
92. Thompson, 'Landownership and Economic Growth in England in the Eighteenth Century' in Jones and Woolf, (eds) *Agrarian Change and Economic* Development, p. 54.
93. R. C. Allen (1998) 'Landlords and Economic Development in England, 1450–1800' in *Aristocracy, Patrimonial Management Strategies and Economic Development, 1450–1800* (Seville: University of Seville), p. 24.
94. M. J. Daunton, *Progress and Poverty: An Economic and Social History of Britain 1700–1850* (Oxford: Oxford University Press, 1995), p. 76.
95. Daunton, *Progress and Poverty: An Economic and Social History of Britain*, p. 76.
96. Cannadine, *Aspects of Aristocracy: Grandeur and Decline in Modern Britain*, pp. 39–42.
97. DHC, D/ANG/B5/45, 15 January 1833.
98. https://www.bankofengland.co.uk/monetary-policy/inflation/inflation-calculator accessed 20 January 2019, suggests that in 2018 this would have equated to around £65 million pounds.
99. DHC, D/ANG/B5/45, 15 January 1833.
100. https://www.bankofengland.co.uk/monetary-policy/inflation/inflation-calculator according to Bank of England inflation calculator this equates to just over four million pounds a year in these outgoings alone.
101. DHC, D/ANG/B5/45, 15 January 1833.

102. DHC, D/ANG/B5/68, 24 December 1833 – held with the sale documents compiled in 1846.
103. Ibid
104. See, Cannadine, *Aspects of Aristocracy: Grandeur and Decline in Modern Britain*, particularly Chapter 2 'Aristocratic Indebtedness in the Nineteenth Century', pp. 37–54.
105. Jones, *The Stalbridge Inheritance 1780–1854.*
106. DHC, D/ANG/B5/36, Castleman to Anglesey on the loan situation, 31 May 1825.
107. DHC, D/ANG/B5/37, 1 February 1826.
108. Ibid., 14 March 1826.
109. DHC, D/ANG/B5/39, 12 April 1827.
110. DHC, D/ANG/B5/42, 3 April 1830.
111. DHC, D/ANG/B5/40, Half yearly statement of interest.

CHAPTER 3

Working Relationships

Overview

The landlord–tenant system depended on the great wealth of landowners, and this provided tenants with both the security and the freedom to make the best of their farms.[1] During the early nineteenth century, the aristocracy were the largest landowners, controlled the terms on which land was let and provided much of the capital and initiative for agricultural improvement.[2] Traditionally historians have bound together paternalism with the idea that landownership brought with it a range of duties which were exhibited through public service. In many ways, paternalism has been recognised as the code of the elite, a system whose protocols had its roots in the vestiges of chivalry and one whereby individuals of status and position were expected 'to behave honestly and humanely towards their dependents'.[3] Eric Jones has more recently questioned this concept and argues instead that many landed proprietors passed much of the burden and risks of husbandry and cultivation onto their tenants. In turn the tenants offset this by laying off their labourers during periods of poor prices and other exogenous events such as long cycles of bad weather.[4] The landed estate is seen as a 'hand-me-down' evolving to safeguard special interests. Jones advocated that as an institution it served to preserve the status and position of a narrow caste and to ensure for members of the group a favourable distribution of income.[5] There is thus a dichotomy at the heart of the

C. Beardmore, *Financing the Landed Estate*, Palgrave Studies in the History of Finance, https://doi.org/10.1007/978-3-030-14552-1_3

debate surrounding the relationship and framework within which landowner and tenant working relationships existed.

The working connexions on an estate reveal that they were governed by complicated rights and duties on both sides and this muddies the waters, but both the traditional historical interpretation and the more modern viewpoints of Jones have become intertwined. Ultimately an estate was not merely a space where money was exchanged for land but was instead a hereditary community of landowners and tenants. The Duke of Bedford as seen in the Introduction believed in both the continued inheritance of the landowner and his tenants whose farms passed from one generation to the next.[6] The interweaving of this dual dynastic system created a common identification within a particular property which lay at the centre of the ideas surrounding the 'moral economy of the landed estate'. This according to Cragoe created a common sense of personal interests which bound and formed the basis of the landowner-tenant relationship.[7] Essentially the Marquis of Anglesey's Dorset and Somerset estate does not fit comfortably into any of these fixed perspectives but incorporates characteristics from each. Undoubtedly the majority of Anglesey's extensive income came from his acres spread across four counties and at times he or his land agents might be mercenary if rents went unpaid or tenants failed to follow the estate line during the election process. This follows Jones' theory of once having passed on the risk he was prepared to distrain and evict when necessary. That said Anglesey was known for his benevolent attitude to both his tenants and the poor of his estate. As will be seen, he fitted the more traditional norm, spending large sums on reinvestment into the estate, supporting the tenants and making numerous charitable payments which are explored in Chap. 6. Yet, the estate was expected to make a profit, and in order to do this, the risks as described by Jones' were split. In the precarious economic climate in the post-Napoleonic period, however, there were times when the landowner was expected to ignore this paradigm and proffer a range of unprecedented financial support. Nurturing good tenants was as important as maintaining the buildings and keeping the soil in good heart. Managing tenant distress was a necessity and needed to be handled with tact and diplomacy, if the estate was to survive. Working relationships were established within a set framework within which each party understood its specific role.

The landowner-tenant relationship worked as a partnership wherein the landowner's financial commitment was to provide all the basic necessities for good farming. Ideally this included an enclosed farm with decent access, buildings in good order and well maintained and the land in 'good heart'. On the other hand, the tenant was expected to provide the working capital and stock. Increasingly, land agents sought men who had sufficient capital not just to purchase seeds and animals but to see them through the lean times until the farm began to make a profit. It was not uncommon, therefore, to turn down potential candidates for empty holdings because they were unable to demonstrate adequate monetary resources. Behind this thinking was the idea that a tenant without sufficient capital would be unable to weather even the smallest of financial crises and quickly revert to the estate for rent reductions and abatements. Trying to limit the number of tenants who might fall into difficulties during times of poor prices or disease in livestock made good business sense. That is not to say that a landowner would not help in exceptional circumstances, but financially buoyant tenants made this less likely or support less expensive. Being able to farm responsibly with suitable skills and an inclination to innovativeness rather than recklessness were taken as a given.[8] As will be seen both here and in Chap. 5, there were, however, more factors to take into account than simply removing a tenant who could not afford to pay his rent. The tenants were the spine of the estate and essential for its fiscal health so picking those who could do this with the minimum of support was vital. Although the Marquis of Anglesey was prepared to share the risks of farming, it was crucial that the situation was kept in check and balanced wherever possible.

Understanding how the various working relationships functioned on a daily basis remains under-researched or difficult to unpick from the wider estate archives. As Susanna Wade Martins' commented on the Holkham estate, the characteristics of the individual tenants are unknown, and only some information remains on the farming practices of the more famous or progressive.[9] In 1968 Eric Jones wrote 'Of the three agricultural classes, landowners, farmers and labourers, it is surprising that we know least about the economic condition of the middle group … the business history of the farm is unwritten'.[10] This statement is as true today as when Jones originally made it. Estate records allow a glimpse at individual tenants but all too often it is those who encounter problems or are themselves problematic that appear in the archive thus often giving an unbalanced view. Richard Hoyle's *Farmer in England 1650–1980* has gone someway to begin to fill the gap, but it still concentrates on the few farmers who did leave a record of some kind.[11] Using a detailed estate study adds another facet to the history of the tenantry. In this chapter three broad themes will be used to explore how working relationships developed and the extent to which they relied on the financial input of the estate itself. These will include, firstly, an exploration of the way in which the estate managed tenant distress; this was particularly difficult in the unstable economic environment of the post-Napoleonic War period. In 1829 the situation was further exacerbated by disease amongst the livestock. Secondly, when the Marquis of Anglesey inherited the estate it had been much neglected. While Cox the previous agent as seen in the Introduction had left matters in chaos, the accounts were incomplete, and as will be seen below, he had made promises to the tenantry and then failed to fulfil his or the estate's commitments. Cox embodied all the perceived problems of absenteeism and a lack of supervision from the landowner. Admittedly for much of Cox's time with the estate, it was either under the control of Anglesey's father or after 1812 Anglesey was involved in fighting wars on the continent and so less likely to have paid attention to this rather distant outpost of his holdings or was simply out of touch. Cox's mistakes proved costly and left a lingering legacy of problems. More importantly a lack of firm management had fractured the trust of some of the tenants, while others sought to capitalise on the confusion. Castleman, however, demonstrated the merits of employing the right agent who could capably manage the daily problems and at the same time keep costs low and the Marquis of Anglesey informed and up to date. On taking up his agency, he found many buildings in a poor or dilapidated state of repair. To try and bring some semblance of order, the estate set out to enforce lease covenants and to make sure that Anglesey's obligations were fulfilled before embarking on a more detailed survey and sustained period of maintenance. Thirdly, the estate constantly sought to improve its capital investment mainly through drainage, which allowed the land to be worked for longer and protected the livestock from water-borne diseases such as liver fluke. The introduction of more up-to-date threshing machines was intended to make the process more efficient but as will be seen were in fact costly to set up and did not necessarily out-perform their predecessors. At the core of the estate's thinking was the retention of good or useful tenants by allowing them the financial space to recover, so that debts were paid and a return to paying rent in full and on time was once again normal practice. Repairing farm buildings and a steady but continual improvement of the land would boost the value of the estate while encouraging the tenants to farm responsibly and so boost profitability. It was, despite the estate's attempts, difficult to manage the debts of their tenantry as they faced long-term poor prices, animal disease and economic hardship.

Tenant Distress

The depression in English agriculture following the Napoleonic Wars was distinctive because it was both severe and long lasting. While landed estates forged a unique local economy, this did not mean that they were immune from national economic downturns. Many tenants had taken on expensive rental agreements during the boom war years and now found themselves unable to meet the rent call. Landowners saw the remuneration from their estates fall as farms which fell into hand brought in less income. Those tenants that clung on requested rent rebates or needed to accumulate a percentage of the rent as low prices left them unable to pay the entire amount outstanding. To fully understand the problems, it is necessary to briefly explore farming in 1800 and the effect the war had on its processes and only then is it possible to appreciate the nature of the economic forces which turned prosperity into depression. The rise in industrialisation and the growing proletarianisation of the workforce meant that the population was no longer able to supply its own food. Consequently, there was a need for radical change in agriculture if the country was to be able to feed itself.[12] The problem was highlighted as early as 1792 by the disappearance and replacement of the balance of grain exports by regular imports. Once England had become reliant on foreign grain, many factors could influence supply and dynamics such as a blockade of the ports were of considerable importance to both farmers and consumers. One of the elements which had boosted prices during the wars was the suspension of specie payments by the Bank of England and the conversion of currency to an inconvertible paper basis.[13] Agricultural prices reached their nadir in 1812 and 1813, with the prices of meat and grain more than doubling during the 22 years of war. A great deal of common land had been brought under private control through enclosure, pastures were ploughed up and waste land reclaimed. While prices continued to rise, there seemed no better investment than land. Competition for farms inevitably forced up rental prices. It has been estimated that in Essex these rose from 10s an acre just before the war started to 45s–50s in 1812.[14] Although emerging victorious from the war, Britain was saddled with a huge national debt, excessive taxation, an unstable currency and a discontented population who were given to rioting. Both landowners and farmers had to accept that prices were not going to rise again to the levels seen during the war years and would have to adjust accordingly.[15]

In consequence of the above problems, prices fell dramatically, albeit the original fall was due to the abundant crop of 1813. This harvest, it has been argued, was one of the best in history, and John Stratton states that wheat prices fell from 123s 10d a quarter in January to 67s 10d by November.[16] To compound the problems, there was another large harvest in 1815, and with continuing low prices, farmers were forced to sell both produce and livestock at a loss. Exogenous factors included the failure of some county banks of which 240 ordered the suspension of cash payments and a depression in manufacturing and commerce that exacerbated the high levels of unemployment caused by the demobilisation of soldiers. There was unsurprisingly an obvious decline in government purchasing food, clothing and equipment for the army.[17] Whatever the cause there can be little doubt that the resultant lowering of prices occasioned a huge amount of distress among the landed classes between 1815 and 1816. Although there was some recovery after 1816, this was short-lived, and a state of depression was again apparent between 1821 and 1823. While these two shortish periods were the worst years, there is rarely a year in the correspondence when the tenants are not requesting monetary aid. It was during this first period of fiscal downturn that William Castleman took up his agency of the Marquis of Anglesey's Dorset and Somerset estate. He immediately found not only were the buildings as seen above in a dire state of repairs but the tenants were struggling to make ends meet.

From the beginning of the Anglesey/Castleman archive, there is an embedded sense of the financial difficulties that many estates faced. This land agent was nothing if not tenacious, and after the Michaelmas audit in 1814, he was able to report to Anglesey 'the Tenants have in general paid better than I expected'.[18] Despite this seeming success, several of the larger tenants were without doubt floundering. In December of the same year, he wrote that Baldwin's arrears are very large, 'I am convinced that he cannot go on with the farm'.[19] By the Lady Day audit in 1815, his outstanding rent stood at £2235 0s 6d, his annual rent was £1500, thus he was around 18 months in arrears.[20] Whereas Abbot's, Oborne's, Welch's and Bournes' accounts were in such a mess that Castleman thought it would be impossible to ever work out a settlement of the amounts still owing.[21] In order to settle the disbursements on each account, a clear sense of what work had been done and what was to be paid by the landowner and or the tenant was essential. In the case of the above four tenants, the repairs and improvements undertaken on their farms had been signed off by Woodhatch. This, however, simply indicated that the works had been completed to the required standards but did not infer that the bills were in themselves due.[22] As seen in Chap. 2, accounting for every penny spent

Table 3.1 Statement of Abbot's arrears and the sums to be paid

Arrears for the farm due at Lady Day 1815	£1790 16s 6d
Due at Michaelmas	
Arrears for tithes to Michaelmas 1814	£225 17s 5d
½ years rent for the farm to Michaelmas 1815	£461 12s 0d
1 years tithes to Michaelmas for 1815	£126 16s 0d
1 years tithes to Michaelmas for 1815—gatehouse	£4 10s 0d
1 years tithes to Michaelmas for 1815	£1 10s 6d
	£820 5s 5d
Received at Michaelmas audit	£200 0s 0d
Sum expected to be paid at the audit besides the half years rent now due	£620 5s 5d

was a vital part of the role of the land agent. A sense of the extent to which rents could accrue was characteristically illustrated by William Abbot's account. On behalf of the estate, a letter was sent out to him in June 1816 which contained a statement of his arrears from Lady Day 1815, it stated that the situation could not be allowed to continue. Overall Abbot owed £1790 16s 6d. At the Michaelmas audit, he had simply paid £200 and now he was required to pay the half year's rent due and the sums remaining from the Michaelmas audit of 1815 (see Table 3.1). This still would not have paid off the full debt but would have made a substantial inroad into the monies owing.[23]

Conditions on the estate remained dire in 1816. As already seen in Chap. 2, Castleman was a great advocate of the lease but even he realised that 'Leases can afford no Security against the Failure of the Tenant' but the advantage was 'to prevent the Tenant or those who may come into possession under him from mismanaging the Farm'.[24] In order to foster a good working relationship with an incoming tenant, it was sometimes necessary (as when Baldwin had originally taken up his farm) to make an initial allowance to counter problems caused by the previous lessee. In this instance he had been allowed £300 in the first year due to the loss of his clover crop as the previous tenant had not sown the required grass seeds.[25]

Baldwin's financial situation was such that his debts had reached such a level that an enquiry revealed that neither he nor his son had the capital to stock the farm and to pay off their outstanding arrears. Baldwin therefore intended to quit his farm at Michaelmas. In order to facilitate this deal and on being granted permission to break his lease, he proposed to pay both his arrears and full rent to Michaelmas. His son who was equally and fully responsible guaranteed the payment.[26] The payment of the £300 which

Baldwin had been granted was a contentious point as he had more of his land in wheat, barley and oats than was usual. He had been ordered and was supposed to follow a four-field course system, but this had not been strictly adhered to and the question arose as to whether he should be fined. Castleman understood why Baldwin had strayed from the prescribed husbandry pattern and admitted that the excess of white straw crops was excusable in consequence of the near total failure of his turnip crop the preceding year. There was still a cost to the estate as Baldwin was now to quit his farm two years early, and it was assumed that it could only be re-let with a considerable reduction in rent. That is not to say that the estate and its land agent were not sympathetic to his plight as shown in the following letter to Anglesey: 'he [Baldwin] had lost a considerable sum of Money on the Farm a great part of which has arisen from the blight in his wheat crops for the two last years'.[27] As already discussed in the previous chapter, the Marquis of Anglesey did not like leases but Castleman's insistence on them being used did give the estate some financial protection in these circumstances. Like Withers in Chap. 2, Baldwin invoked another tirade from Anglesey, who stated '… there is nothing of which I am so certain as the futility of a Lease. It is binding only upon the Landlord never upon the Tenants. If the times are good the Tenants alone profit. If they are bad it is the Landlord who suffers'.[28] Baldwin became the focus of his annoyance. He argued that this man was greatly in arrears and yet the estate had made great accommodation to keep him on his farm with an allowance made for his bad entry. Exasperatingly he then decided to quit with no thought to the impact that this would have on finding another tenant. In the end he left the amount to be allowed, if any, to his land agent's discretion.[29] Although it seemed this was the end of the matter, the situation continued to rumble on and still remained unresolved in 1817. The allowance of £300 was still a sticking point but the overriding concern remained that if the 'principle' was adopted, it would open the flood gates to other tenants seeking similar deals and this could be financially ruinous for the estate. Realistically Castleman was not comfortable making a decision that he believed was based on Anglesey's 'liberality'.[30] Ultimately the estate stood to lose considerable sums of money, and this was a responsibility beyond that which many agents were prepared to accept. This volume has argued extensively that an absentee landowner relied heavily on a good land agent to make reasonable fiscal decisions but there were occasions when accountability for his employer's finances went, as here, beyond his remit.

For this estate and many other areas of the country, 1816 was particularly difficult.[31] The extent of the agricultural distress was discussed in parliament, and there was general agreement that it was the result of the lower prices of both farm produce and farm properties. There was less consensus as to the factors responsible for this decline although oversupply of grain was at the top of the list of measures which if they so chose parliament should consider.[32] The extent of the estate's problems became apparent in July at the audit, when arrears after it was complete stood at £13,166 10s 10½d.[33] Consequently Castleman wrote, 'the tenants have paid less than I expected; but the times are such as will not admit of a resort to conceive Measures without great Risqué of severe loss'.[34] Matters were exacerbated by two factors, firstly, the Hanley tenants always paid their mid-year rent late, to allow them time to sell their sheep at the August sale. On this occasion the usual sale was moved to September, and secondly, a late harvest meant the December audit had to be postponed until January 1817. He hoped this would allow the tenants time to sell their crops and raise the monies to pay their rent.[35] In 1815 at Christmas, the estate had granted allowances of 7½ per cent for the grass farmers and 10 per cent for the corn farmers as the former were not quite so badly off. By the end of 1816, however, all the farmers were in the same situation, and the rent allowance was raised to the higher rate for all. At Milborne Port there was a suggestion that the reduction should be even higher and range from 10 to 15 per cent. Although these were high, there was a huge worry that the tenants would simply quit, and the estate could not hope to re-let without a greater abatement to that which was now proposed. Local knowledge here formed an essential element of the decisions made, and Castleman reported that Mr. Bankes for whom he also worked had had a farm worth £1100 per annum in hand for more than six months. Hardly surprising therefore that Anglesey commented 'I have no doubt of the necessity of what you herein propose & I therefore agree to it'.[36] In a further attempt to reduce pressure on the estate, Castleman offered to take a reduction of 10 per cent in his salary. This Anglesey would not contemplate and stated, 'I am much gratified, but I decline'.[37]

Over the course of 1816 to 1818, the general price level according to the indices of Jevons and Silberling rose by about 12 per cent reaching a peak in 1818.[38] Improvement in the general economics of the country was reflected in improved rental returns. At the end of December 1817, he recorded 'the corn farmers are beginning to recover but the Grass farmers are very much distressed'.[39] Consequently, the time was now right to reduce the corn farmers rent allowance and to increase that of the grass farmers hoping that this would prevent a change of tenants. Overall the measures put in place by the estate had helped to increase the amounts paid by the tenants from £5700 to Lady Day 1816 to £7727 10s 3d at Lady Day 1817. During the same period, rental arrears fell from £12,483 2s 9d to £8044 18s 10d.[40] Nowhere is the sharing of the risks of farming more evident than here in the outstanding amounts owned. In effect Anglesey was acting as a money lender without the benefits of guaranteed interest rates. All he could hope was that they would eventually be repaid. Arrears were always problematic for a land agent, and Castleman was keen to reassure Anglesey that their continued high levels were not for want of trying on his behalf. He reiterated that he had already distrained on those tenants whose arrears had reached levels where their outstanding debts were no longer tenable.

The problem of arrears and low agricultural prices was ongoing, and the most serious recession of the post-war period occurred in 1821–1823 when a return to the gold standard had a deflationary effect on prices.[41] The correspondence of 1822 was littered with sorry tales of tenant distress, examples include Biles at Hanley who had not 'a sixpence of money to reduce his Arrears'.[42] The farm despite his financial problems was in excellent condition, and two years previously it would have been possible to guarantee an increase in rent by a new tenant if it had been necessary to remove the present one. However, in the economic conditions now prevailing, all he could promise was to obtain the best terms possible. Fortunately, there was more than sufficient capital in the farm to pay off the outstanding debt.[43] Local networks revealed that wheat which should have been fetching £18 per load was now selling at just £8 for the same quantity of grain.[44] Even long-term tenants were not immune to the financial climate, Samuel Harris who had followed his father failed owing debts of £297 10s 10d.[45] The moment at which the estate decided to distrain against a tenant varied accordingly to the risk the tenant posed, but there came a point when the debt would no longer be recoverable from the farm's assets of livestock, crops and equipment. Deciding to distrain was not a simple option as the effects of the tenant needed to be valued and then sold and this came at a cost to the landowner. Harris had at the time of his failure 64 sheep legally belonging to another person, but under the current law these were classed as being part of the farm's stock. Anglesey, however, refused to lay claim to these animals, and they were returned to their original owner.[46] Altogether when sold Harris' effects reached £200 and did not fully cover the outstanding monies owed. Harris had a large and sickly family and having considered the number and distressed state of this kinship group, it was decided to return their few household belongings and to leave them out of the sale altogether.[47] The family were not left homeless as the estate rented to Harris a dwelling house and three lime kilns and took sufficient securities to cover the rent to prevent the same situation developing again.[48]

In the majority of the case studies above, the tenants remained in place and on their farms. Even Harris who was forced to quit was found an alternative way of making a living within the confines of the estate. One of the biggest concerns was to find ways which would prevent a tenant absconding with the stock so that it might be sold at any price for ready cash. In such cases there was little hope that the monies raised would be used to pay outstanding arrears. Bishop, the tenant at Wyke Farm, was a worry and it was thus necessary to keep 'a constant watch on his Proceedings'. Bishop had repeatedly failed to meet the agreed payments in respect of his arrears, and in February 1822 it appeared he was disposing of the farm's produce. Immediately Castleman dispatched his son to level a distress but found instead that the missing two ricks of old wheat had merely been moved into the barn so that they might be threshed in order to raise money for the rent.[49] This did not, however, stop him from valuing the farm: the livestock had a total value of £1437 and included 7 cart horses, 1 hackney, 20 working oxen presumably for ploughing, a small number of milking cows and poultry, nearly 700 sheep and 200 pigs. Stored crops probably intended as feed are recorded as old wheat, new wheat, barley, oats, beans, peas, vetches, hay and potatoes. Standing crops were again a mixture of 72 acres of wheat and 10 acres of vetches and the two combined equated to £1239 5s 0d. The implements of husbandry were listed as 4 waggons; 5 dung pots; 7 ploughs; 4 pair of harrows; 2 pairs of drags, harness, yokes and chains; and a threshing machine, winnowing machine, barn tackle and sacks and were altogether worth £124. Household furniture was recorded as being in very good condition and contained 10 feather beds and priced at £150.[50] The value of this entire estate was estimated at £2950 5s 0d. Bishop also had a number of sheep out 'at keep'. This inventory is significant because it gives a sense of the value of capital invested by the tenants and aids in understanding the way they farmed the land.

While as with Bishop the estate was successful in keeping him in place, this was not the case for all. One tenant who did abscond was Phillips and in doing so deliberately removed and hid the stock so that it could not be distrained against it. Outstanding in rent and tithes was £1630 so the estate had no choice but to make an example of this fraudulent tenant to try and prevent others doing the same. A bigger picture can be obtained through contemporary newspaper accounts which reported that William Phillips had in September 1821 driven off more or less the whole of his stock and household effects. W. Dyke of Suddon, Henry Dyke of Wincanton, Charles Phillips of Burton's Mill and Thomas Dowding of Cuckington and N. Norrish all appeared on 4 July 1822 before Rev. H. F. Yeatman and the R. J. Monkhouse to answer the charge that they had assisted in the removal of part of Phillips effects. All but Dowding were fined for double the value of the goods they had in their possession. Dowding was acquitted only because it could not be proven that the goods he was holding had been on the farm at the time the arrear of rent had become due.[51] Phillips was never prosecuted because he had not stayed in the area but disappeared quickly to America, to escape any form of justice. However, Castleman had a long memory and in 1828 Phillips was rumoured to have returned to England to claim a £1500 legacy.[52] He started an enquiry amongst his networks and wrote to Anglesey that should Phillips be found he had in place all the necessary paperwork to recover the now long-outstanding debt. This money belonged to his employer and could not simply be written off.

The plan of making an example of Phillips was not exactly successful and certainly did not deter Drake who farmed at Stalbridge from removing a considerable part of his stock, household goods and other items with a clear intention of defrauding the Marquis of Anglesey of £92 8s 9d. This was the outstanding arrears of the rent paid at Lady Day. Drake had been much more careful or perhaps learnt from the mistakes made by Phillips because it was noted, 'Immediately I made the best enquiries I could on the subject and the Business seemed to have been conducted with so much Art and Skill that I see no prospect of being able to recover the Property'.[53] Consequently, Castleman arranged for Drake to be arrested and 'lodged in Dorchester Gaol'. About £30 of the debt was recovered and it was feared that the rest would simply become a loss against the estate. Despite Drake's attempts to get himself released from both prison and his debt, he failed; the Magistrates ordered him to be imprisoned for 12 months. In many respects Drake was used as another visible example of the estate's attempts to enforce the notion that absconding would be met with legal action. That said, Castleman was happy to swap the year's prison sentence for something shorter if that meant he could obtain payment for the greater part of the debt. Anglesey was not quite so forgiving. He suggested that the final decision should be left to his land agent, but if after Drake had served three months of his sentence and most of the monies could be recovered, then his release should be considered.[54] Financially the estate could not afford to lose tenants in this way, therefore keeping an eye on proceedings as with Bishop was essential, if it was to avoid being defrauded by more struggling tenants. The level of tenants who behaved in this way was relatively small but does show the effects of high levels of debt and its impact on both the estate and the men who farmed it.

Dawes and Barrett were perhaps the highest profile case of absconders the estate faced. Together they had rented Gibbs Farm at Stalbridge since 1821 at a rent of £420 per annum. They were known for paying their rents regularly till Michaelmas 1829.[55] At this point they had upwards of 40 head of cattle. By the Michaelmas audit of 1829, however they owed £486, they paid £50 and gave notice to quit at the next audit. On 29 January they had visited Castleman assuring him of their solvency and promised to shortly reduce their arrears. In fact, on the same day, they drove off about 20 heifers and had other property removed and hidden.[56] On approaching the pair, they freely admitted that they had driven some of the cows to different markets in order to sell them and raise the money to pay their rent but had not been offered anything for them. The correspondence recorded that they seemed to be 'perfectly honest Men but struggling under the pressure of the general Distress'.[57] A good land agent was one who understood how tenants might act during hard times, and consequently he ordered William Burge to 'keep a sharp look out on the Farm and if he saw anything wrong to distrain immediately'.[58] On 2 February Burge reported that Dawe and Barrett had driven off ten more of their cows to Salisbury Market. An immediate distraint was placed on the farm, and a special messenger was despatched who discovered that Dawe and Barrett had in fact driven off the whole of their cattle and absconded. Without hesitation the Marquis of Anglesey demanded that they be prosecuted. In fact, under this threat both men surrendered themselves to the Fleet Prison where they then applied to be discharged under the Insolvent Act.[59] On 22 July *The Dorset County Chronicle and Somersetshire Gazette* reported that the 'Chief Commissioner' stated:

> It was evident the insolvents represented to Mr Castleman their solvency on purpose to lull him to sleep as they might more easily effect a removal of their whole property … there was a gross preference to a relation, by hand-

> ing over 9 beasts for an old debt, and the other 9 beasts had been fraudulently made away with other the arrest … the insolvents were adjudged to *eight calendar months imprisonment* at the noble Marquis's suit.[60]

There was a worry that Dawe and Barrett heralded the beginning of a new wave of tenants secretly selling of their livestock and fleeing with unpaid rental arrears. This was a particular concern as the levels of distress were described as unparalleled. It was, therefore, essential to make a thorough example of this pair. The estate managed to crawl back some of the missing stock because a substantial reward of £5 for information leading to its recovery had been offered. Robert Brooks detected the missing stock and was paid this reward after the stock had been collected and sold.[61] The biggest issue the estate faced came in 1829 and the epidemic which swept through large numbers of the sheep caused a major financial crisis. This was perhaps the biggest threat to the estate's viability.

There was little idea of what caused the disease which ravaged the sheep flocks of some of the largest farmers in 1829. Causes were attributed to beasts eating the 'coathe plant', others believed it was precipitated by the decomposition of grasses aided by warmth and moisture, to the taking in of the flukes which then developed in the livers and stomachs of the sheep. It was, however, believed that wet boggy lands which had been flooded were especially dangerous to sheep. Importantly, it only appeared in the summer and autumn months and this led to further confusion.[62] Fluke is now known to come from water snails. Undrained or wet land in south western England during periods of warm damp weather was particularly prone as it provided the perfect breeding conditions for *Lymnaea truncatula*, the host of the liver fluke. When sheep are grazed on infected land, they ingested the snail and they then came under attack from the fluke and failed to thrive, mortality rates are often extensive. Financially the disease was disastrous for the tenants on two counts, firstly, they lost their main source of income and this left them in a precarious pecuniary state. Secondly, they lost the means of manuring their land which added to their misery and meant they either had to purchase some form of fertiliser or accept much lower yields. Those who did not have the capital to reinvest would be forced to quit their farms with their debts unpaid and the estate left out of pocket. Those who had the money to buy new stock were taking a huge financial risk as there was no guarantee that these new beasts would not also succumb to the same disease.

The outbreak of coathe which hit the estate in 1829 was exacerbated by several other factors which had led to some of the largest tenants facing financial ruin. The problems had begun in 1828 when incessant rain caused considerable damage to some of the farm buildings. Repairs could not begin until the land had dried out in the spring.[63] Despite the early problems, the Michaelmas audit of 1828 was reasonably successful with most of the tenants paying according to expectations. Even those tenants who were known to be defaulters of old had agreed to pay their rents within the month, albeit with the threat of distraint. As a result, the arrears in the accounts at Michaelmas stood at £1953 4s 10d.[64] The early rains continued throughout the year and resulted in a crop of corn which was deficient in both quantity and quality. The hay crops had been either severely damaged or washed away in the floods.[65] Both the summers of 1828 and 1829 have been described as wet with disappointing harvests.[66] Although seemingly reasonably stable within six months, the financial landscape for the estate, the tenants and agricultural labourers had deteriorated significantly. By Lady Day of 1829, there were signs that there was a serious problem as alongside the agricultural difficulties there was a more general economic decline. *The Sherborne Mercury* reported that 'It is with the deepest regret we are compelled to state, that in all the manufacturing districts of the country the greatest distress prevails'.[67] It argued that not since 1793 had the population 'been more impoverished or more embarrassed … In fact, more general distress never did prevail'.[68]

The full horrors of this problem began to emerge in August of 1828 when Highmore, one of the largest tenants on the estate, reported that his entire flock of about 900 sheep had been attacked with the 'coathe' and some 600 were now dead and the remainder in a poor state.[69] Unfortunately the disease had struck so quickly and as Highmore's flock had not previously been coathed, he was overcome before he realised the depth of the problem. Symbolically the narratives surrounding Highmore's case are indicative of the exogenous problems the tenants faced but which they were powerless to solve. He wrote to the estate stating that the value of the sheep lost was in the region of £1200. Further information revealed that a great part of his hay and grass had been spoiled in 1820 by heavy rains and again in 1829 when much had been washed away. As the farm was low lying, extra monies had been spent in the annual clearing of the river, trenches and ditches. Other beasts, Highmore claimed, had been lost because they had become chilled by the 'coldness and dampness of the lands' and his spring crops for the last two years had been miserably bad.[70] Although Highmore had been allowed a 25 per cent reduction in his rent for the loss of his livestock as had the other tenants who had been significantly affected by the coathe, there had been nothing allowed for the loss of his hay and grass. Highmore had made the stipulated payment at the recent audit to reduce his arrears; however, Castleman believed that he had borrowed the money. This is an indication of the extent to which even the largest farmers were facing financial disaster. The problems suffered by the tenants were reflected in a sharp increase in rental arrears which in October 1829 stood at £3720 16s 2d.[71]

Ultimately Highmore attempted to get a greater reduction in his rent, and as he was one of the biggest and most skilled tenants on the estate, it was prepared to review the situation. To have lost a tenant of this stature would have been catastrophic for the estate as he was both a good farmer and a vocal political supporter of the Marquis of Anglesey. To try and alleviate the situation, it was suggested that his farm should be revalued and the annual casualties which had not previously been included taken into consideration. As to a further immediate allowance on his rent, there was a sense that this should be at the behest of the Marquis alone, because it would make an exception that could lead to the other tenants making similar requests.[72] Diseases such as the coathe could have significant long-term implications, and in 1832 Highmore had resorted to buying lime at a heavy cost in order to replace the natural manure which his sheep would normally have produced. Consequently, there was no quick recovery and for Highmore his misfortune was ongoing, and in 1832 his flock had been twice coathed and now a member of the third flock had been found dead again of the same disease.[73] The conditions which caused the problems faced between 1828 and 1830 were much more localised than the economic depressions of the early 1820s but nonetheless caused enormous problems for the estate's tenantry.

Generally, there was little improvement in the state of farming until after 1837, and not until the mid-nineteenth century did agriculture move on to a more secure and prosperous footing.[74] Overall in the latter part of the 1820s the estate had experienced a much more stable period. For example, in January 1827 Castleman reported that 'my Clerks succeeded in collecting the arrears at Milborne Port beyond my expectations'.[75] Rental arrears gradually reduced until in 1836 the rents assessed and paid reached parity. That is not to say there were not blips and the economic volatility of the period remained a constant and present problem. There were concerns over the price of wool in 1827 when the land agent reported, 'the best South Down fleeces in Somersetshire will only realise 9d p[er] pound and the long Wools I find are decreasing both in demand, and in value'.[76] Rental arrears peaked in 1830 at £4185 15s 0½d and then began to fall, in October 1830 to £3378 8s 5d, and by 1831 at £1841 4s 9d they stood at around the same level as seen in 1827.[77] There was a lack of tenants who attempted to abscond compared to ten years earlier, perhaps because of the prominence of the Dawes and Barrett case in 1830. Of course, there were glitches, but as the situation in 1844 illustrates, while some sections of the estate might be affected, others escaped relatively unscathed. This was different to the all-encompassing depression that struck in the immediate post-Napoleonic war period. On this occasion it was the smaller tenants who struggled while the larger ones seemed better prepared to weather the changing storm.[78] Castleman on taking up his agency had set about improving working relationships by undertaking a schedule of repairs and improvements which ensured that the tenants' farm buildings and land were once again fit for purpose. Maintaining the estate was essential and an important factor in keeping and attracting tenants.

Maintaining and Repairing the Estate

There was, by the early nineteenth century, a considerable volume of literature available for a land agent to consult when faced with a neglected estate and this clearly explained the importance of keeping it in good repair. For example, William Marshall advised that if a landowner maintained his properties, it would augment personal income and increase the value of landed interests.[79] As seen in the Introduction, absenteeism did not necessarily mean an estate was neglected but could instead, under the right management, thrive. There were no laws to force a proprietor to farm or rent his land and an estate could be left to lie waste with impunity provided this did not impact on any other private property. Land could be left unproductive but generally landowners were bound not just by the ties of interest but also of a perceived duty to keep their land in good repair.[80] The role, however, played by individual landowners in improving the agricultural practice of their estate has been much debated, and it has often been assumed that a few great and well-known men played a critical role in spreading new ideas which culminated in the Agricultural Revolution.[81] Thomas Coke at Holkham was one such landowner and the audit books for this estate include both new buildings and lists of repairs to existing ones. The years

1774–1804 reveal an expenditure of some £80,000. On top of this sum must be added the materials which the estate supplied and perhaps Arthur Young's suggested expenditure on improvements of £100,000 is closer to the truth.[82] Few landowners would have spent anywhere near these sums. Problematically estate archives are widely dispersed and often incomplete, and it is impossible to ascertain the full extent of the monies expended. Coke was often accused of seeking publicity, and while this may or may not be the case, he unashamedly exhibited his status and position. In so doing he demonstrated his wealth and the vast amounts of money he had available to spend. The visual result of his expenditure placed him in the top echelons of the landowners of his day.[83] Others such as the fifth Duke of Bedford, the fourth Duke of Portland and the third Earl Spencer have all been recognised as great agricultural improvers.[84] Without being detrimental to the men mentioned here, there is a general sense that as a group landowners were not overly important as agricultural improvers.[85]

Not all landowners had the wealth of Thomas Coke and many such as the Marquis of Anglesey lived beyond their means, yet maintaining their estates was essential if they were to continue to attract good quality tenants. Land brought status and power and therefore neglecting it was not really an option. The secret was for the landowner to behave in such a way as to suggest that money was plentiful and never in short supply. While a farm might be let, in effect the landlord owned the soil and, through his agent, made sure that it was farmed efficiently and skilfully by carefully observing the tenants and the methods used.[86] Land had to be well drained and the farmhouse and buildings, which were usually the responsibility of the landowner, kept in good repair. While Eric Jones argues as seen above and in the Introduction that the risks of farming were placed on the tenant, it might be argued that these were willingly swapped through the landlord's capitalisation of the holding as this allowed the tenants to use their monetary resources for implements, seeds, fertilisers and the purchase or hire of better livestock.[87] The basis of the landlord–tenant contract was therefore that properties should always be in good condition at the time of entry.[88] If at the point of signing the lease any outstanding works remained uncompleted, these needed to be carefully detailed and recorded and care should be taken to expedite the repairs. In other words no excuse should be given to the tenant to either allege neglect or rid himself of his own liabilities. Charles Curtis argued that repairs were always a difficult subject, but if the premises were in a good state of repair when the lease was signed, the tenant was less inclined to neglect his maintenance duties. This would ensure the execution of any necessary works throughout the duration of the lease, thus saving on expensive and extensive works when the lease came to an end. It was commonplace to supply some of the required materials, but the tenant was expected to haul any of these resources lying within a reasonable distance of his farm, often defined as a ten-mile radius.[89] In the correspondence and vouchers, timber in particular is described as 'rough' that is unsawn and needed to be converted into usable lengths by the tenant.[90] Supplying wood in this state allowed the estate to save the expense of preparation and with the tenant arrangement the transportation cost of haulage. It was not unusual to insert a clause within the lease which allowed the landowner or his agent to inspect the building at any reasonable time. This ensured tenants complied with their lease covenants and saved the estate considerable expense. It also helped to prevent wilful neglect on the part of the tenant particularly as a lease came close to expiry. An agent could save the estate both time and money by viewing repairs as an important criterion in the landowner-tenant working relationship. When this relationship lacked trust or stopped working, it could have serious financial repercussions.

At the beginning of his agency, Cox who was discussed in the Introduction created a range of problems not least of which impacted on the maintenance of the estate. He had promised some of the tenants new buildings to replace those which were no longer fit for purpose. By the time Castleman took up his agency, these guarantees had not been fulfilled and some of the tenants were in a state of agitation. Biles, one of the tenants at Hanley, for example, in 1814 owed more than 18 months' rent with arrears in excess of £800. He claimed that the failure to supply the new buildings promised by Cox had caused him financial loss and he had no intention of paying any of his outstanding debt until sufficient recompense had been agreed. Understanding the mindset of tenant farmers was an essential part of the land agent's role in the day-to-day management of the estate. In this case it was presumed that Biles was being coerced by Cox into creating trouble. Using his extensive range of local networks, Castleman wrote that he had found 'by unquestionable Testimony the means taken by Cox to influence Biles and some of the other Tenants to resist paying their Rent'.[91] The situation had been exacerbated because Biles was a known troublemaker. Anglesey stated, 'Biles conduct is infamous', and he ordered immediate steps must be taken to recover the outstanding debt and to remove him from his farm. The estate was worried that if Biles was not quickly silenced then the monetary cost to the estate would be enormous as other tenants would stop paying their rents and would likewise demand the repair of their existing buildings or the construction of new ones. Thus, Biles was to be punished as an example to others.[92] There is no doubt that a good land agent was essential if the maintenance was to be kept up to date. Cox did not leave the estate in the best of shapes and this had to be rectified quickly.

An experienced land agent understood that tenants expected to move into a farm which was in a good state of repair. Undoing years of neglect could be costly but necessary if a new tenant was to be found for an empty farm. In many cases when the outgoing tenant had struggled to pay the rent or had become too infirm or old to farm efficiently, it was the repairs which had been left undone. As a result, properties were often left to fall into a state of dilapidation. In these cases, the landowner had no choice but to pay for the work to make good the farm's buildings both domestic and agricultural. For example, when Mr. Piper quit his farm at Hanley in 1844, a repair schedule to put the property back into a lettable state was set up in short order. John Kendall supplied a whole range of materials including the following: oak for 'scantling' and wall plates along with red pine, deal for weather board, new oak gate posts in the fields, elm fence rails for the farm yard, new joists were placed in the parlour, iron ties were placed across the roof of the kitchen and milk house weighing 80 pounds, the cow house door was repaired, gate hooks and staples for fastening were replaced, and the stable loft was mended as well as the doors and stairs. All in all, the estate spent £33 15s 8¾d.[93]

Shortly after taking up his agency, Castleman undertook a cursory survey of the properties under his management and reported that having spent the 'whole of last week' looking over part of the estate, he was sorry to report that 'many of the farms are in a shocking state'.[94] This was best illustrated in the description of Adams farm at Hanley where the report stated the 'farm house and some of the other Buildings on this farm are in Ruins'.[95] This was a long-standing problem. An estimate had been made two years previously for rebuilding the house and repairing the rest of the premises which amounted to some £500–600. The work had not been carried out and as the tenant was considered a bad farmer, the intention was to combine the land with Biles farm, who could afford to raise the money for stock. By combining the two properties, the farmhouse and many of the other buildings were no longer necessary and the estate spared the expense of carrying out the work to make them usable.[96] Biles' farm buildings were in a tenantable state with little needing to be done. There was a further incentive to this decision as Biles would want a new barn and cottage as an inducement to take Adams farm especially as his present buildings were two miles from his land. Moreover, this would mitigate the problems caused by Biles in the latter part of 1814. It would give him the outbuildings promised by Cox, but without seeming to bend to his threats of withholding rent. Nothing, however, was left to become waste and the materials that would arise from the demolition of the derelict buildings would be used in the construction of any new ones. Not only does this demonstrate the ability of the land agent to consider the most effective means of maintaining the land but also the ways in which his decisions were dominated by financial factors.

Other farms on the estate were in an equally ruinous condition; Castleman reported, for example, that Slocombe's premises at Bradford were 'in a most miserable state'. One of the barns had fallen down shortly after he had taken the lease. Slocombe did not live in the farm house but instead rented another property from Anglesey for one life which was not only sound but had good farm buildings attached. As the whole farm was expected alongside a number of other premises to 'fall into hand' within a few years, a deal was negotiated whereby rather than expending £200 in repairs, he would allow a yearly reduction on the rent of £30. This was the same amount that Slocombe paid for the house in which he resided. In order to cover the estate from any repercussions surrounding this decision, Slocombe signed a document exonerating Anglesey from his side of the repairs except on the labourers' cottages.[97] In early 1818, to try and get on top of the problem, a much more detailed survey of the estate was undertaken with a view to putting it finally into a suitable state of repair. Consequently, in August a notice was sent to every tenant which reported on the examination and laid out the repairs that were needed. In effect this was a general order but all those who leased property were asked to 'sufficiently … thatch, glaze, drain, cleanse and repair the buildings, windows, hedges, ditches, banks, trenches, water courses, gates, posts, bars, stiles, rails, pales and fences on the farm which you rent'.[98] This was a comprehensive list and demonstrates exactly the extent of the problem and the scope of works that everyone was to undertake. Tenants had an expectation that their landowner would provide some form of financial aid and this is clearly represented in the surviving schedule of works for Robert Davies at Yenston Farm. In this instance the estate shared the cost. Both parties undertook an agreed amount of thatching alongside the renovation of walls, and roofs to put both the house and farm buildings into a decent state of repair.[99] Altogether the estate spent

£41 12s 8d.[100] The split in the schedule illustrates the blurring of landlord and tenant capital whereby there was a shift to sharing the burden of refurbishment of both domestic and agricultural buildings.[101]

The motive in carrying out this huge round of repairs was entirely pecuniary. Part of the process was to ensure that the tenants themselves met their contractual obligations and this would result in a saving in the future. Castleman was not, however, taking chances and leaving everything to trust. He intended to employ Pearman and Ford who were in 1818 assessing works undertaken on Mr. Bankes' estates to check the bills before they were paid.[102] Furthermore, he argued 'I am sure' this will 'prove a material saving in the article of repairs & will I trust ensure their being done in a proper and workmanlike manner'.[103] This programme was successful and took around three years to complete finally in 1822, a report sent to Anglesey stated:

> … the general management of the Farms under my agency is very good … that the state of Repairs of the Farms is in general very satisfactory as will appear from the very small amount of the disbursements allowed for the last year and I can with confidence state that (subject to Accidents) these Disbursements will be considerably decreased in the Current year.[104]

Besides attempting to put right existing dilapidations, uncontrollable elements such as the weather and the damage it might cause were one of the few factors that the estate was unable to regulate, and high winds in particular could cause extensive damage. The estate vouchers across the period contain numerous examples of repairs needing to be carried out after episodes of inclement weather and are far too numerous to give more than a taste of the type of destruction that might have been caused. In 1823, for example, James White was paid £1 13s 9d for the labour required in providing sawing and nails to repair the roof of the barn at Mr Barn's Upper Farm on account of it blowing off in a recent storm.[105] In order to ensure cost effectiveness, tenants were themselves encouraged to carry out work on behalf of the estate. John Highmore, for example, was paid £13 17s 2d for repairing the river bank on his land which had been damaged by flood.[106] Perhaps the most notorious storm in Dorset occurred on 29 November 1824, and the estate was badly hit with roof tiles and thatch being blown off in the wind. In order to get repairs done quickly, the estate paid workman on behalf of tenants such as Goodridge who was ordered to 'make good the pan tile on the farm stall that was uncovered by the tempestuous weather that happened on the 22 & 23 Nov' on Highmore's farm. In other instances, tenants such as Biles were allowed the interest of £39 6s 0d on the cost of building a new barn because the existing one had been blown down.[107] In 1837 another storm of sufficient magnitude as to appear in the correspondence hit the estate. On that occasion the storm had 'been very destructive' to the timber. Some of the 'fine old Elms' in Stalbridge Park had been blown over with one falling on the gates at the entrance and had in the process destroyed them. Others had fallen on to several parts of the park wall, causing extensive damage. Fortunately, the principle buildings of the estate had in the main escaped. Even a storm could result in a fiscal gain and the timber blown down was quickly measured and sold. Any property which had been affected was surveyed and immediate remedial work actioned, and any repairs that could wait until the spring were left.[108] While the weather was unpredictable and could not be financially planned for, it was in the estate's interest to act quickly when such events occurred to protect the integrity of the capital investment of both landowner and tenant. There was little point in leaving buildings in a derelict and unusable state as this would encourage tenants to quit and move off their farms or to leave timber lying on the ground at the risk of being stolen. Repairs overall coupled with improvements were major contributors to estate expenditure and together underpinned the financial commitment of the landowner to his tenants. Improvements ensured the land remained in good heart and were a vital element in forging a successful working relationship. By sharing the cost of repairs, the bonds of landowner and tenant were in some ways strengthened as tenants investing in their farms looked to a long-term return on their investment rather than simply farming for high profits and then quitting. Alongside maintaining the integrity of the farm buildings, a landowner was expected to explore ways in which to improve the estate, and in the early nineteenth century, this revolved around two core factors, namely, drainage and the introduction of mechanisation in the form of the threshing machine.

Capital Investments

The improvements which took place within British agriculture from around 1750 until about 1880 are now regarded as being part of an Agricultural Revolution. This terminology is somewhat problematic because there was no sudden explosion of technology nor a rapid improvement in the means of growing crops or breeding livestock. In fact, there is a level of disagreement among historians as to when the changes actually took place. Eric Kerridge argued that the Agricultural Revolution took place much earlier occurring somewhere between the mid-sixteenth and mid-eighteenth centuries. He suggested that a mixture of land hunger and population growth resulted in an increased demand for food and made a reorganisation of agriculture necessary.[109] J. D. Chambers and Gordon Mingay are the most recognised exponents of a later revolution arguing that increased output in agriculture was not as in industry the result of massive mechanical innovation. In most cases improvements concentrated on existing traditional machinery, and it was not until the mid-twentieth century that the drive towards a fully mechanised industry began. The main departure from this course was the introduction of the threshing machine where horse-drawn machinery began to replace manpower. As will be seen in the next chapter, there was a Luddite-type rebellion against its impact on the employment of agricultural labourers. It is not therefore on the grounds of technological innovation that English agriculture experienced a revolution. Mark Overton takes a different approach and advocates that whether or not an Agricultural Revolution took place during a specific time frame is 'both a conceptual and an empirical issue'.[110] The timing of a revolution is in many senses immaterial as English agriculture was successful in responding to the challenges of feeding a growing population in both the sixteenth and early seventeenth centuries and again in the period after 1750.[111] There is little doubt that the processes of change in agriculture were slow, taking many years to germinate and reach maturity.[112]

Agriculture was hampered by the backwardness of biological sciences and thus the remarkable achievements made in increasing output came through the insights of men of genius as well as landowners and agents who were prepared to experiment. Drainage had long been recognised as an important component of improving the quality of the soil especially in heavy clay soil because it effectively removed any excess water from the land. It was of benefit to any wet areas because well-drained land meant that sheep and cattle could be put to pasture for longer periods and it improved the ability to tend crops during winter and spring. Kerridge, however, refuted the effects of drainage and stated that it was of 'limited application' with trench drains being already known.[113] Contemporary agricultural writers were though in no doubt of its worth. John Henry Charnock argued that:

> Unquestionably the concurrent testimony of every tolerably executed work, and a vast variety of soils, has proved, beyond a doubt, that the operation *of thorough underground Draining* is the one from which the land derives the most immediate and permanent advantage – that it is, in fact, the *only* basis for the real improvement of land.[114]

Using fertilisers of any kind including lime (which must be burnt in order to be useful) costs money either to the estate or tenant or both, and their use on wet undrained land was both ineffective and a waste of capital.[115] Within the Anglesey/Castleman archive, there is no sense of rapid change which equated to an Agricultural Revolution; there is instead a consideration of factors and improvements that would aid the estate in being more profitable. As seen above wet land in Dorset and Somerset was detrimental to livestock. The estate took drainage seriously and the vouchers contain yearly amounts expended on this activity. It was not just the physical work of the farmers and their labourers who were relied on to carry out this work. There is evidence that under Castleman the estate used extensively a mole plough as part of the drainage commitment to the tenants, and he wrote in February 1816:

> This machine which for a considerable time before the commencement of my Agency had been suffered to be idle has been this winter and is now very actively employed and I have been using every means in my Power to proceed in other Improvements of the property.[116]

To which Anglesey has written in the margin of the letter, 'I am very glad to learn that this useful implement is at work'.[117] Using a tool of this kind which was presumably horse driven would have saved greatly on the time required to physically dig out drainage ditches and trenches. That is not to say that more traditional methods were ignored, and it is possible to see evidence of a variety of methods being employed. The amount spent overall is impossible to determine but tenants were granted allowances against their rent for drainage works which they had carried out across the year. Emblematic examples include 'Mr Chs Toop' receiving the sum of £3 15s 0d for walled draining at his farm at Charlton Horethorne which he rented jointly from the Marquis of Anglesey and Ralph Ironside. In 1830 for 96 lugs of underground draining in a field called 'Hams Moor' in the occupation of James Snook, an allowance of £1 12s 0d was given. Payment was not necessarily swift, and it was not until 1832 that Snook signed the voucher which finally ensured the monies were paid.[118] On top of the cost of physically creating the drains, the estate had the expense of checking its quality before the allowances were granted. In 1832 William Taylor who undertook much of this kind of surveying work was paid £5 0s 0d for examining the underground draining on different farms which were rack rented.[119] Perhaps the best example of how of a landowner/tenant drainage agreement worked in practice is the surviving indenture between the Marquis of Anglesey and Ralph Ironside.

Bradford Leaze was a patch of commonable pasture land fed by a number of springs off the nearby hill and which the estate believed would benefit and be improved by draining. The document clearly lays out what Ironside was to be paid for each part of the works, stating that he was to 'dig the carriers at eight pence per Grad'. The small work was priced at 'two pence three farthings per grad', and finally the underground drains were quoted at eight pence per Grad. The indenture distinctly stated that the 'said drains' were to be of a proper width and depth and were to have been dug in a 'workmanlike manor'. Once the drainage had been completed satisfactorily, Ironside was to receive a further ten pounds. Furthermore, the maintenance of the system was to be his responsibility, and he guaranteed to keep the 'Carrier's small work or arms and underground drains … in good and efficient repair'. The initial work and the ongoing contract were to 'effectually answer the purposes of the said Drainage for the Term of Ten years from the date thereof'. As part of his contractual commitment, the Marquis was to provide at his own cost the stone and any other 'proper materials' for making the carriers and the underground drains. He was also to cover the expense of carrying these materials to the places where Ironside needed them. As part of the agreement, those who used this piece of common land were to continue to strive towards its better management and improvement. Alongside his commitment to provide the materials, the Marquis of Anglesey promised:

> that he will before or as soon as the said Drainage shall have been completed by the said Ralph Ironside make at his Expence such Arches or Trunks as may be necessary for the better effectuating the said Drainage and also for the Cattle to pass over the said Drainage or Carriers without Damage.[120]

While the indenture lays out the schedule of works, it gives no sense of how much the estate spent overall, these hidden sums are found separately in the estate vouchers. John Custard was paid £2 0s 0d for measuring the open and underground drainage and drawing the leading carriers to the principle springs. Cridling the Mason was paid for his and a boy's labour to draw up the large cover stones to go over the top of the large carriers. In total Ralph Ironside was paid £91 18s 0d, Cridling received £6 15s 0d, Woodhatch was paid £53 0s 0d for superintending the works, and John Spencer who kept the cattle while the work was being undertaken another £4 12s 0d, when all the sums are added together the overall cost was £205 19s 8d.[121] This indenture and the resultant vouchers really explore the financial implications of the landowner and tenant partnership as a working relationship. Neither party was responsible for all of the work or carried the risk of the expense. Instead they worked together and the Leaze once drained would allow the tenants to graze their cattle for much longer periods. These works had improved the value of the land, made it more workable and reduced the chances of liver fluke amongst the livestock. This indenture and its resultant vouchers demonstrate the cost of draining even a small piece of land. While drainage was the main improvement carried out by the estate, they did allow tenants to invest in threshing machines and provided support when they were malfunctioning.

The threshing machine was according to Phillip Miller writing in 1835 the most valuable implement in the farmer's possession.[122] They were originally worked by horses, water, wind and latterly steam, and it was possible to adapt the size and power dimension of the machines to meet the farm and its needs. Miller suggested that the preferred method of powering the thresher was water where available. Using a threshing machine should, if working correctly, thresh the grain cleaner than the flail and save considerably on the cost of labour. The first effective machine was constructed in 1786 in Scotland by Mr. Meikle. While expensive to set up a powerful machine could thresh and dress the grain at the same financial outlay of dressing alone, when done by manual labour. The corn 'is more completely detached from the straw' and much more could be preserved in a bad season which would otherwise have spoiled in a stack. Economically it saved money on labour, 5 per cent more grain was gained from the straw, the process was much quicker, petty pilfering could be lowered, the grain was less injured, seed for sowing was much more easily procured and finally if the grain was dried beforehand then a whole stack could be threshed in a day.[123]

The introduction of the threshing machine had coincided with a shortage of labour during the Napoleonic Wars. An indication of its spread can be gained from the Board of Agriculture Reports. By the early 1790s, it had moved into north east England and by 1808 threshing machines could be found in just about every county in England although the greatest concentrations were in the north east and south west.[124] Mark Overton suggests that most were permanently installed in barns and were horse drawn, that said some of those on the Marquis of Anglesey's estate were as in Miller's preferred method water driven. There is no record of exactly how many threshing machines were on the estate, as they appear in the correspondence in relation to other matters; for example, when Bishop's farm was surveyed in 1822, one is listed amongst the farm implements.[125] Threshing machines were neither cheap to buy nor install and in August 1814 the tenant at Clifton Farm was complaining that the new threshing machine which had been recently installed at a cost of £1500–£2000 was useless. Oborne, the tenant, had stated that he preferred his old machine despite the enormous expense of setting it up. One of the problems was that it would hold no more than four loads of corn. It is hardly surprising that Oborne was unhappy because the estate had lent him the money for the machine on the proviso that it was paid back in seven annual payments. As part of the working partnership between landowner and tenant, the estate had paid for all the works connected to installing the machine. In May of the following year, the problems with Oborne's thresher remained unsolved. It would still not thresh the corn clean. As the mechanism had a tendency to lock, there was a worry that it posed a very real fire risk. Oborne was ordered to find and call in the best millwright in the area in an attempt to solve the problem once and for all. Even when the construction costs were withdrawn, it left Oborne with a machine that was still not as good as the one which he had previously owned. The machine at Clifton was also problematic in that there were difficulties with the water supply. A temporary wooden trough was built by Taylor the estate's surveyor although he was to later refute his own idea as unsatisfactory.[126] Abbot to whom the machine belonged agreed to wait until the spring for the estate to build a new wall which would be frost proof and hopefully get the thresher working. Over the winter this project was considered against the fiscal expense but in the end as Abbot had decided to quit his farm and the machine was owned on the same principle as that of the Oborne's, it was decided the works were not worth the outlay.[127]

In order to make the machine at Clifton Farm more profitable, a scheme was devised whereby Messrs. Thompson who owned a nearby manufactory would employ the water wheel when the machine was not needed for threshing. Firstly, the wheel had been examined by two different mechanics to ensure that this idea would not cause any unnecessary damage.

Porter the tenant was to receive £2 2s 0d a week when the machine was used during the summer months and when the water in Thompson's mill was scarce. During 1821 under this agreement the sum paid equated to 42 guineas. Once it was established that the usage might be quite high, an agreement was drawn up whereby Thompson would indemnify against repairs or mischief to the machine. As the access was across Porter's land, he was allowed two-thirds of the monies paid by Thompson and Anglesey would receive the rest.[128] Without a doubt the fire risk as mentioned above was real as demonstrated in December 1824 when a blaze destroyed Porter's threshing machine and some of the adjoining buildings. The damage was estimated at £500 and it was assumed that as the tenant had been using the machine the whole of the proceeding day the fire originated 'by neglect of proper attention to some of the wheels'.[129] Castleman's insistence that Thompson was under a covenant to insure the buildings and machine against fire meant that the estate would not be out of pocket. However, in the flooded labour market of the early 1820s, it was now easier and cheaper to once again thresh by hand; therefore, while the barn was to be rebuilt the threshing machine would not.[130] The introduction of the threshing machine had been a financial decision by the estate in the light of labour shortages created by the Napoleonic Wars. By 1824 replacing the destroyed machine no longer made sense. The working relationship between landowner and tenant is amply illustrated with this form of mechanism whereby the landowner provides the necessary buildings and the tenant the capital albeit through a loan to purchase the machinery. While threshing machines are often viewed through the lens of the Swing Riots, they are as much part of the financial history of the estate as they are labour history.

Conclusion

Working relationships on the landed estate were complex, they relied on a number of factors not least of which was an established framework within which both landowner and tenant had certain responsibilities. Although unwritten it was expected that the tenant on entry into a farm would be provided with a set of well-maintained farm buildings and soil in good heart. On his part the tenant agreed to farm responsibly and in accordance with any husbandry clauses within the lease and to maintain the farm in a good state of repair. Agriculture post-1815 went through a series of deep depressions which meant this relationship was sorely tested. In the case of absentee landowners like the Marquis of Anglesey, a good, trustworthy land agent or steward was essential. William Castleman emphatically understood the local community within which he practised both law and managed a successful land agency business. There has been a dearth of research into working relationships within an estate due to the seeming lack of available data. In this case and in many other estate histories, under-utilised or under-researched archives contain a wealth of information relating to how estates worked and functioned or not when run by recalcitrant agents. Castleman's letters present many of the tenants not as the Anti-Corn Law League's dullard servile retainers but as men who were able to negotiate the terms of their leases, force rent rebatements and improvements, and as will be seen in Chap. 5, they did not meekly follow the Marquis of Anglesey's lead in politics and county affairs but understood the price of their voting loyalty. Thus, the financial history of the estate was a two-way process.

Financially the tenants were the spine of an estate, it could not survive without men and more rarely women who paid their rent on time, in full and did not fall into arrears. When the Marquis of Anglesey inherited the estate, it was in a dreadful state of repair. The previous agent Cox had failed to maintain the landowner's side of the bargain and Castleman quickly set about a schedule of works. In many respects this aided in keeping tenants in place during the difficult economic period in the immediate post-war period. As seen in this chapter, managing the tenant's arrears was a juggling act, because at the end of each audit day, monies were needed to pay the estate disbursements and to contribute to the life-style of the Marquis of Anglesey. Allowing rental arrears to accumulate was a risk worth taking providing the tenant could survive long enough to overcome the specific exogenous factors affecting prices. It was not uncommon, as seen here, for tenants to take matters into their own hands and to abscond selling off their goods for their own uses rather than paying their debts. Where possible the estate prosecuted in the severest of manners to act as an example, in the hope that this would prevent others following the same path. For the majority of tenants, it was a case of weathering the storm, but even the larger tenants such as Highmore suffered through no fault of their own. Every decision undertaken had a financial reason behind the process. While both repairs and improvements meant that the tenants benefited, ultimately it increased the value of the estate and meant that when prices improved farms could be rented at a higher price or in the case of a sale more monies raised. As seen in the Introduction, the Marquis of

Anglesey was constantly in debt, and he owed considerable sums of money to a range of people, thus collecting rents on time and in full was essential. The future of the estate was always unsure, and consequently maintaining the standard of the estate was paramount simply because Anglesey was never sure when a sale might be forced. As Castleman had arranged many of the local mortgages, he was in no doubt of either Anglesey's finances or the precarious nature of the economics surrounding estate management. The fact that the Dorset and Somerset estate of the Marquis of Anglesey survived owes much to his agent's entrepreneurial skills and his innate understanding of the tenants, the sums needed to be paid out and the monies which were likely to be received on audit days. An estate, however, was more than the sum of its working partnerships, equally social relationships formed part of the daily means of social control and were a vital part in the linkage which bound together a diverse range of peoples.

Notes

1. T. W. Beastall (1981) 'Landlords and Tenants', in G. E. Mingay (ed.), *The Victorian Countryside Vol. II* (London: Routledge & Kegan Paul), p. 428.
2. M. Cragoe (1996) *An Anglican Aristocracy: The Moral Economy of the Landed Estate in Carmarthenshire, 1832–1895* (Oxford: Clarendon Press), p. 2.
3. Ibid., p. 4.
4. E. L. Jones (2018) *Landed Estates and Rural Inequality in English History: From the Mid-Seventeenth Century to the Present* (London: Palgrave Macmillan), p. 115.
5. Ibid., p. 117.
6. Ibid., p. 4.
7. Ibid.
8. J. D. Chambers and G. E. Mingay (1982) *The Agricultural Revolution, 1750–1880* (London: B. T. Batsford Ltd.), p. 21.
9. S. Wade Martins (1980) *A Great Estate at Work: The Holkham Estate and its Inhabitants in the Nineteenth Century* (Cambridge: Cambridge University Press), p. 107.
10. E. L. Jones, *The Development of English Agriculture, 1815–1873,* Studies in Economic History (London, 1968), p. 25.
11. R. W. Hoyle (2016) 'Introduction: Recovering the Farmer' in R. W. Hoyle, (ed.), *The Farmer in England 1650–1980* (Abingdon: Routledge), p. 1.

12. L. P. Adams (1965) *Agricultural Depression and Farm Relief in England 1813–1852* (London: Frank Cass & Co. Ltd), p. 2.
13. Ibid.
14. Ibid.
15. Chambers and Mingay, *The Agricultural Revolution*, p. 16.
16. J. M. Stratton (1969) *Agricultural Records* (London: John Baker), pp. 96–97.
17. Adams, *Agricultural Depression and Farm Relief*, p. 69.
18. DHC, D/ANG/B5/15, 21 December 1814.
19. Ibid.
20. DHC, D/ANG/B4/1/23, Accounts to Lady Day 1815. Abbott and Oberne together owed nearly £4000 in arrears.
21. DHC, D/ANG/B5/15, 21 December 1814.
22. Ibid.
23. DHC, D/ANG/B5/21, 25 June 1816.
24. DHC, D/ANG/B5/21, 23 May 1816.
25. Ibid.
26. DHC, D/ANG/B5/21, 15 May 1816
27. Ibid.
28. Ibid.
29. Ibid.
30. DHC, D/ANG/B5/22, 29 August 1817.
31. See, for example, Adams, *Agricultural Depression and Farm Relief.*
32. Ibid.
33. DHC, D/ANG/B/4/1/28.
34. DHC. D/ANG/B5/21, 1 July 1816.
35. Ibid., 16 December 1816.
36. Ibid.
37. Ibid.
38. Quoted in Adams, *Agricultural Depression and Farm Relief*, p. 88.
39. DHC, D/ANG/B5/22, 20 December 1817.
40. Ibid.
41. F. M. L. Thompson (1963), *English Landed Society in the Nineteenth Century* (London: Routledge & Kegan Paul), p. 231.
42. DHC, D/ANG/B5/31, 17 July 1822.
43. Ibid.
44. DHC, D/ANG/B5/31, 20 July 1822.
45. Ibid., 22 February 1822.
46. Ibid., 18 April 1822.
47. Ibid.
48. Ibid.
49. DHC, D/ANG/B5/31 14 February 1822.

50. C. A. Beardmore (2015) 'Landowner, Tenant and Agent on the Marquis of Anglesey's Dorset and Somerset Estate, 1814–1844', *Rural History* 26:2, p. 191.
51. *Public Ledger and Daily Advertiser.* 16 July 1822.
52. DHC, D/ANG/B5/40, 10 July 1828.
53. DHC, D/ANG/B5/31, 16 November 1822.
54. Ibid., 9 December 1822.
55. *The Dorset County Chronicle and Somersetshire Gazette,* 22 July 1830, p. 3.
56. Ibid.
57. DHC, D/ANG/B5/42, 5 February 1830.
58. Ibid.
59. DHC, D/ANG/B5/42 17 and 25 June 1830.
60. *The Dorset County Chronicle,* 22 July 1830, p. 3.
61. DHC, D/ANG/B5/54 Estate Vouchers for 1831.
62. *The Farmer's Magazine, Vol. 19* (1861), p. 487.
63. DHC, D/ANG/B5/40, 7 February 1828.
64. DHC. D/ANG/B/4/1/50, Accounts for October 1828.
65. DHC, D/ANG/B5/41, 6 April 1829.
66. Stratton, *Agricultural* Records, p. 102.
67. *The Sherborne Mercury*, 6 April 1829.
68. Ibid.
69. DHC, D/ANG/B5/42 Letter from Highmore 11 August 1830.
70. Ibid., 25 August 1830.
71. DHC. D/ANG/B/4/1/50, Accounts for October 1829.
72. Ibid.
73. Ibid.
74. See, Adams, *Agricultural Depression and Farm Relief.*
75. DHC, D/ANG/B5/39, 27 January 1827.
76. DHC, D/ANG/B5/37, 7 April 1827.
77. See DHC. D/ANG/B/4/1/52, Accounts for October 1830 and DHC. D/ANG/B/4/1/55, Accounts for October 1831.
78. DHC, D/ANG/B5/61, 11 November 1844.
79. W. Marshall (1804) *On the Landed Property of England: An Elementary Treatise* (London: G. and W. Nicol and J. Robinson; R. Faulder; Longman and Rees; and Davies; and J. Hatchard), pp. 28–29.
80. Ibid., p. 28.
81. J. V. Beckett (1989) 'Landownership and Estate Management' in J. Thirsk (ed.), *The Agrarian History of England and Wales 1750–1850* (Cambridge: Cambridge University Press), p. 569.
82. See S. Wade Martins (2009) *Coke of Norfolk 1754–1842* (Woodbridge: The Boydell Press), p. 97.

83. Ibid.
84. Beckett, 'Landownership and Estate Management', p. 569.
85. Ibid., p. 570.
86. Beastall, 'Landlords and Tenants', p. 428.
87. Ibid., p. 429.
88. C. E. Curtis (1901) *Estate Management: A Practical Handbook for Agents and Pupils* (London: Horace Cox), p. 41.
89. Ibid., p. 42.
90. Ibid.
91. DHC, D/ANG/B5/16, 21 December 1814.
92. Ibid.
93. DHC, D/ANG/B4/4/67.
94. DHC, D/ANG/B5/17, 22 May 1815.
95. Ibid.
96. Ibid.
97. Ibid.
98. DHC, D/ANG/B/6/2, Stewards Notebook.
99. Beardmore, 'Landowner, Tenant and Agent', p. 194.
100. DHC, D/ANG/B5/25. Schedule of repairs at Yenston Farm 1819.
101. For a general overview of repairs, see J. Lawrence (1806) *The Modern Land Steward* (London: H. D. Symonds, T. Ostell, J. and J. Richardon); Thompson *English Landed Society in the Nineteenth Century;* J. Thirsk (ed.) (1989) *The Agrarian History of England and Wales 1750–1850* (Cambridge: Cambridge University Press).
102. Castleman also acted as land agent to the Bankes family.
103. DHC, D/ANG/B5/23, 7 March 1818.
104. DHC, D/ANG/B5/31, 25 April 1922.
105. DHC, D/ANG/B4/4/47 Estate Vouchers for 1822–1823.
106. DHC, D/ANG/B4/4/49 Vouchers for 1824 of J. N. Highmore.
107. Ibid.
108. DHC, D/ANG/B5/60, 1 January 1837.
109. See E. Kerridge (1967) *The Agricultural Revolution* (Abingdon: Routledge) and E. Kerridge (1969) 'The Agricultural Revolution Reconsidered', *Agricultural History*, 43:4, pp. 463–476.
110. See M. Overton (1996) *Agricultural Revolution in England: The Transformation of the Agrarian Economy 1500–1850* (Cambridge: Cambridge University Press), p. 7.
111. Ibid., p. 7.
112. Chambers and Mingay, *The Agricultural Revolution*, p. 5.
113. Kerridge, *The Agricultural Revolution*, p. 37.
114. J. H. Charnock (1843) *Suggestions for the More General Extension of Land Draining* (London: Longman, Brown, Green and Longman), p. 5.

115. A. D. M. Phillips (1989) *The Underdraining of Farmland in England During the Nineteenth Century* (Cambridge: Cambridge University Press).
116. DHC, D/ANG/B5/20. Report on the estate from William Castleman to the Marquis of Anglesey 28 February 1816.
117. DHC, D/ANG/B5/20, February 1816.
118. DHC, D/ANG/B4/4/54. Estate voucher relating to James Snook December 1830 and signed July 1832.
119. DHC, D/ANG/B4/4/54. Vouchers for 1831.
120. DHC, D/ANG/B5/26. Drainage indenture dated 21 February 1820 and Beardmore, 'Landowner, Tenant and Agent on the Marquis of Anglesey's Dorset and Somerset Estate', pp. 181–199.
121. DHC, D/ANG/B5/45. These figures are contained within the vouchers for 1821.
122. P. Miller (1835) *The Gardener's Dictionary, Vol. I* (London: G. Henderson), p. 223.
123. Ibid.
124. Overton, *Agricultural Revolution in England*, p. 125.
125. DHC, D/ANG/B5/31, 14 January 1822.
126. DHC, D/ANG/B5/16, 17 September 1814.
127. DHC, D/ANG/B5/16, 22 May 1815.
128. DHC, D/ANG/B5/31, 18 April 1822.
129. DHC, D/ANG/B5/34, 15 December 1824.
130. Ibid.

CHAPTER 4

Social Relationships

Overview

At the heart of both social and working relationships was the landowner. When he was absent or simply missing for short periods, for example, in attending to his political responsibilities, the role was taken up by his agent. Social leadership, historians have argued, was rarely challenged.[1] There is a theme which runs throughout the rural literature of the nineteenth century that rural communities were held in thrall to the landed classes and lived in fear of the consequences of disobedience. Under this theory agricultural labourers and other minority figures within the rural community harboured a dislike for and hatred of any person in authority. For much of the time, this discontent rumbled away underneath the surface occasionally erupting into violent words or deeds. A second strand portrays the relationships within the rural community as one of conflict which is contained by coercion and which is dealt with by social leadership and conditioning mixed with paternalism.[2] In this type of relationship, there is an underlying sense of tension. The Swing Riots of 1830 have in recent years through the research of Carl Griffin formed part of a much longer and wider period of rural unrest.[3] There is a third viewpoint that praises the rural community as a happy harmony of village life nourished by landlord kindness, but this is an idealised myth that in the light of modern research does not hold true. Eric Jones contends that the estate system was 'cold and cruel' no matter how many acts of charity or bowls of soup

C. Beardmore, *Financing the Landed Estate*, Palgrave Studies in the History of Finance, https://doi.org/10.1007/978-3-030-14552-1_4

were distributed. He argues that property, not people, was the 'watchword'. Outside observers such as Prince Hermann von Puckler-Muskau who visited many estates in the 1820s found the upper classes to be 'hard, exclusive and often philistine'.[4] Often landlordism is seen as something wicked with thoughtless landowners oppressing their tenants.[5] In reality there were both good and bad landowners and whether resident or absentee they exhibited a great interest and concern for both their tenants and others in the rural community.

Much of our understanding of how the different interactions within the agrarian society of the early nineteenth century worked relies heavily on the work of Gordon Mingay and like much else of this now dated literature remains generalist in content.[6] More recently Rab Houston has explored social relationships within estates and suggests that the way historians have sought to explore these interactions has changed. He argues that the emphasis a generation ago was mainly focused on the upper echelons of society and thus constituted a history from above. In contrast the local or village studies of the 1970s and 1980s explored the daily life and the interactions of peasant life. There was an emphasis on the relationships of ordinary people particularly the poor and the middling sorts.[7] Social interactions run across the different spectrum of societies and include everything from the provision of audit dinners for the tenants to coal and food for the poor. The fate of the agricultural labourer was tightly bound with the economic fortunes of the farmers for whom they worked. While an estate worked on many different levels, it was above all else an integrated whole. The Marquis of Anglesey and his agent understood the financial and political benefits of keeping the poor rate low—this encouraged the payments of rents on time and aided in the employment of any surplus labour. Social relationships within an estate were as individualistic as the landowners who owned them. There was not in other words one set of experiences which fitted the tenants, farmers and agricultural labourers. The standard nucleated settlement has tended to dominate studies of rural areas, and the evidence suggests that village identity was strong.[8] Yet as argued by Alun Howkins, many boundaries are much harder to define and are infinitely more porous than is often assumed, and this was particularly so with diverse estates such as that of the Marquis of Anglesey's. As seen in the Introduction, Peter Walter had put together the estate by buying up land as it became available; it had not been consciously built up over time as a single functioning estate of nucleated villages. In that sense perhaps the most cohesive locality was Milborne

Port bound together by its political identity and landscape which will be taken up in Chap. 5. For the rest of the population, William Castleman acted as a unifying force and the focal point of estate relationships whether socio-economic or political.

This chapter will explore social relationships between the estate and tenant and the estate and the poor who could not be controlled through access to politics and the vote. It will, firstly, explore the tensions created by the estate's decision to veer away from traditional expectations, which included hunting on court leet days, the contested ownership of trees and the right to pick firewood from hedges. Secondly, the estate illustrates the long-term impact of rural unrest which was not simply about low wages and unemployment issues but encompassed the loss of common grazing rights through enclosure and the disenfranchisement of Cranborne Chase and rural incendiarism. Thirdly, for the lower sections of agrarian society suffering from abject poverty, the estate made charitable payments, in the form of food, clothing and coal and these are the subject of Chap. 6. There was as much a financial cost to the estate in managing social relationships as in working ones. While the sums expended may not have been as large, they still made an important contribution to the rural community or stopped its members from undertaking activities which would have undermined estate profitability. It is often difficult to separate out different aspects of estate life, and they remain in many respects closely intertwined.

Traditions

Most academic historians of the countryside since the industrial revolution have according to Jeremy Burchardt, put agriculture at the centre of their accounts, but this is to view the history of the rural community in the narrowest possible terms.[9] Consequently, it is often forgotten that although reliant on farming, landed estates were communities with people at their heart. Like much of agricultural and rural history, it is the lack of records from below that hampers research and fails to provide the narratives and discourses which are an essential component of estate history. Elsewhere the pauper letters explored by Thomas Sokoll and Steven King provide at least a brief and narrow glimpse into the poverty suffered by the poor during periods of economic downturns but due to their nature fail to provide a wider or clearer picture.[10] Neither do they, as estate records might, provide a sense of changing fortunes which rested on the success of the tenant farmers. Contemporary writers argued that the established laws of an estate even though they might be imperfect should be adhered to, and only when a better tradition could be established should these be introduced.[11] Estate records while still providing a snapshot of a small area express the ways in which the tensions within the community were bound with its identity. Nowhere is this more evident than when exploring traditions. As will be seen here, part of the tensions surrounding an expected right was the financial cost to the estate and on occasions this was one which neither the Marquis of Anglesey or his land agent was prepared to bear.

Both tenant farmers and labourers had preconceived ideas over their customary rights. For example, the tenants expected a good and appropriate dinner on audit day. This event acted as the cement of the landlord and tenant relationship and was a convivial affirmation of the landowner's accessibility or offered at the very least access to his representative. Besides paying his rent on audit days, this was a time to present bills for improvements and to ensure that they were allowed against sums assessed. William Marshall argued that fixed rent days should be such that they allowed the tenants to 'make the most of their produce', in other words setting dates after specific sale days so that monies were readily available to meet the rent call.[12] On the Marquis of Anglesey's Dorset and Somerset estate, traditional audit days were Lady Day and Michaelmas although these dates were fluid and could be changed according to the state of agricultural prices or the date of harvest, for example.[13] Setting an immoveable date made no financial sense. Yes, an inflexible owner could force his tenants to sell their produce at a loss, but this would mean no profit and little chance of discharging all or indeed any of their debts. In the end actions such as this would simply create animosity and increase the number of tenants choosing to quit their farms or worse abscond with the stock and implements. The estate's vouchers contain numerous receipts for audit dinners, and as the estate was so dispersed audits were held in central places such as Stalbridge and Milborne Port on different days. The dinner and often bed and breakfast were paid for by the estate. For example, the 1816 Michaelmas audit for Stalbridge was held in late January 1817 at the Red Lion and cost the estate some £47 14s 6d. The bill included payments for coffee, tea, suppers, glasses, beds, breakfasts, fruit, servants, sugar, writing paper, tobacco, fire and lights and alcohol in the form of beer sherry, port and punch.[14]

When Castleman started working for the estate, he had noticed that the audit expenses seemed excessive; moreover he had been surprised to find that the large hall at Stalbridge had been full of people of which perhaps only half were recognisable. A consequent enquiry revealed that the invitation to dinner had been extended by Cox beyond the tenants to include bricklayers, carpenters and others who had been employed in repairing the estate. Tenants would only attend dinner on the day that they came to pay their rent, but these extra persons had been sanctioned and did attend for dinner on each of the three days over which the audit was spread. This seemed a 'wanton enhancing of the Expenses', and so an immediate directive was issued that none of these tradesmen should be allowed to attend in the future, thus restricting audit dinners simply to the tenants. Castleman intended, however, to reduce costs even further by omitting from such occasions those whose rent was below £10 per annum. Instead this group would be compelled to pay their rents at the Manor Court at the same time as the Lords Rents were received.[15] Castleman was a landowner in his own right, but it was presumably easier and less expensive to collect his own rentals at the same time as he did his employers. Accounting for even minute sums as seen in Chap. 2 was vital, and in order to be above board, he declared his own tenants at the audit dinner in 1844. It clearly and specifically states to 'deduct 4 dinners for Mr Castleman's Tenants paid for by Mr Castleman'.[16] Providing food and drink was closely interlinked with the political landscape of the time, and this will be taken up again in Chap. 5. The tradition of the audit dinner on rental day ensured that the estate had a visible presence in agrarian society—paying rent was a public affair. These occasions reiterated and reinforced the power of the local landowner but also acted as the glue which cemented the community together. Dinners had in the past also been provided at court leets, for example, at Henstridge. When it was decided to stop this event, the tenants were incensed—they put together a petition to Anglesey which stated 'in this Parish times have been a good Dinner & Punch used to cheer our hearts'. The estate they claimed had often paid £5 for this event, but in late years this had fallen to an allowance of £2 2s 0d for 12 'respectable Men for to cheer themselves'.[17] There is no doubt that these men felt one of their customary rights had been taken away. The estate faced a continual dichotomy of financial expediency balanced against maintaining the status quo in the eyes of the tenants. Other traditions were much more controversial and could heighten already existing tensions and easily erupt into unexpected violence.

Balancing the rural community like all aspects of estate management relied on choosing a land agent who was level headed and had good people skills. Employing someone with these capabilities could pay dividends as he either defused or handled difficult situations. In 1818, for example,

Castleman refused to allow the usual hunt to take place on the opening day of the Court at Hanley. An anonymous letter sent to the Marquis of Anglesey in 1819 stated that this event had 'been practised and deemed a right in the memory of Persons near a hundred years of age most living and without doubt many years beyond any memory'.[18] The crux of this matter lay in the phrase 'deemed a right'; in other words Castleman was not entitled to interfere in something that was beyond his remit. In the past and as observed by old Mr. James, it had been traditional for the estate steward to open the court early in the morning at eight o'clock. This had allowed the tenants and others attending the court to go deer hunting before the proceedings began. This time he had refused to open the court until one o'clock 'clearly on purpose' to prevent the hunt from taking place. Castleman was accused of 'insolent Tyranny'. It was claimed the agent's actions in forbidding the tenants to hunt meant he had failed to give them due satisfaction for the injury the deer caused to their lands. The author of the letter had been further angered because Castleman had stated that the courts were to cease from now on in, thus bringing to an end an event that had at least in living memory been taken for granted. The author advocated that if for some reason Anglesey had conceded to his agent's actions, then he had 'given up the most Valuable rights of your estate and your Court will not be deemed legal'.[19] If, however, it had been his agent's idea, then he had marred Anglesey's reputation and should be sacked immediately.

On its own this letter might have been the opinion of one single malcontent tenant but as ever nothing in estate history is simple. With his return letter, Castleman attached a bill for 30 guineas which was the sum he was out of pocket for trying to establish the legality of the hunt. His attempt had failed because the Court of the King's Bench had moved towards a new trial which was defeated being of the opinion the custom of hunting on Court day was bad in law.[20] In reply he stated that he had held the court the previous year at 'the risqué of my life'. On arrival he had been mobbed by 400 to 500 'lawless fellows' who were upset because the court had not been opened two hours before the posted notice. To demonstrate their anger, the jury had as soon as they had been sworn in walked out with the rest of the mob to go deer hunting. It was therefore impossible to conduct the legal business of the court and it had therefore been immediately closed—this meant that none of the officers for the following year had been appointed. When Castleman in 1819 had considered whether to hold the proceedings, he had been informed that the local populace intended to behave in the same manner according to their perceived customary rights. Part of the problem with this tradition was that it did not take place solely on Anglesey land but infringed on that of Lord Rivers. This would have brought the two landowners into conflict, a risk this land agent was not prepared to take, at least not, without written affirmation from Anglesey himself. In 1818 Rivers had taken one of the hunters to court, and although the enquiry had ended after the date of the anonymous letter, it was presumed Rivers would have the man committed to gaol. In order to protect himself from allegations of bribery, Castleman admitted to having received some venison from Lord Rivers since the case had ended.[21] Financially establishing whether the hunt was legal had been time-consuming and costly rather than difficult. It was not a case of being hampered by tradition, but instead a conscious decision was made whereby neither the landowner nor his representative would be dictated to by the tenants. In other words, it was an opportunity to manage social relationships between the local populace and to bolster and promote those with other landowners in the locality. Remaining on good terms with neighbouring landowners was essential, especially when borders were intertwined and not necessarily clear.[22] It was of far more important to placate Lord Rivers than the unruly population of Hanley.

Timber Rights and Traditions

The Court at Hanley was not the only area were the local populace clashed with the estate. Tensions arose over who owned the timber on estate lands; the taking of it for domestic use and maiming or shrouding the trees was used as a form of protest. Contemporary writers argued that the rental and intrinsic value of an estate could be enhanced through the maintenance and production of good timber. John Lockhart Morton suggested that woods should not be allowed to extend to encroach on profitable agricultural land as crops planted in the shade did not grow well.[23] It was essential that if wood was to be cultivated for profit, then Morton argued that it was important to match the right species of tree to the soil and climate. Plantations needed careful management as without proper care, they would cease to prosper, and consequently any profit could easily become a loss.[24] This predicament was evidenced in 1815 when Castleman inspected the plantations at Clifton and Bradford and found them 'in a miserable state', stating, 'indeed there was hardly a living tree'.[25] Thus caring for any plantations was an important part of estate management as timber in the erratic economic period of the post-war period brought in welcome income, especially when rental monies were slow in being paid and arrears continued to rise.

Carl Griffin argues that the maiming of trees particularly in Southern England falls within the remit of rural protest. He suggests that these deliberate acts were not an attempt to effect an immediate transformation in circumstances, but instead speaks to a wider discourse on the everyday processes of social change, or the sense of dislocation which had been created through rapidly altering economic circumstances and the intensification of agricultural practice. Tree maiming instead illustrates how wider social pressures were expressed by those without a political voice and were intended either to cause terror or to monetarily attack the capital of those who were seen as oppressors of the poor.[26] In many respects this was covert rather than overt protest, but one that would be instantly understood and recognised. Moreover, there has been little debate over the ways in which tree maiming fits into the wider debates of protest history. The Black Act of 1723 created a whole new range of capital offences, and amongst these were new offences which pertained to the cutting down or destroying of trees.[27] Timothy Shakesheff in his work on rural conflict, crime and protest in Herefordshire between 1800–1860 argues that it is almost impossible to ascertain the true extent of wood and crop theft or even wilful damage to hedges, fences and trees.[28] The law was changed again in 1825 which benefited the victims of crop theft, and consequently anyone found entering an orchard and carrying away trees, plants shrubs, fruit or vegetable was committing a crime that was now punishable by transportation.[29] The almost total absence of tree maiming in accounts of popular protest is according to Griffin unsurprising as the recording of such attacks was often fragmentary and in most instances little more than cursory.[30] Protest history has concentrated on larger outbreaks of dissent such as the Swing Riots rather than smaller and more localised events such as those which will be discussed below. That Castleman saw fit to write about the individual occurrences gives a sense of the importance the estate placed on these perceived outbreaks of violence and disgruntlement. For any estate it only took small pockets of dissatisfaction to quickly escalate into something much bigger, such as the rapid formation of the mob as seen above at Hanley court.

The importance placed by the estate on its timber was apparent from the beginning of Castleman's agency, not least because timber grown on the estate besides being sold was an important commodity for repairs and improvements. This left the estate open to theft and fraud by both contractor and tenant. Castleman debated with Anglesey whether it was better to let the contractor find his own timber, for which the estate would then remunerate him, rather than leaving the estate open to deception.[31] Nowhere is this better demonstrated than by Harding, a carpenter employed by the estate. He had been engaged by the errant agent Cox not just to carry out repairs but also in the cutting, felling and sale of Anglesey's timber. Harding stated that he had paid the money he had received for timber sales to Cox, who in turn was adamant that he had not received any a penny. An investigation was commenced, and it was suggested that no further monies were paid to Harding for work carried out until a better understanding of the situation had been reached.[32] Contemporary advice suggested the agent should mark each tree to be felled with different colours for each lot. A sketch plan should then be made which detailed the various divisions within the wood and the number of trees within it.[33] A fraudulent agent and an absentee landowner was a recipe for disaster, and with poor accounts, it was a problem that seemed to have no solution and given the different economic circumstances of the post-war period a loss the estate could ill afford. Next on the list was to ascertain the condition of the standing timber on the estate.

An inspection of the various plantations in 1814 revealed the condition of the timber on the estate was very mixed. At Clifton the wood had been badly 'pruned', and although some 40 acres out of 200 had received this treatment, the smaller trees had escaped with little damage. There was a suspicion that the larger ones might become rotten especially where large branches had been removed.[34] On the south east of Clifton Wood, the plantation was in 'a compromising state'; it appeared to have been planted with trees unsuitable for the soil, many of which were now dead. At Stalbridge and Wyke, the situation was even worse, and the report stated that 'the destruction committed by felling of the Timber on the estate … has been very great and on the latter estate [Wyke] there is scarcely a tree left'.[35] At Hanley in order to prevent further damage to the woods, it was proposed that building a small cottage for a resident woodsman would prevent further trespasses and thefts.[36] Employing a good agent meant one with the skills to recognise what might prove profitable. Certainly, surveying the timber to see what was required to bring the woods back to health was one means of increasing financial viability; the other was to recognise potential income streams. In 1818 Castleman realised that the ironwood coppice might, by placing a small cottage on it, become rentable.

In fact the Overseers of Yenston offered a net rent of £60 per annum, and he thought with a little persuasion, they could be persuaded to increase their proposed rent. At that time Anglesey's policy was not to let the coppices, but this principle had been put in place much earlier, and it was now suggested that it should be let. It was a relatively simple process to arrange a series of regulations which would ensure its proper management. The estate had refused to pay either the poor rate or any other taxes due on the land because Castleman had suggested that these were unfairly charged, and this would present a good solution to the problem.[37] Indeed his plan was executed, and an update on the coppice revealed that by 1822, it was 'getting into good order by the Protection offered to it by the Woodman's residence'. Importantly, it had turned from land that had not made enough to pay the taxes charged against it to one that had now become a good source of income.[38] Likewise, the regulatory measures put in place at Clifton Wood meant that it was now much more productive than heretofore. These above emblematic examples emphasise how decision-making and even change were underpinned by financial objectives and ultimately to an improvement in estate revenue.

Fraud and theft were ever present threats, and as seen above the estate had sought to mitigate these at Hanley by putting a woodsman in residence. It also sought to protect its timber from unauthorised ownership and prosecuted those who were caught stealing. Carl Griffin argues that there was a vast difference between those who took wood for domestic use and those who removed it for commercial purposes.[39] In the event of provable theft, the estate had no hesitation in prosecuting offenders and did not differentiate between domestic and commercial cases. So, in 1819, for example, there were two cases recorded in the correspondence. The first took place early in January when Castleman reported 'I have been under the necessity of making a severe though I trust salutary example of the Persons who insisted on the right of cutting down Timber on a Leasehold estate at Stalbridge'. This it was noted had been common practice and the tenant had then refused to pay for the timber used. On this occasion the offenders had been summoned before a magistrate and convicted with costs of £20. They were ordered to pay within the week or else they risked being committed to gaol for a period of not less than six months.[40] It was not just timber trees but fruit trees that the estate worried over; when attending to a change of tenants at Milborne Port in October, Castleman found that John Thorn, John Hallet and Sam Gregory had stripped their gardens of almost every tree including apple trees. Hallet had cut down a 'fine young Pear Tree the body of which is from 10 to 12 inches in diameter purely out of mischief'. To make matters worse, their leases sought to protect the trees on their properties, and the land agent suggested that legal advice should be considered.[41] The fact these were seen as criminal acts rather than a series of protests may explain why tree maiming does not appear as an element of protest history. With Hallet the tone is much more one of disgruntlement and acting to upset the estate rather than making any implicit statement of protest. Problems with timber theft remained ongoing, and as late as 1844, the situation was still not fully under control. Castleman wrote to Anglesey: 'Notwithstanding the utmost efforts on my part by employing persons to discover offenders by cutting and stealing the Timber and Saplings at Stalbridge a considerable Depredations are committed'.[42] Only one of the offenders was prosecuted as the other was protected by limitations contained in the Act; the overall effect was to break up the gang who was responsible for the damage. In effect this was definitely not a case of protest but undertaken for profit and gain actions the estate were keen to stop, nonetheless.

Timber was a saleable item and the estate was not prepared to miss out on the financial benefits it could bring. Knowing the value of the stock, the estate claimed ownership of all old, standing and fallen trees. Where these assets were perceived by the local population as being part of their intrinsic rights or where there was disputed ownership, the potential for considerable dissent existed as will be seen through the following case studies. For example, in 1827 Castleman wrote to the Marquis of Anglesey that there was a considerable quantity of ash on the waste of Hanley Manor which was 'getting' into a state of decay. To realise its capital value, he had sold much of it to Kendal, a carpenter in the village. This immediately raised issues over who had the rights to the timber; consequently as soon as the sale became common knowledge, Castleman declared that 'the whole mob in this riotous place announced that the timber was theirs'.[43] In this sense the crowd are exerting the notion of legitimisation, their actions informed by what has become known as the 'moral economy'. Consequently they conceived that in fighting the estate's decision, they were defending their traditional rights, and in this they definitely had the consensus of the wider community.[44] The trees were morphed by Mr. Streatfield, the local curate, into 'a fine avenue of Ash Trees which for many years has been [the] greatest ornaments of our Village and which local associations have endeared to ye people'.[45] Yet this 'great ornament' had escaped Streatfield's attention when Adams cut off one of the Trees and one of the rioters had 'shrouded' another, while others were cut down in the night and two more were stolen.[46] This incident was more about a local power struggle than stealing for commercial purposes and revolved around whether Anglesey, who was not Lord of the Manor, still owned the timber rights. This was not just a riot of agricultural labourers as already seen by the inclusion of an ex-naval captain and the local curate but one that encompassed a much wider section of the community. The bailiff at Withers' farm in the area probably expressed the general sentiments of the local population when he stated:

> they were not going to be frightened by the Marquis or his Bullies the General cry from the Mob was the Marquis and Mr Castleman had taken away the hunt from them and now they wanted to take away the rest of their rights.[47]

By guarding the timber overnight, the rioters were stopped, and Castleman sent his son the next day to remove the timber by force if necessary. Adams was the only person prosecuted and imprisoned. He was, however, 'truly penitent', and with a wife and four children who now had to be supported by the parish, there was a sense that Lord Anglesey would consent to his release from gaol after he had served a month of his sentence. While this seems a simple dispute over a smallish quantity of timber, it was in essence something much more serious. An earlier riot over the same issue at Hanley had occurred in 1811, and Cox, the then agent, had refused to fell any more trees in the area for the length of his agency. Castleman acted in much the same way as when he failed to open the court early in 1819; in doing so, he was exerting both his and the estate's authority and power. While it was usual to find the land agent rather than the landowner negotiating through the minefield of customary rights, when the landowner was an absentee, winning in this type of situation could mean the difference between a well-managed estate and one that descended into chaos. Attempts to socially control the local community will be picked up again in Chap. 6.

This was not the only instance when cutting and taking away trees created tensions over who owned the timber rights. The riot at Hanley illustrated both the moral economy in practice and the way in which local opinions could quickly turn into something more serious, but the second was perhaps the most worrying coming in the wake of the Swing Riots. In both outbreaks of dissent, local unruly elements of the population sought to challenge the power of the estate, while the actions of the estate were underpinned by the value of the timber which was at risk. The tempest of 1837 mentioned in Chap. 3 which had brought down several elms in Stalbridge Park elicited an attempt by the labourers in the area to take away the fallen timber. There was a precedent for this incident which had occurred six or seven years earlier. On that occasion a great number of labourers had congregated in the park with hooks and 'carried away a considerable part of the tops and persisted until they were overpowered'. The same behaviour had once again been exhibited by the lower sections of the community, but perhaps being now much more aware of the contentious nature of the crowd, the estate had been better prepared, and although the horde were resisted with difficulty, they were turned out of the park. The motive behind this action was the belief that they 'were entitled to the Tops of the Trees'.[48]

Timber was important for two main reasons: it provided building materials for repairs and improvements but needed to be protected for the financial benefits it remunerated to the estate. These came under threat in 1842 when the government in trying to reduce the price of timber had changed the tariffs on that which was imported. Colonial timber was allowed to come into the country with a nominal duty, while that on Baltic timber had been greatly reduced.[49] Castleman suggested to Anglesey that this was an 'apparently ruinous measure to the landed estate'. It was without doubt a financial worry as he expected the price of timber to fall by at least a third. So, when selling, the estate would make a loss. There was, however, an upside to this situation and one which could be fully exploited. By arranging to complete some new buildings and extensive ongoing repairs, it was estimated that it would be possible to reduce the carpenter's charges by as much as 30 per cent.[50] A good land agent was adaptable and was able to modify situations to his employer's advantage, and as here while the estate might lose money on the one hand, it could save considerable sums on the other. Timber was a vital component to both the estate's finances and to keeping the costs of repairs down; thus it sought to oversee, preserve and conserve its supplies. The full force of the law might be used to enforce protection of timber supplies, but this could also be achieved by putting in place resident woodsmen or renting out areas of woodland as seen above. The ownership of timber could invoke bitter disputes and threaten social relationships between the landowner and local population. The biggest breakdown of social relationships, however, occurred in 1830 when Castleman was called upon to use the full extent of his managerial and people skills to avert disaster when the estate was faced with destruction as a result of the Swing Riots.

Swing Riots

Since Eric Hobsbawm and George Rudé's groundbreaking work on *Captain Swing* published in 1969, there has accrued a significant historiography on rural protest.[51] Peter Jones, however, argues that much of the new literature still relies on the methodological and historiographical model established by Hobsbawm and Rudé.[52] Carl Griffin is one of the exceptions and has challenged social and economic historians to take a new and fresh look at instances which on the surface appear simplistic but that might in reality fit into the wider histories of rural unrest. In doing so Griffin advocates that *Captain Swing* is no longer 'archivally, analytically or conceptually' correct even though it remains a relevant and highly readable account. Problematically *Captain Swing* now appears to have seriously underestimated the scale of the disturbances in terms of not only the number of crowd actions and arson attacks but also their geographical spread.[53] The research of Katrina Navickas, for example, sets Swing within a northern context arguing that events which took place in Carlisle, Cumberland, on 30 November 1830 were seen locally in newspapers and witness reports as the work of *Captain Swing*. This is highly significant because Swing is usually associated with the arable flatlands of Southern England rather than a northern phenomenon.[54] Many of the cases in counties, such as Yorkshire Navickas argues, were proven to be the product of local grievances. In many respects this is also true of the outbreaks in the south and certainly was the case when the impact of Swing is examined on the Marquis of Anglesey southern estate. Furthermore, these ideas link with the question of whether or not Swing constituted an actual movement.[55] Overall Swing did not follow a recognised pattern nor does it appear to have been a function of any controlling influence. Earlier historians such as Gordon Mingay argued that the speed at which the disturbance spread meant that there had to be some form of inherent organisation even if only at the local level.

Most historians from Hobsbawm and Rudé onwards have argued that Swing contained the attributes of a loosely cohesive movement. In this, Peter Jones argues, lies a paradox, because precisely those factors which form a movement such as focus, co-ordination and a specific end goal are all missing from these riots. It is, however, perhaps easier to see Swing in the way that Jones does, conceptualised as 'meta movements', whereby the incidents were interrelated and took place within a broad canvas across England but at the same time were defined by an intense localism. This was at the expense of anything that resembled an overarching set of demands, guiding principles or a figurehead beyond the fictitious Captain Swing.[56] The machine breaking that took place in 1830 was not new, and counties such as Norfolk, Suffolk and Essex had experienced such episodes before in 1816 and 1822.[57] While these riots were hostile to the threshing machine and were the work of agricultural labourers, they have not elicited the same amount of research as the Swing Riots. In fact, most historians suggest that this outbreak was confined almost exclusively to East Anglia, and yet an incident in the estate village of Charlton Horethorne in this year suggests that the unrest spread over a much wider area which sits outside that covered by current research.

In November placards appeared in the village which stated 'Woe to the Farmers that use Threshing Machines'. This was followed shortly after by a fire in the rick yard of Mr. Took who unsurprisingly used a threshing machine in the daily work of the farm. As a result, a barley rick was destroyed, and it was reported that it was only through the 'unremitting exertions' of the local population that more damage was not incurred. Newspapers reported that when the fire was at its height, the same words from the placard were heard from a voice in the crowd.[58] A reward was offered of 50 pounds, and consequently Barnett came forward and provided information that himself and a father and son named Talbot were all involved. In the end the younger Talbot was acquitted as he could prove an alibi. The evidence against the elder provided by Barnett was so implausible that he was also discharged. Barnett on the other hand was committed to Ilchester gaol.[59] Castleman, however, was not convinced that they had got 'to the bottom of this infamous business'.[60] He left instructions in the parish that if any further information came to light, it should be conveyed to him immediately. Anglesey who from his political position would have been aware of other incidents commented, 'It is very desirable to snip in the bud this first incendiary spirit & if you think it necessary you will send for a Bow St Officer'.[61] There was thus already a model in place which Swing then used to great effect. Incendiarism hit at the very core of the estate's financial heart, by destroying the produce which the tenants would ultimately use to pay their rent. Incendiarism according to Hobsbawm and Rudé was only a characteristic of rural unrest after 1830.[62] In fact, as seen here, it was used almost a decade earlier. It did not though have the same impact as the wider outbreak of Luddite-like destruction which took place during Swing.

No one has yet reached a definitive answer as to why Swing occurred in 1830 rather than any other year. For much of the preceding 25 years, William Cobbett realised that the farm workers had due cause to turn to violent insurrection. By the mid-1820s, he had come to prophesy a major rural rebellion which by 1828 he prophesied would occur in 1830–1831. He predicted that the outbreak would not be as localised as the bread and wage riots of 1816 or the machine breaking of 1822. Instead Cobbett argued this revolt would be wider and has a much broader mandate than anything that had come before. Although historians such as Ian Dyck have suggested that neither hunger nor unemployment was any higher than in the previous periods, Cobbett predicted that both the above factors had now been joined with a new political consciousness.[63] The causes of Swing are in many ways as individual as the localities themselves, but there is a general consensus that a number of factors were common to all. Hobsbawm and Rudé argued that the average labourer in the south of England was in a dreadful and demoralised condition. They argued that it needed the right kind of trigger to provoke a reaction. Revolution on the continent and political crisis at home had begun to create a sense of expectation, tension and hope. David Kent's idea that there was nothing complicated about the causes of the Swing disturbances and that they simply sprung from the grinding poverty which faced most agricultural labours is too simplistic.[64] Peter Jones, however, maintains that the reasons behind the protests were much more complicated than the simple projection of the labourers' issues surrounding increasing poverty. Instead he suggests that the problem in ascertaining the causes of the riots lies in the diverse nature of local factors.[65] Undoubtedly though contemporary evidence suggests that poverty and low wages were a common cause and one which the Reverend Mason at Hanley would have agreed.[66] Roger Wells argued that unionist mentalities were central to Swing especially in the frequent demand for higher wages. He argues that the recurrent campaigns of agriculturalists for concessions from successive Tory governments between 1815 and 1830 exaggerated the geographical and chronological events of the depression.[67]

The Hammonds looked in 1911 to the threshing machine as being at the centre of the disturbances. They argued that the labourers relied on threshing by hand during the winter months to keep their standard of living just above starvation level.[68] The Hammonds highlighted the extent to which winter employment impacted upon agricultural labourers. Their research revealed that a landowner and occupier near Canterbury had written to the *Kent Herald* arguing that in each barn where machinery had not been installed, around 15 men were employed until May threshing corn. If it is assumed that each man had a wife and three children, then one barn was responsible for supporting the lives of 75 people during the leanest part of the year.[69] Joyce Burnette has suggested that the changes where threshing machines were used are even more significant than simply a reduction in the number of labourers employed. It allowed for the employment of more women and boys at a lower rate of pay and shifted the period in which they worked from the first quarter of the year to the fourth.[70] The latter factor meant that employment was reduced during the period which was the quietest part of the farming year. Griffin suggests that by the turn of the decade, applications for poor relief had reached record levels.[71] Other historians such as Keith Snell while recognising that the Swing Riots were diverse both in terms of causes and manifestations maintain that opposition to the threshing machine was a common thread that ran throughout the disturbances.[72] The *Rural Queries* dispatched in 1832 revealed that local correspondents attributed the riots to a variety of causes which included under- and unemployment, the antipathy of paupers to Overseers, game preservers, the parish system of poor relief as well as the threshing machine. Together these factors formed the general reasons for unrest but do not take into account the individual grudges and grievances held by the local populace.

By 1829 a range of specific factors were beginning to affect the Marquis of Anglesey's Dorset and Somerset estate, and these highlight the localism of the Swing outbreaks. The wet summers of 1828 and 1829 as seen in Chap. 3 meant that many of the larger farmers lost large amounts of their livestock, hay and grass crops and laid off their labourers simply to survive. The winter was truly dreadful, and many labourers were unable to work (and were therefore not paid) as the ground froze solid. Dorset was synonymous with low wages, and it is suggested by Kevin Bawn that the earnings of agricultural labourers in the county during the late 1820s and 1830s ranged from between seven and eight shillings per week.[73] When these are compared to Martin Daunton's figures for Northumberland where wages ranged between ten and twelve shillings, the meagreness of the Dorset wages becomes even more apparent.[74]

The problems in the latter part of the decade of local under- and unemployment were exacerbated by a more general countrywide economic downturn. To emphasise the difficulties faced by the estate, Castleman sent Anglesey a newspaper clipping which stated:

> This embarrassment is not confined to one particular department of industry. It pervades all the trading and manufacturing districts of the country. It depresses alike the cotton-manufacturer, the woollen cloth-manufacturer, the iron-smelter, the silk-weaver and all other leading manufacturers of the empire. The resources of the nation are actually paralysed and as the capitalist is pursuing an unprofitable business, the operative is starving from inadequate wages. In fact, more general distress never did prevail.[75]

At Milborne Port where the glove industry provided vital employment for women, it was noted that the importation of French gloves had forced owners to reduce their workforce to around a half. As family income rarely relied on just the male breadwinner's income, this was a real blow. At nearby Corfe Castle in 1790, it had been estimated that at least 30 per cent of the income of a labourer's family came from the earnings of women and children; thus anything that reduced women's employment could have a dramatic impact on family incomes and sustainability. Contemporary newspaper reports stated that the stock held by the glove manufacturers was higher than any in their history as the finished product had become unsaleable. Consequently, the *Bath Chronicle* and *Weekly Gazette* wrote: 'The distress among the lower classes, arising from this depression, is in the highest degree lamentable'.[76] The correspondence of 1830 consisted of two mains themes: distress amongst the tenant farmers in the early part of the year and the Swing Riots at the end.

William Castleman first became aware that the rural disturbances which had begun in Kent had reached Dorset while at home in Wimborne on 24 November 1830. Once the spark had been ignited, the riots had quickly spread causing great fear and panic amongst the landed classes. As already discussed above, while the individual riots shared many themes, it was the specificity of local concerns that stood out. At Hanley the grievances were intermingled with disgruntlement surrounding the changes in common rights over Cranborne Chase.[77] The estate was attacked in several places. *The Sherborne Mercury* reported that a body of rioters had burnt a 'threshing machine belonging to Mr Grey' at Henstridge and the group had then moved to 'Yenstone' where the machine of Mr. Davis had been destroyed.[78] At Hanley around 60 rioters had gathered, where they levied contributions on money and provisions and subsequently destroyed the whole of the agricultural machinery.[79] At Stalbridge the magistrates had tried to enlist special constables to aid in policing the area and to prevent any further damage to property. On 2 December when reaching the town on his journey from Milborne Port and seeing the magistrates surrounded by a 'great many persons', Castleman seized the moment. He wrote to Anglesey: 'taking the Testament in my hand I said I did not wish to involve others in a personal danger in which I was not willing to participate; upon which I was sworn a special Constable'.[80] After this the local populace quickly took the oath and were enrolled. The secret to this success may also lie in the estate vouchers with a receipt which recorded 16s 8d for brandy for the special constables during the riots.[81] It is possible that this action saved Stalbridge from the same type of loss seen elsewhere on the estate.[82] Consequently, the threshing machine which had stood in Stalbridge Park for many years remained undamaged. Ultimately the actions taken were as much financial as they were about maintaining public security and ensured that the local populace were now duty-bound to fight the rioters and to defend property. By protecting the agricultural machinery of the tenant farmers, he was ensuring that the poor economic situation would not be exacerbated and less leeway would need to be given in terms of compensation or rental reductions. While the Swing Riots are often seen as relatively minor, the seriousness of the violence was highlighted by Castleman when he wrote, 'they must be put down or we shall very shortly have them for our governors'.[83]

The estate needed to come up with an immediate plan to relieve both the tenants and the labourers. There was a realisation that financially all elements of the rural community needed to be included in some form. When looking for reasons for the outbreak of violence, Castleman had stated that 'I do not believe there are many more Persons out of employ than has generally occurred at the season of the year', and as shown in Fig. 2.1 in Chap. 2, rent arrears were beginning to decrease again.[84] Stalbridge was around two thirds pasture and had never accordingly provided full employment during the winter months. There was an awareness that over the last two years some of the tenants had discharged labourers during the winter months 'merely for want of money to pay them'.[85] While this had enabled the tenants to cut costs, their farms had suffered as a result, and in an attempt to keep the poor in employment, he had issued notices to 'make Hedges, cleanse branches &c'.[86] Labourers who were thrown out of work became a burden on the parish, and as will be seen in both the Introduction and Chap. 5, there was a balancing act to be achieved between the level of poor rate and ensuring voter loyalty. While on paper tenants usually voted in line with the landowner's chosen candidate, it will be seen that deference needed to be fought for and was in effect much flimsier than is often assumed. To grasp the extent of the problem, an order was issued to the tenant farmers requesting that by 10 am on the 8 December, a statement should be submitted describing the number of labourers both men and boys who could additionally be employed.[87] The actions then implemented had a fiscal price, for which the estate agreed to meet the cost. For the tenants there was an immediate ten per cent rent abatement from which would be deducted the sums paid in extra labour. When the additional labourers were unable to work due to poor weather such as frost, they were to receive parochial relief 'as in ordinary cases and be in public works as usual'.[88] This would keep the men occupied and paid, rather than descending back into absolute poverty. For those who had recently taken up a lease, there would be a smaller reduction that had yet to be agreed. The women were to be found where possible work in the glove manufacturers owned by the estate at Milborne Port.[89] John Sanderson, the agent-in-chief, proposed building eight or ten cottages at Stalbridge, each was to have half an acre in land. They would be let to the 'best Labourers with families at fair Rents'.[90] These houses were constructed of a higher standard than any others in the town with stone walls, slate roofs, privies, iron window frames and pipes to carry water to the cottages, and altogether the costs amounted to £1004 10s 3d.[91] In many ways this part of the scheme was inspirational as in time the cottages could become a source of income in their own right as they were assessed for Church, Waywarden and poor rates. Using the labourers in the construction of the properties ensured they stayed off the parish. It was further suggested that maybe some form of winter work in the form of basket weaving might be found for the labourers during the winter evenings, but this never materialised.

Swing was responsible for two additional charges to the estate. There was a legal bill for collecting the 'Depositions of John Davis, Robert Stay, John Stay Elisha Legg and Charles Hooper' 'against George Eavis, James Samson otherwise Chippett, Edward Turner, Charles Bilbin otherwise Day, John Biss, Joseph Seymour and William Condon' for their part in the riot at Henstridge of £19 15s 0d. At the trial Seymour was acquitted and of:

> The other Prisoners – Cordon and Biss found not guilty – Eavis convicted and Transported for 7 years – Samson, Turner and Bilbin Convicted and sentenced to 3 Months Imprisonment and hard labour.[92]

At Hanley, Stokes, Anstey, Samuel Zillwood, Robert Zillwood, John Read and James Hick were all indicted for breaking a 'threshing machine'. As a result, Stokes and Read were sentenced to one year's imprisonment and Zillwood to six months.[93] The final bill was from the men who had acted as night watchmen at Bradford Abbas. A petition on their behalf from the Vicar, Overseers and churchwardens stated:

> Mr Joyce gave certain of us reason to understand that the Marquis of Anglesey would defray the expences the Men were hired on that consideration and understanding, and we trust that you will see fit to make good the promise which was held out.[94]

The bill was relatively small; 12 men had spent a total of 30 nights protecting this area of the estate giving between one and four nights each and charged their time at the rate of two shillings per night. All in all, they were asking for £3 0s 0d, a seemingly small expenditure for the protection of machinery where the outlay and set-up could be in excess of £1000.[95]

The countryside returned to a reasonably peaceful state fairly rapidly, and by 11 December, the correspondence states '… at Stalbridge everything is quiet there and I hope before tomorrow night that Bradford [Abbas] will be quieted also'.[96] When Swing actually ended remains a much-debated topic. Hobsbawm and Rudé suggest as does Carl Griffin that the unrest continued with outbreaks of localised violence.[97] A more sustained revival of rural unrest broke out in 1834–1835 when the implementation of the Poor Law Amendment Act gave a new focus to the labourers' grievances.[98] The estate did not escape in this second wave of disturbances although events were confined to Bradford Abbas where there were a number of incendiary attacks. In June 1835, fires which had broken out in a number of buildings the previous winter were now deemed to have been deliberate. Mr. Grant, the local vicar, and some of the inhabitants working in cahoots with the estate had attempted to find the offenders. Two women were apprehended and after a long investigation were committed for trial but were then acquitted. On 19 May, three cottages which formed part of Mr. Andrews' farm were burnt down. The middle cottage in which the fire started was unoccupied and it was commonly believed to be the act of an incendiary. To try and nip this disturbance in the bud, hand bills were distributed offering a reward on conviction of the offenders, while the local populace issued other bills detailing a further reward. This was all to no avail. The labourers and others in the vicinity had been effective in extinguishing the blaze, and without their efforts the damage would have been extensive. In order to show the estate's appreciation, five pounds were sent to distribute amongst the firefighters. On 17 June, news arrived that yet another wilfully started fire had broken out on the previous Saturday. It was suggested that now a 'proper person' should be sent from London who might discover the perpetrator.[99] Thinking about future proofing the estate in light of the three recent fires, there was a growing idea, that some thought should be given to insuring the principle farm buildings against future conflagrations. This seemed especially prudent as many of the buildings were thatched and the premiums likely to be high but still much less than having to replace them. He suggested that the insurance might be stopped once the offenders had been caught or 'when their evil dispositions shall appear to have subsided'.[100] While the rush of incendiary attacks lessened in the area, there was another fire in 1837 which once again occurred on Andrews' land. This time it was an old farmhouse which burned 'with uncontrollable fury', and although attempts were made to extinguish the fire, the building was destroyed. *The Morning Chronicle* reported 'there seems to be little doubt that this is a repetition of the fearful system which for a long time has been carried on in Bradford'.[101]

The Swing Riots and the rural unrest which rumbled away in the background meant the estate and its land agent needed to keep a close eye on unravelling events. The management of social relationships meant being a visible member of the rural community, and as demonstrated by Castleman enrolling as a special constable at the height of the unrest, could have a considerable impact. Although seemingly an act of publicity, it probably did more to protect the threshing machine at Stalbridge than any other action. Overall the aim had been to prevent any further loss of the estate's or its tenants' capital. While there is a substantial historiography surrounding Swing, a local meticulous case study still has much to offer to the development of a wider understanding of the local nature of protest. Navigating social relationship was part and parcel of the role of the land agent, but at the core there was an implicit understanding that there was a price which the estate had to pay to be effective. Power and authority had to be maintained while balancing the processes through which the community lived and functioned.

Negotiating Social Relationships

Until relatively recently estate studies have concentrated on the landowners themselves, the people who were supposedly society's natural leaders. In the 1970s and 1980s, there was a movement towards local or village studies which examined the way in which communities interacted with each other, with a particular emphasis on relationships between the 'middling sort' and the poor.[102] At the same time, agricultural historians concentrated on a broader history of agriculture and farming during the period covered by the Agricultural Revolution.[103] There have been a number of estate studies such as that on Holkham estate by Susanna Wade Martins, which at least examined the tenantry, but in general they all consistently failed to explore the social relationships which existed between the estate and the people who lived within its borders.[104] To some extent the gap in the literature has started to be filled by Rab Houston, but even this does not explore social relationships across the various societal divides nor does it consider the financial implications which underpinned many of the decisions made.[105] Houston argues that in most estate studies, the tenants normally take centre stage which is not unsurprising as it is from this group that most income was derived. More recently Eric Jones has suggested that landowners regarded the 'last labourer's revolt' in 1830 with dismay. He argues that they had headed, governed and reigned over patriarchal societies where they had mistaken deference for approval.[106] As will be seen in the following chapter, deference was quite fragile and something that was both given and taken away at will. Only the richest of landowners could have afforded to have evicted all their tenants in the event that they unilaterally removed their support. Allegedly landlords were most annoyed with tradesmen and artisans who owned some form of small property and which gave them a minor stake in society. Frequently it had been this group who sided with the ringleaders in the revolt.[107] The Marquis of Anglesey was renowned for his benevolence, and there is no sense of a desire to punish anyone other than those who could be identified as having played an integral part in the damage to machinery or ricks. Instead both landowner and agent innately understood that the estate needed to act as mediator in disputes, traverse local arguments and, if necessary, spend monies which benefited either the local community or as explored in Chap. 6 contributed towards the social control of the unrulier elements of agrarian society.

An emblematic demonstration of the estate's intervention to the advantage of the local populace was evident in the weighing engine which was situated near the Old Red Lion at Stalbridge. When first erected by Admiral Aylmer, it had required an outlay of some £70–£80. In the beginning the estate had charged a toll to use the engine, but this had created very little return on investment. Consequently, the estate had taken the decision to let out the engine for a fee of £5 per annum subject to occasional repairs. Overall it had been a loss-making exercise especially as engines of this type had a relatively short working life of perhaps some 14 or 15 years before they were worn out. An enquiry found that it would cost as much to repair the old machine as to purchase a new one. A more modern one had been located which would suit the estate's purposes for £68 and from which would be deducted the value of the old machine. Having the machine in town was a benefit to the tenants and the local population, but it would never produce a profit. This did not mean that the estate would not replace the now outdated equipment. In response to Castleman, Anglesey had returned his letter having written in the margin, 'If this machine is not a matter of profit as it is one of accommodation to my tenants provided it is not one of [extensive] loss I do not object to its continuance'.[108]

One area where the estate and tenant relationship came close to breaking down was over the rabbit population. Blood sports were ancient pastimes of those who had access to land, but this pastime was formalised by the Victorians and the game laws which came to dominate rural society.[109] Deference to the landlord's interests in sport and personal interests could be irksome, but in return the community could expect their welfare to be of paramount interest. Tenants, consequently, were expected to protect the game and this included rabbits, and usually they could not be destroyed without the express permission of the landlord. In return occupiers of land were expected to rely on the estate to employ regular drives against this pest to keep numbers down and to protect their crops.[110] In fact, the contemporary writer Robert Brown suggested that if landed proprietors would 'look to their own interests', they would destroy all rabbits and hares on their estates; this would not only help to protect young plantations but would be of benefit to the tenants. Brown argued that if the rabbits were not given over to the tenants, then 'proper rabbit-trappers' should be appointed.[111] This remained a contentious issue and could add unnecessary pressure to both working and social relationships.

An example of the problems which could arise concerned Mr. Yeatman, the rabbit population and hunting on the estate. The sporting rights of Stalbridge Manor were leased to the said Mr. Yeatman, who was also, 'an active magistrate and a man of considerable property and some influence in the Neighbourhood'.[112] By early 1844 matters had reached crisis point with the tenants surrounding this manor complaining about the damage being caused by the rabbits which Yeatman should have controlled. An indication of the reaction was inherent in Castleman's comment: 'I fear that this will lead to a lengthened if not an unsatisfactory and unpleasant correspondence'.[113] In order to deal with the problem quickly and swiftly so that good social and working relationships could be re-established, it was suggested that a circular was sent to the tenants allowing them to take upon themselves the destruction of the rabbits. This, however, did not meet with Anglesey's approval; he stated: 'I have great repugnance to do anything in the least degree unkind or offensive to a brother sportsman'.[114] Understanding that something needed to be done or he risked the tenants either quitting their farms or asking for rent reductions neither of which was ideal, it was decided that Yeatman must be ordered to destroy the rabbits as per the clause in his lease.[115] Mr. Yeatman's compromise, which was acceptable to the estate, was to pledge to pay the tenants a fair restitution for any losses which they incurred.[116] Of course the sums had to be agreed and Yeatman wanted the damages to be assessed by his own surveyor.[117] As well as making payments Yeatman sought to control the pests, writing that he had held three parties 'to shoot Rabbits in the Park [Stalbridge] this Season'. He reported that since Castleman's last letter, they had killed 104 rabbits and his keeper with traps and ferrets nearly 200 more.[118] Although Yeatman now seemed to be complying with the estate's demands, Mr. Blake was sent to examine Mr. How's wheat near the Stalbridge Weston Coppices. He argued that the injury would not have been so bad if Yeatman had dealt with the rabbits when requested in late November 1843. Now he argued that 'the tenants will no doubt press for a remuneration for the serious damage they will sustain in their Crops, and I scarcely know how this claim is to be evaded'.[119] This argument was to rumble on with Yeatman playing for time. Realising that he needed to step in to placate the tenants, a provisional arrangement was reached whereby the tenants paid the estate the same rent as Yeatman, and in return they accepted the present stock of game and rabbits in compensation for the damage that had been sustained.

If, however, they let Yeatman remain until Lady Day, the estate would escape having to personally remunerate for the injury to the crops.

The narrative surrounding Yeatman dragged on, not least because William Castleman died in the middle of the debate. There was subsequently a slight lull in estate business to allow for the ensuing discussion as to whether his son should take up the agency which is indeed what happened. It was not unusual for sons to follow their fathers into the profession, and Edward had already been working alongside his father. It thus made sense for him to carry on. In late December Edward Castleman went to Stalbridge to meet with those who rented the sporting over the manor. He communicated that Anglesey wished Yeatman to be allowed to follow his game but not to beat for it. The tenants one and all refused to comply arguing that 'they might as well give up their rights altogether to Mr Yeatman and allow him merely to follow his game as they would sustain as much damage by that as by allowing him to beat'.[120] This was a baptism of fire for a new land agent. He would have needed to have drawn on all the knowledge he had learnt working alongside his father to find a deal that was fiscally acceptable to the tenants and the estate. Eventually after four hours of intense negotiation and subject to Lord Anglesey's approval, it was agreed that the tenants would allow Yeatman, to beat for game over any part of the manor, except those areas rented by Parsons who refused to join the scheme. In return Anglesey was to allow each of the tenants who were affected one half of the reserved rent for the sporting. The tenants complained bitterly that Yeatman annually caused immense damage to their crops and fences, and although he promised to pay compensation, this never materialised. Hay crops in the spring suffered too especially from late hunting. Edward Castleman, however, stated 'I fear from the very strong feeling expressed by each tenant, that even in case of the above arrangement being carried out they will take the Law into their own hands & destroy every hare on the Manor'.[121] Matters remained tense, ultimately Parsons threatened to quit his farm, the tenants had great animosity towards Yeatman which it seemed little if anything would appease. Juggling such relationships was difficult; to some extent Anglesey sympathised with Yeatman 'his sporting brother' but he could not afford to do so at the expense of his tenants. Using his land agents to mediate on his behalf ensured that he did not appear to favour one side over the other. Both types of tenants in this case paid the estate rent; it was a case of working out which would cause the smallest financial burden to the estate. It should be noted that the amount of time that was spent trying to sort this out meant that other areas of estate management might be neglected. It does though reveal just how many problems one troublesome tenant might cause. This was not the only area where the estate needed to take the lead in dispute management.

References to roads and turnpikes are common in the estate's archive and performed an important role in the transportation of heavy materials such as stone for drainage, timber for repairs, manure to replenish the soil and crops and to move livestock to and from the farm or to market. Lord Ernle argued that even when parishes were active in road repairs, many of those in rural areas were in a deplorable condition.[122] The contemporary writer, Edward Laurence, stated that 'A Steward, upon his Surveys, should observe whether the Tenants keep the Bye-roads leading through their Grounds in good repair'.[123] For John Lawrence the reputation of the landowner and the interest he invested in his lands were apparent in the state of the roads.[124] In those areas where there was an abundance of hard materials, poor roads he argued revealed a 'most contemptible and churlish indolence'.[125] Roads Lawrence warned require constant attention, and although large sums of money might be expended, they might never reach a fair and passable state for any length of time.[126]

Roads without doubt were important to the smooth running of the estate, and improving these facilities was an effective way of putting to work the unemployed. At the end of the Swing Riots, the estate as seen above had taken up the expense of employing those labourers who were out of work. At the autumn audit of 1832, the tenants had again asked that the estate continue to guarantee wages of 30 to 40 men. This request was refused for two reasons: firstly, the women were earning nine shillings a week in the glove factory, and secondly, the tenants had once again begun to throw their labourers off the land. Subsequently, there was an ongoing fear that the proper management of the farms was being neglected. Although it was made clear to the tenants that they must comply with all the repair covenants in their leases, he proposed an alternative. Similar to many rural areas, Castleman stated that:

> some of the private Roads to the farms are almost impassable in the Winter and during part of the Summer, this of course materially affects the value of the Land and precludes Improvement for want of the means of conveying manure &c in the Winter.[127]

To both rectify the problem of the roads and to create work, a contract with the Overseers would be drawn up whereby they would take labourers off the parish and put them into useful employment. While this would be a relatively small expense on the estate, it had a number of benefits that made the expenditure worthwhile. It would keep the parish rates low, improve the value of the estate and importantly ensure that the labourers' thoughts did not turn again to riot or the destruction of further agricultural machinery.

At Stalbridge in 1835, new roads had been created across parts of the parish to which the Marquis of Anglesey contributed £20. Castleman stated that 'they are done extremely well', and as a result, the rich lands on either side to more than a mile in distance were now accessible. This meant for the first time that they could be manured and dressed as they ought to be—not only would production improve, but in the long-term so would rental and land values.[128] Cleverly this road served a dual purpose and acted as a drain to a 'considerable proportion of the adjoining lands'. At the beginning there had been a sizeable resistance to the road from the tenants, but by its completion they were in agreement that it had been one of the greatest improvements in the parish in living memory.[129] Taking advantage of the change in the mindset of the tenants, further improvements to other roads in a similar state which were not public were planned. So, convinced was Castleman by the soundness of this decision; he had engaged a surveyor from his own salary to employ the surplus pauper labourers in making new roads across 'Drews' land. Of course, he hoped that Anglesey would sanction the monies he had personally spent to the value of £30.[130]

Roads were also an area of rural disputes. In such disagreements the land agent was expected to act as an impartial conductor representing the sentiments of the tenants but without taking sides.[131] This could test the negotiating and management skills of even the best of agents. Roads are often considered as Eric Jones has recently argued in terms of diverting traffic away from the main house or out of view of the landowner himself, but not in terms of estate relationships.[132] Given the enormous areas covered by estates, the opportunity for meddling with rights of way was enormous. The problems created over who had the right of way over the road on a neighbouring estate further complicate the issue as seen in the following example. Tenants would turn to the landowner or his agent for help, and this could prove both time-consuming and expensive. Shortly before his death in 1844, William Castleman found himself embroiled in an argument concerning the right of the tenant of Pidgeon Farm House to use the road passing over Lord Westminster's land to the High Road. This had been done without issue by the tenant since 1829 when he took up the farm's lease. To try and establish the facts in the case, a great number of witnesses were interviewed in the hope that these testimonies would establish the right of way. Unsurprisingly in a time when borders and boundaries were fluid and often unwritten, there was a 'great deal' of conflicting information. Correspondence between Anglesey's and Lord Westminster's agents revealed that the other side denied so much as a footpath across the road. In order to use the evidence gathered and to see whether the right did indeed exist, the matter needed to be laid before the counsel which of course came at a price.[133]

After a series of letters between the barrister and the estate, more evidence needed to be gathered. Richard Meatyard, the tenant at Pidgeon Farm, in a statement reiterated that he had used the road with a waggon, cart, bridle drift and foot byway without any interruption. A bridge which had crossed a ditch had been removed by Westminster's tenant about five years previous, and although it was now impossible for either a loaded waggon or cart to get across, the road had still been used as before. Although this route saved Meatyard time, it was suggested that he should not cross it except on foot while the dispute remained ongoing.[134] In order to try and solve the problem, repair relationships with Lord Westminster and prevent incurring any further expense, Castleman wrote: 'I have opened a communication with Lord Westminster's solicitors which I hope will effect a Settlement of the dispute by Reference'.[135] This case in itself demonstrates how a land agent working on behalf of the landowner was required to undertake complex and time-consuming negotiations. They were made more difficult by the lack of written agreements and even maps which recorded customary rights. The system although unwritten worked well until they were challenged by one of the parties. The process of mediation is often hard to follow through the estate correspondence, and consequently the final decisions are often missing, but an effective manager clearly understood that disputes of this nature would take up a considerable amount of time and could get very expensive if they ended in a court trial. The estate thus sought to try and arbitrate the problem with Westminster's solicitor to the benefit of both sides.

Conclusion

The final case in this chapter illustrates how social and working relationships were closely intertwined. The picture becomes even more complicated and complex when these become mixed with customary rights. As seen here the withdrawal of the hunt at Hanley and the dinner and punch at Henstridge Court Leet caused considerable dissonance amongst the tenants. The audit dinner as will be seen in the following chapter alongside election dinners was part of the farming calendar. In trying to lower estate outgoings, everyone other than the tenants was forbidden to attend audit suppers, and this seems to have been accepted with little complaint. The ownership of timber was the most controversial issue and one which created unrest on more than one occasion. As a local attorney, William Castleman was able to quickly draw up essential paperwork and to use his networks to protect the estate's assets. Rural unrest frequently bubbled beneath the surface, but unlike Carl Griffin who suggests that this manifested itself in dissent, this volume argues that the local population were simply keen to maintain their customary rights. It was not so much as wanting change through rural unrest but a desire to maintain the *status quo* whereby perceived rights were allowed to remain in place. The Swing Riots which affected areas of the estate were more Luddite in nature than a desire to overthrow the estate's power. The outbreaks of violence destroyed farm machinery and sought to improve their living conditions. As will be seen throughout both this chapter and the volume as a whole, incendiarism was already a problem and one which continued long after 1830. Swing did not unite the whole population against the Marquis of Anglesey and his land agent, but instead ensured that the estate took the labourers into account when putting together schemes to alleviate tenant distress.

The estate and its agent sought to navigate the tensions which arose throughout this period as the land agent pursued the most cost-effective route to reach a conclusion that worked for the estate. This frequently meant resorting to the law and prosecuting those who appeared to be the ringleaders or those whose demise would have the most effect. Sometimes as in the case of Adams at Hanley, it meant letting him serve enough of his sentence to be a deterrent but not so much as to allow his family to become a burden on the parish and the rate payer. At no point could the needs and desires of the population be allowed to become more important than the requirements and financial viability of the estate. The land agent of a large estate needed a whole range of skills not least of which was an inherent understanding of the worth of its resources and the rights of the land-owner in the ownership of those assets. Besides maintaining both social and working relationships, the estate sought to socially control its unrulier elements, through tangible means, such as schools, churches and charity payments. This volume will return to these ideas in Chap. 6.

Notes

1. P. Horn (1980) *The Rural World 1750–1850: Social Change in the English Countryside* (London: Hutchinson), p. 225.
2. See, F. M. L. Thompson (1981) 'Landowners and the Rural Community' in G. E. Mingay, *The Victorian Countryside Vol II* (London: Routledge and Kegan Paul), pp. 457–458.
3. See C. Griffin (2012) *The Rural War: Captain Swing and the Politics of Protest* (Cambridge: Cambridge University Press).
4. Quoted in E. L. Jones (2018) *Landed Estates and Rural Inequality in British History: From the Mid-Seventeenth Century to the Present* (London: Springer International), pp. 40–41.
5. R. A. Houston (2014) *Peasant Petitions: Social Relations and Economic Life on Landed Estates, 1600–1850* (Basingstoke: Palgrave Macmillan), p. 12.
6. See for example, G. E. Mingay (ed.) (1981) *The Victorian Countryside Vols. I &. II* (London: Routledge & Kegan Paul); G. E. Mingay (1977) *Rural Life in Victorian England* (London: Heinemann) and G. E. Mingay (1989) *The Rural Idyll* (London: Routledge).
7. Houston *Peasant Petitions*, p. 10.
8. A. Howkins (1992) 'The English Farm Labourer in the Nineteenth Century: Farm, Family and Community' in B. Short, (ed), *The English Rural Community: Image and Analysis* (Cambridge: Cambridge University Press), p. 85.
9. J. Burchardt (2002) *Paradise Lost: Rural Idyll and Social Change in England Since 1800* (London and New York: L.B. Tauris), p. 1.
10. See T. Sokoll (2001), Essex Pauper Letters 1731–1837 (Oxford: Oxford University Press) and S. King (2019) *Writing the Lives of the English Poor, 1750s–1830s* (Montreal & Kingston: McGill-Queen's University Press).
11. W. Marshall (1804) *On the Landed Property of England: An Elementary and Practical Treatise* (London: G. and W. Nicol; O. and J. Robinson; R. Faulder; Longman and Rees; Cadell and Davies; and J. Hatchard), p. 354.
12. Ibid., p. 397.
13. Lady Day is the 25 March and Michaelmas 29 September.

14. DHC, D/ANG/B4/4/37, Estate Vouchers for 1816/1817.
15. DHC, D/ANG/B5/16, 23 December 1814.
16. DHC, D/ANG/B4/4/67, Estate Vouchers 1844.
17. DHC, D/ANG/B5/44, 11 October 1832.
18. DHC, D/ANG/B5/25, 21 October 1819.
19. Ibid.
20. Ibid., 9 November 1819.
21. Ibid.
22. D. R. Hainsworth (1992) *Stewards, Lords and People: The Estate Steward and His World in Later Stuart England* (Cambridge: Cambridge University Press), p. 109.
23. J. Lockhart Morton (1858) *The Resources of Estates: Being a Treatise on The Agricultural Improvement and General Management of Landed Property* (London: Longman, Brown, Green, Longmans and Roberts), p. 22.
24. Ibid.
25. DHC, D/ANG/B5/15, 14 June 1815.
26. See C. Griffin (2008) 'Protest Practice and (tree) Cultures of Conflict: Understanding the Spaces of 'Tree Maiming' in Eighteenth- and Early Nineteenth-Century England', *Transactions of the Institute of British Geographers*, 33:1, pp. 91–108.
27. For an overview of the Black Act and its impact, See E. P. Thompson (1975) *Whigs and Hunters: The Origins of the Black Act* (London: Allen Lane).
28. T. Shakesheff (2003) *Rural Conflict, Crime and Protest: Herefordshire, 1800 to 1860* (Woodbridge: Boydell Press), p. 114.
29. Ibid., p. 117.
30. Griffin, 'Protest Practice and (tree) Cultures of Conflict', p. 95.
31. DHC, D/ANG/B5/15, 27 July 1814.
32. Ibid., 2 August 1814.
33. Lockhart Morton *The Resources of Estates*, p. 349.
34. DHC, D/ANG/B5/15, 13 August 1814.
35. Ibid.
36. DHC, D/ANG/B5/17, 22 May 1815.
37. DHC, D/ANG/B5/23, 6 June 1818.
38. DHC, D/ANG/B5/31, 18 April 1922.
39. C. Griffin (2014) *Protest, Politics and Work in Rural England, 1700–1850* (Basingstoke: Palgrave Macmillan), p. 52.
40. DHC, D/ANG/B5/25, 18 January 1819.
41. Ibid., 15 October 1819.
42. DHC, D/ANG/B5/61, 15 April 1844.
43. DHC, D/ANG/B5/38, 14 February 1827.

44. See, E. P. Thomson (1971) 'The Moral Economy of the English Crowd in the Eighteenth Century', *Past and Present*, 50, p. 78.
45. DHC, D/ANG/B5/38, 12 February 1827.
46. Ibid., 16 February 1827.
47. Ibid., 12 February 1827.
48. DHC, D/ANG/B5/51, 1 January 1837.
49. *The State of the Country: Sir Robert Peel's Speech in the House of Commons, Feb. 17, 1843* (London: W. E. Painter, Church and State Gazette Office), p. 7.
50. DHC, D/ANG/B5/60, 18 April 1843.
51. Although this list is not exhaustive see for example, E. Hobsbawm and G. Rudé (1960) *Captain Swing* (London: Phoenix Press); Griffin, *The Rural War;* P. Jones (2009) 'Finding Captain Swing: Protest, Parish Relations, and the State of the Public Mind in 1830', *International Review of Social History* 54:3, pp. 429–458; P. Jones (2007) 'Swing, Speenhamland and Rural Social Relations: 'The Moral Economy' of the English Crowd in the Nineteenth Century' *Social History*, 32:2, pp. 271–290; A. Randall (2009) 'Captain Swing: A Retrospect' *International Review of Social History*, 54:3, pp. 419–427 and C. Griffin (2014) *Protest, Politics and Work in Rural England, 1700–1850* (Basingstoke: Palgrave Macmillan). For the full extent of Swing see K. Navickas (2011) 'Captain Swing in the North: The Carlisle Riots of 1830 *History Workshop Journal*, 70:1, pp. 5–28.
52. Jones, 'Finding Captain Swing', p. 429.
53. Ibid., p. 430.
54. Navickas, 'Captain Swing in the North', p. 5.
55. Ibid., p. 7.
56. Jones, 'Finding Captain Swing', p. 434.
57. J. E. Archer (2000) *Social Unrest and Popular Protest in England 1780–1940* (Cambridge: Cambridge University).
58. *Leicester Chronicle,* Saturday, 22 November 1822.
59. Ibid.
60. DHC, D/ANG/B5/31, 30 October 1922.
61. Ibid.
62. Hobsbawm and Rudé, *Captain Swing*, p. 12.
63. See I. Dyck (1992) *William Cobbett and Rural Popular Culture* (Cambridge: Cambridge University Press), p. 152, and Griffin, *The Rural War*, pp. 67–69.
64. D. Kent (1997) *Popular Radicalism and the Swing Riots in Central Hampshire* (Winchester: Hampshire Papers Series), p. 1.
65. P. Jones (2007) 'Swing, Speenhamland and Rural Social Relations: 'The Moral Economy' of the English Crowd in the Nineteenth Century' in *Social History*, 32:2, p. 274.

66. See DHC, D/ANG/B5/42, Letter from the Rev. Mason, 7 December 1830.
67. R. Wells (1988) 'Tolpuddle in the Context of the English Agrarian Labour History, 1780–1859' in J. Rule, (ed), *British Trade Unionism 1750–1850: The Formative Years* (Harlow: Longman), pp. 118–119.
68. J. L. Hammond and B. Hammond (1912) *The Village Labourer 1760–1832* (London: Longman, Green, and Co.), p. 245.
69. Ibid., p. 245.
70. J. Burnette, 'The Seasonality of English Agricultural Employment: Evidence from Farm Accounts, 1740–1850' in R. W. Hoyle, (ed.), *The Farmer in England 1650–1980* (Farnham, 2013), p. 157.
71. Griffin, *The Rural War*, pp. 67–69.
72. S. Williams *Poverty, Gender and the Life-Cycle Under the English Poor Law, 1760–1834* (Woodbridge: Boydell and Brewer), p. 99.
73. K. P. Bawn (1984) *Social Protest, Popular Disturbances and Public Order in Dorset, 1790–1838* unpublished thesis, University of Reading, p. 158
74. M. J. Daunton (1995) *Progress and Poverty: An Economic and Social History of Britain 1700–1850* (Oxford: Oxford University Press), p. 427.
75. D/ANG/B5/41, 6 April 1829 to which is attached a clipping from the *Morning Journal.*
76. *Bath Chronicle and Weekly Gazette*, 16 April 1829.
77. See, C. A. Beardmore (2016) 'William Castleman and Sons: Agents to the Marquis of Anglesey 1814–1854' in C. A. Beardmore, S. A. King and G. L. Monks, *The Land Agent in Britain: Past, Present and Future* (Newcastle: Cambridge Scholars), pp. 87–106.
78. *The Sherborne Mercury*, 6 December 1830.
79. DHC, D/ANG/B5/42, 25 November 1830.
80. Quoted in Beardmore, 'William Castleman and Sons', p. 103.
81. DHC, D/ANG/B4/54 Estate vouchers for 1831.
82. It should be noted that the correspondence dealing with the Swing riots are dated 2 December 1830, but Irene Jones in *The Stalbridge Inheritance* states that the incident at Stalbridge took place on 29 November 1830.
83. DHC, D/ANG/B5/42, 2 December 1830.
84. Ibid., 4 December 1830.
85. Ibid.
86. DHC, D/ANG/B5/42, 2 December 1830.
87. Ibid., 12 December 1830, minutes of the minute held at Uxbridge House.
88. Ibid., 7 December 1830.
89. Ibid., 12 December 1830, minutes of the minute held at Uxbridge House.
90. Ibid.

91. I. Jones, *The Stalbridge Inheritance 1780–1854* (Dorchester: Friary Press, 1993), p. 80.
92. DHC, D/ANG/B5/53.
93. *The Morning Chronicle* 14 January 1831.
94. DHC, D/ANG/B5/53.
95. See set up rates for threshing machines in Chap. 3.
96. DHC, D/ANG/B5/42, 11 December 1830.
97. Hobsbawm and Rudé, *Captain Swing*, p. 283 and Griffin, *The Rural War*, pp. 295–296.
98. Hobsbawm and Rudé, *Captain Swing*, p. 283.
99. DHC, D/ANG/B5/48, 17 June 1835.
100. Ibid, 22 July 1835.
101. *The Morning Chronicle*, 20 September 1837.
102. Houston *Peasant Petitions*, p. 10.
103. See for example: Mingay, *Rural Life in Victorian England;* J. Thirsk (ed.) (1989) *The Agrarian History of England and Wales VI 1750–1850* (Cambridge: Cambridge University Press); Mingay, *The Victorian Countryside Vols. 1& 2* and Horn, *The Rural World 1750–1850.*
104. See for example: R. A. C. Parker (1975) *Coke of Norfolk: A Financial and Agricultural Study 1707–1842* (Oxford: Oxford University Press), S. Wade Martins (1980) *A Great Estate at Work: The Holkham Estate and Its Inhabitants in the Nineteenth Century* (Cambridge: Cambridge University Press) and J. Wordie, (1982) *Estate Management in Eighteenth Century England: The Building of the Leveson-Gower Fortune* (Woodbridge: Boydell and Brewer).
105. Houston, *Peasant Petitions.*
106. Jones, *Landed Estates and Rural Inequality in British History*, p. 35.
107. Ibid.
108. DHC, D/ANG/B5/75, 23 October 1826.
109. Jones, *Landed Estates and Rural Inequality in British History*, p. 75.
110. T. W. Beastall (1981) 'Landlords and Tenants', in G. E. Mingay (ed.), *The Victorian Countryside Vol. II* (London: Routledge & Kegan Paul), p. 437.
111. R. Brown (1869) *The Book of the Landed Estate* (Edinburgh & London: William Blackwood and Sons), p. 86.
112. DHC, D/ANG/B5/48, Copies and extracts of correspondence between Mr. Yeatman and William Castleman. There is a considerable amount of correspondence between these two men and Yeatman had a reputation for being difficult.
113. DHC, D/ANG/B5/61, 4 January 1844.
114. Ibid., 2 January 1844.
115. Ibid., 5 January 1844.

116. Ibid., 24 January 1844.
117. Ibid., 22 January 1844.
118. Ibid., 12 January 1844.
119. Ibid., 20 January 1844.
120. Ibid., 29 December 1844.
121. Ibid., 29 December 1844.
122. Lord Ernle (1919) *English Farming Past and Present*, 2nd ed. (London: Longmans Green & Co), p. 285.
123. E. Laurence (1743) *The Duty and Office of a Land Steward* (London: J. and P. Knapton, T. Longman, H. Lintot, and J. and H. Pemberton), p. 123.
124. J. Lawrence (1806) *The Modern Land Steward* (London: H. D. Symons, T. Ostell and W. J. and J. Richardson), p. 310.
125. Ibid.
126. Ibid.
127. DHC, D/ANG/B5/44, 20 October 1832.
128. DHC, D/ANG/B5/48, 18 April 1836.
129. Ibid.
130. Ibid.
131. E. Richards (1981) 'The Land Agent' G. E. Mingay (ed.), *The Victorian Countryside Vol. II* (London: Routledge & Kegan Paul), p. 440.
132. See Jones, *Landed Estates and Rural Inequality in British History*, particularly chapter 5 'Road Capture'.
133. DHC, D/ANG/B5/61, 9 February 1844.
134. The statement is undated but filed in DHC, D/ANG/B5/61.
135. DHC, D/ANG/B5/61, 14 August 1844.

CHAPTER 5

Politics and the Landed Estate

Overview

Elections were an important part of the financial landscape of the estate. The landowning elite endowed their tenantry with voting rights which allowed them to participate in the political decision-making process. While such authority was rarely challenged, an election was an opportunity to either endorse or overthrow the local balance of power. In turn this provided at least some measure of check on the landowning elite. Although a landowner might not personally stand as a candidate, they still had to regularly consider their position in the rural community, and when sanctioning, a chosen candidate pick one who was prepared to both fulfil his responsibilities and to represent his patron's interest in parliament.[1] Elections on one hand provided the disgruntled and neglected the opportunity to complain, while on the other the grateful were able to express their appreciation. Frank O'Gorman suggests that at the very least, the proximity or chance of an election must have concentrated the 'paternalistic minds' of those involved. For landowners this might mean keeping the poor rate low, allowing rents as we have seen in Chap. 3 to accumulate for faithful and loyal political supporters and the eviction of those who could not be relied on in a contest. Political ambition was about local relationships which revolved around local elites with local ambitions and obligations. Historians such as O'Gorman and David Moore argue that

C. Beardmore, *Financing the Landed Estate*, Palgrave Studies in the History of Finance, https://doi.org/10.1007/978-3-030-14552-1_5

deference played a significant part in unreformed politics, although.[2] Moore's thesis is not without its critics.[3] Historians such as Gordon Mingay argue that deference was based on the recognition of rank and station and was not simply servilely given despite this the ruling class of English landlords generally expected it. Undoubtedly farmers welcomed a landowner who took a personal interest in their affairs.[4] J. R. Fisher suggests by expanding the basic sociological model utilised it is possible to demonstrate the existence of an 'agricultural community'. This group, he argued, consisted of small landowners, tenant farmers, rural tradesmen and those propertied elements of the community whose income depended on agricultural profitability.[5]

When it came to the role of organising elections, many stewards and land agents found they had acquired a new duty as election agent and this was added to their already bulging list of jobs. If landowners were to assert and preserve their political hegemony within a borough, even a small one, such as Milborne Port, they must control the poll, and often this meant spending money in order to court the loyalty of the leasehold tenants. While it might be presumed that those men who were reliant on their landowner to earn a living would vote according to the landlord's choice of candidate, there was always a chance they might not.[6] Patronage in the parliamentary boroughs extended beyond the electorate to the candidates themselves. Overall it prevented controversial or important members of the Commons from the caprices of electioneering.[7] The majority of England's parliamentary constituencies returned two members to the House of Commons, and as such each voter had two votes to cast. This dual vote meant that political behaviour could be hard to judge. An elector thus had a number of options. On one hand he could choose to cast both votes for two candidates of one party, in other words a straight party vote, or he could split his votes and support a single candidate of each party. On the other, he could decide to use just one vote and discard the other, a system known as 'plumping'. Where a single candidate was proposed, then plumping was the only option.[8] As there were two votes to cast, the electorate expected to be canvassed. Long term this could save the expense of an election contest, but the methods used all came at a price which if not successful could extend into the election itself. Consequently, the voter was aware that his vote had a value, and there are numerous examples of a patron or a candidate purchasing votes. The amounts that a single vote fetched varied, but the following examples reveal the sums involved. For instance, at Leicester it was £1 or £2 and at York £2 for a plumper and £1 for a single vote. In 1832 at Stafford the price started at £2 10s 0d for a single and £5 for a plumper, but as the election approached the price rose to between £7 and £10. Here it was suggested that of 1049 voters, 852 had received some form of bribe. When the Clive family sought to control the pocket borough of Ludlow, it is alleged that as much as £30 was paid for a single vote.[9] Norman Gash argues that while the figures bandied around may be exaggerated, election bribery was rife and commonplace.[10] It was not, however, just about purchasing votes; there were a myriad of ways to attract voters, and as will be seen on this estate, at the centre of the process was its land agent.

There has been considerable discussion as to the role of the election agent in pre-reformed politics. David Hainsworth argues that the gradual shift of 'selections' to 'elections' meant that it was inevitable that the role of the estate steward/agent would be expanded to fulfil the role of election agent.[11] This view is not held by all historians, and E. A. Smith argues that it was impossible to define the term 'election agent before the statutory codification of his duties in the Corrupt Practices Act of 1883'.[12] Smith is, however, somewhat contradictory, and alongside this lack of prescribed duties, he suggests that the business of an election agent had been well understood for many years.[13] Ultimately he was expected to protect the electoral interest, construct the poll list, canvass the voters, organise supporters, arrange the appropriate inducements to ensure loyalty and generally represent the interests of the candidate. In boroughs where the local landowner held patronage, this meant ensuring that he won. As well as maintaining the electorate, election agents were expected to raise funds and to co-ordinate the election process. Curwen argued that the election agent was the person 'immediately known and connected with the electors in small boroughs' as well as 'assisting the candidate with all their wants and necessities'.[14] With his local knowledge and networks, an understanding of the law and regional politics and an innate financial acumen, it is hardly surprising that the land agent was the man for the job.

Using the estate correspondence, it is possible to view politics as an economic consideration as much as a political entity. As the working and social relationships seen in Chaps. 2 and 3 were underpinned by financial considerations, so too was the electoral process. There existed here as elsewhere an expectation and a framework within which the tenants expected to be treated and feted both between elections and on polling day itself. Someone who could be trusted had to control the finances and pay the bills, keep an eye on any opposition, compile the poll books and ensure that the right people were registered to pay the poor rate.[15] For a man like Anglesey who held the patronage of more than one borough, Milborne Port feeds into a wider story of power, status and economic stability as seen in the Introduction. It is possible to discern the cost of maintaining his patronage and the impact this had on the landscape of the borough and the people within it. Three aspects of elections lay at the core of this chapter and include the political landscape of Milborne Port and the contested election. The petitions which were presented to parliament by the opposition reflect the unseen and unrecognised costs of owning the patronage of a borough. Secondly, the election process and the construction of the election campaign both of which entailed a financial commitment and needed a manager who understood where and how to spend money in a way that would have the most effect. Under the Great Reform Act of 1832, the borough was disenfranchised and became a financial burden rather than an economic asset and consequently was sold off in short order. This last act demonstrating that politics as much as any other activity on the estate had to be value for money.

The Political Landscape of Milborne Port and the Contested Election

While some areas particularly in the midlands and north of England had expanded rapidly during the late eighteenth and early nineteenth centuries, Milborne Port remained a tiny borough in the Hundred of Horethorne in Somerset. It continued to return two men to the House of Commons until the Great Reform Act of 1832. County and borough politics were inherently different. The former contained a more standardised electorate and a clear demarcation between members and electors. The latter consisted of distinctly individual political personalities, with a diverse franchise and representative capacity, which made it 'messier'. Despite their differences, the destinies of both sections were closely linked to the political fortunes of local landowners. To maintain this equilibrium took up time and effort. The landed elite needed the electorate to remain in power and herein lay a problem that had to be overcome, as only a small percentage of those eligible to vote were completely reliant on the elite class either politically or economically.[16] To a greater extent, the pattern of electoral control varied with the social and economic make-up of each constituency. In most and certainly in Milborne Port, a seemingly settled regime of control by the landed interest prevailed.[17] Frank O'Gorman, however, argues the ruling order was neither 'settled' nor 'fixed', and its institutions and interests whether personal, family, social or political often found expression at the electoral level.[18] When placed under a magnifying glass, the constituent families, interests and institutions were rarely ever completely reconciled, and these tensions played out locally rather than nationally.

Exploring electoral behaviour O'Gorman argues is best viewed not by categorising the franchise but through determining the basic elements of control exerted over the electorate. He splits these into four: venal, proprietorial, corporation and patronage boroughs. In venal boroughs, politics was reduced to the status of a purely financial transaction, in which electoral support was given in response to fiscal persuasion. In proprietorial boroughs, the vote was treated as a form of property, and the voting process formed part of the transaction in property relationships. For example, in scot and lot boroughs such as Milborne Port, it was possible for a patron to buy up the majority of properties wherein residence conveyed the vote. Getting and maintaining a majority position was reliant on owning the largest share of appropriate property. Mounting a challenge to the current patron was simply a case of having enough money to buy up 'voting houses' or to own the land upon which to build suitable properties. Thus, politics were determined by property transactions rather than political conflict. Tenants were simply expected to vote according to the wishes of the landlord. It was in these boroughs that some of the worst abuses of the unreformed system occurred. Towns which had been granted charters were also boroughs. Some of these developed into corporate towns which had the right to return Members of Parliament, and these were known as corporation boroughs. The majority had small electorates which were controlled by patronage, and consequently contested elections were rare. After 1775 a relatively small number perhaps around 15 per cent necessitated the calling of a poll. Patronage boroughs were the most common type. These were boroughs in which 'natural' interests were at the forefront based on the foundation of landed property, services to the constituency and the goodwill of the electors. In this environment deference was expected and voting against the prevailing wishes of the patron could be classed as hostile and brought with it the threat of eviction. The structure of patronage boroughs was not static nor universal but adaptable, constantly shifting and changing as needed. Although there might be just one patron who dominated the political landscape security was still bought by showering the voter with generous gestures. The amounts spent could increase expediently if another landowner mounted a challenged to the establish patron. Voter loyalty was important and purchased either through cash or specific inducements. When these factors are combined with the expense of managing the borough and the cost of holding an election, this political borough changes from being simply a political interest to one which has economics at its core. In this sense as seen in the Introduction and elsewhere in this volume, the political landscape of the borough was no different to many other aspects of managing the estate. Financial factors were even more important for Milborne Port as it sits between the divide of scot and lot, proprietorial and patronage boroughs.[19] Consequently, while Anglesey wished to maintain control, he had to be prepared for the immense expenses that might be incurred; thus patronage cannot be seen as simply a political state but must be viewed as an inherent economic cost to the estate.

The Marquis of Anglesey held the patronage of Milborne Port from 1812 to its demise in the Great Reform Act. This did not, however, mean that matters always ran smoothly. The precedent for challenging results had already been set, when, on 20 January 1775, the petition of Edward Walter and Isaac Hawkins Browne against the return of the Honourable Temple Luttrell and Charles Wolseley was tried by a committee of the House of Commons. Altogether three petitions were read; it was alleged that three returns had been made by three different people each claiming to be returning officers. The offending returns had been attached to the writ by the sheriff, who had then returned them to the Clerk of the Crown. The individual petitions each claimed victory with a majority of the legal votes, and all made mutual allegations of bribery. The petition of Walter and Browne purported that Luttrell at the time of his election and return 'had by himself or some person in trust for him, an office, place or employment, touching or concerning the farming, collecting, or managing his majesty's customs', meant that he was incapable of being elected. After hearing all the evidence, the court decided that the return made by John Newton and John Peckham on behalf of Luttrell and Wolseley was an illegal return. Given the complicated nature of the other two returns, the committee thought it was their duty to 'go upon the merits of the election', rather than try and decide between them. Part of the hearing centred on whether rates set and collected by 'illegal' officers (or rather those who had no authority to do so) had actually paid and were entitled to vote. This raised the issue as to whether these persons should be treated equally under the law as those who had legally paid scot and lot. The counsel of Walter and Browne concluded that this should indeed be the case and the committee eventually came to the same decision. Once everything in the petitions had been scrutinised and the evidence heard, the committee decided that the original election result should be allowed to stand.

A further petition was heard on 6 April 1819. The election had been held on 18 April 1818 at which Sir Edward Paget, Robert Matthew Casberd, Richard Sharp and Samuel Moulton Barrett were candidates. The petition claimed that James Noke Highmore and John Highmore illegally took it upon themselves to act as both the sub-bailiffs and returning officers at the said election; by taking the poll it was alleged they had consequently and dishonestly rejected the votes of several persons:

> who had the good right and title to vote and had tendered their votes for the said Richard Sharp and Samuel Morton Barrett, Esqrs. and admitted other persons to vote for the said Sir Edward Paget and Robert Matthew Casberd who had no right to vote at the said election.[20]

It was alleged that by using these tactics, the Highmores had fraudulently manipulated a majority for Paget and Casberd, and they had subsequently been illegally returned to parliament. Yet again there were charges of general bribery and corruption and of unduly closing the poll, although this latter charge was later abandoned by the counsel for the petitioners. The numbers who voted for individual candidates are detailed in Table 5.1 which really emphasises the smallness of the electorate.[21]

William Castleman's correspondence gives a wider sense of local sentiments that it is impossible to gain from official reports. He had been informed by William Payne in late October 1818 that the petition had been signed, but the opposition were prepared to wait until the last minute to present it so that they might gain the largest possible number of opposition members.[22] It was suggested that Sharp and Moulton Barrett

Table 5.1 List of candidates and votes polled

Sir Edward Paget	39
Mr Casberd	33
Mr Sharp	15
Mr Barrett	21

had been 'put up' by Lord Darlington who was a Whig borough-monger and 'egged on' by John Henning, a glover in the town who had a grudge against the Pagets. As a result, Lord Darlington had purchased land in the borough from Grime, and on which he embarked in a house building programme with the aim of challenging Anglesey's stranglehold.[23]

The official record and the estate's correspondence give a sense of the complex nature of politics within the borough as Darlington mounted his challenge. On this occasion there was an additional accusation which accused Anglesey's supporters of preventing voters from 'freely attending the poll'. Thomas Fooks in his deposition stated that the supporters of Paget/Casberd were holding a meeting of their followers at the King's Head when members of the opposition accused them of confining some of their allies within the room. The opposition demanded admittance on the grounds that it was a public house. Fooks rebuked their request stating that the room had been privately hired, but he agreed that the door would be left open and the opposition could call out asking if anyone wanted to leave. This was duly done but there was no reply.[24] Other protests included an objection to some of the votes. It was claimed that these men had sworn that they were in possession of their property and had paid the poor rate for at least six months but had not been resident for six weeks. There were questions raised as to George Longman's vote on the grounds that he was not legally of an age to vote. The opposition alleged that Mr. Hallet had stated to Payne that the Blues would purchase a public house to be licenced for him. They would lay in a stock of beer while also arranging for the licence of the Queen's Head to be transferred to him in otherwise an explicit act of bribery. Henning told Payne he would give him £50 if he would not disclose the bribery by the 'Blues'. Henning then went home and returned and offered him £20 in part which Payne stated he had refused to accept. Feaver who was Lord Darlington's agent had been placed in Grime's cottage. It was alleged that the Blues relied on the oppression by Mr. Castleman towards some of the votes advocating that when he delivered their leases, the tenants were warned by him: 'We take your rent off so much a year on account of not giving you the Bag. Now we grant you a favour before we ask for yours'.[25] In other words the electorate were offered monetary incentives in return for voter loyalty. These allegations all revolve around some form of financial gain, and while the amounts paid in cash seem small, any significant reductions in rent ate into the estate's overall profits. The reasons behind the shared risks of farming discussed in the Introduction and elsewhere in this volume are clearly visible in borough politics.

Despite the petition containing multiple objections, many of them centred on illegal financial payments, the committee decided that their attention should concentrate on the case of the nine voters who formed the capital bailiffs. At Milborne Port there were nine capital bailiwicks who each had a capital bailiff, but due to a system of rotation, only two were in office at any one time. These were known as the reigning bailiffs, and at the Michaelmas court leet, those in office appointed a deputy or sub-bailiff. It was these men who were in effect the returning officers. The petition had objected to the capital bailiffs because they did not reside in the borough. It was argued that the appointments in respect of which they voted were thus illegal and void. However, Mr. Serjeant Pell on behalf of the sitting members argued that the petitioners had not properly specified their objection in the list as required by an act of parliament.[26] As a result this point was not a valid reason for complaint. At the end of the sitting, the committee came to a number of conclusions. They resolved that the votes of the nine people who were part of the complaint were to remain on the poll. It was agreed that George Longman had not been resident for the prerequisite six months. The evidence, however, stated that his father had died in testate, more than six months before the election, and George Longman had been granted letters of administration over his goods and property, and this, therefore, entitled him to vote. The opposition argued that he could not vote by proxy, and in fact his mother had equal rights to the property. As a result, the committee decreed that this vote should be discarded. Having dealt with all the issues in the petition, the committee determined that the sitting members had in fact been properly elected.[27] Now that the business surrounding the complaints had been concluded, it was time to compile the accounts and assess the amount spent by the Marquis of Anglesey in defending the original ballot. Castleman advocated that before any monies were paid out, all the briefs and other papers connected with the petition should be lodged at Uxbridge House.[28] This suggestion was 'not a distant notion' but one of 'common security and caution' because if something were to happen to Mr. Lowe, the estate's barrister, the papers might get into the wrong hands.[29] This underpins the idea that anyone taking up the patronage of a borough was in effect taking on both a financial and economic responsibility that went beyond the case of simply putting up a candidate when an election was called.

An exploration of the political landscape through contested elections reveals that despite the Marquis of Anglesey's patronage, local tensions and grievances created an unsettled and oft-contested battle ground. The situation was further complicated when Lord Darlington attempted to grab power. During this period Castleman as land and election agent was expected to watch over the electorate and to weed out any that could not be relied on. This took him away from other areas of the estate during a period of economic instability when his time would have been better spent supporting the tenants in places such as Stalbridge which were more profitable in terms of rental income. The unsettled and antagonistic nature of borough politics was thus time-consuming and added to Castleman's already heavy and complex workload. The borough was important and needed to be watched; the huge investment in housing stock, the encouragement of new industries and the monies spent on entertaining and courting votes meant that Anglesey could not afford to let Darlington succeed. This created a difficult and tense situation that will be explored further in the next section. It illustrates more than anything else the financial implications of mounting a takeover, and the sums Anglesey spent in thwarting him are indicative of why politics was an economic issue for this estate and why all the decisions made had financial implications. Elections followed a set procedure that included organising the voters and the payment of bills; getting the timing right was essential and the responsibility of William Castleman.

The Election Process

The election process is most usually constructed as a political process, but all the decisions made were based on an economic and financial basis. As will be seen, an estate had to weigh up the importance of their political power against the cost of maintaining the electorate and fighting off any opposition. Borough politics was often personal; to know and be known by those who were governed was a central theme of English paternalism. There were according to David Roberts three main principle sets of duties that the conscientious superior paternalist felt he must perform: ruling, guiding and helping.[30] Essentially this meant a commitment to rule firmly and supervise appropriately. In order for this system to work, the tenants and others who formed the electorate had to give their consent; they expected to be advised on who to vote for, but their accord was not given freely. Tenants expected to be feted and canvassed; any landowner who attempted to avoid the customary system did so at his peril. This became increasingly important as the eighteenth and nineteenth centuries witnessed the expansion of political awareness which extended politics beyond issues of parochial concern.

There were three main elements to the development of this new conscious interest, firstly the role of the press. As a medium for the communication process, newspapers were indispensable and their usefulness was enhanced by growing literacy rates. They carried advertisements, opinions, letters and increasingly versions of candidates' speeches.[31] Historians have long understood that newspapers were circulated among friends and families, were kept for reference and information and used as a source of knowledge. Much less though is understood about their circulation.[32] What is known is that provincial newspapers could have a substantial readership, with each copy being shared, discussed and valued. In order to emphasise its spread and reach, *The Sherborne Mercury* stated it was 'chiefly distributed by men and horses hired on purpose, in a very regular, expeditious and expensive manner'.[33] It claimed that it was distributed 'in every direction, over four counties, extending from the town of Poole, to the eastern extremity of Dorsetshire to Penzance and land's end in Cornwall'.[34] More than 80 agents resident in towns were employed in both vending and receiving advertisements and communications. For electoral purposes newspapers countered parochialism and placed the election process in both regional and national contexts.[35] Secondly, the bureaucratisation of the political process had less impact in small rural areas. While in larger urban conurbations, the press had acted as a general agency for electoral mobilisation, this had in turn led to the creation of election clubs. Although they varied in size, the average membership was around 150–200. To put size into context, the typical number who signed up to one of these urban clubs was more than the entire number of voters in Milborne Port. The third and final reason was a more politically aware electorate which it is argued was seen as the development of and escalating phenomenon of petitioning. Despite there being a customary precedent for this process, it became increasingly fashionable to petition parliament. For example, in the hundred years between 1750 and 1850, the constituency of Reading sent 432 petitions, each was the result of a public meeting, a canvass and frequently considerable local agitation which all incurred a financial cost.[36] Even small boroughs took part, and amongst other petitions from the borough of Milborne Port, there were two relating to anti-slavery: the first was sent to the House of Commons in 1824 and the second to both

Houses in 1826. In the same year, a petition against the importation of foreign gloves was sent to the House of Lords. Anti-Catholic sentiment is often represented as one of the main causes of the growing political cognizance of the electorate locally, regionally and nationally and Milborne Port was no different; consequently, Protestant dissenters petitioned for the repeal of the Test Acts in June 1827 and anti-Catholic petitions followed in February 1829. The latter two petitions caused considerable upheaval in the borough because Lord Anglesey had been recalled from his post as Lord Lieutenant of Ireland just a month earlier for his Catholic sympathies.[37] Uncharacteristically Castleman wrongly assessed the situation in 1825 when he had written to Anglesey about Mr. Portman, one of the candidates in the upcoming Dorset election:

> I have despatched a clerk to canvas all your Lordship's Tenants at Stalbridge, Bradford &c, &c against Mr Portman or any other Candidate supporting Catholic Emancipation and to with hold a promise of their votes in the present.[38]

In response Anglesey had returned the letter writing in the margin 'Do not let the Catholick question be named by me as any ground for opposing any vote'.[39] While in 1825 Castleman had underestimated his employer, in 1829 he failed to capture the mood of the tenants. As a result, he was caught off guard when one of his clerks informed him of the intended anti-Catholic petition. Once he knew of its existence, he still did not want to be associated with any aspect of it, because once presented to parliament he stated, 'it will be my duty to account to Lord Anglesey for the part I have taken in it'.[40] It appeared that the tenants had been totally unaware of the change in Anglesey's political sentiments. Castleman's attitude was very much one of restraint suggesting that out of respect for their landlord, the tenants should have refrained from making a public demonstration of their own beliefs. Petitions while at times problematic were often signed by both the franchised and unfranchised electorate and gave a voice to both men and women, especially those who did not have the vote. As a source they do much to demonstrate an expanding interest in politics at all levels of society and suggest the 'political nation' encompassed a large body of people who took an interest in all aspects of government.[41]

In contrast F. M. L. Thompson advocated that most English tenants did not have strong political views or indeed particularly cared about the political process.[42] This lack of interest was created by the domination exerted by landowners and the influence they exerted over electoral candidates and the elections themselves. For the electorate, Thompson argues, politics was not about choosing a party or policies but voting for someone from the same landed class that already exerted a considerable influence on their lives.[43] While the landowner might have taken great interest in the choice of candidates, Thompson assumed that whoever stood was an irrelevance in the minds of the tenants because they would simply vote as they were instructed.[44] If true, then canvassing would have been unnecessary, and the estate spared much expense. In fact, as already discussed, the two-vote system created a degree of autonomy, and in the Introduction and throughout this volume, the partnership between landowner and tenant was unwritten but based on mutual trust. There is a danger, according to Martin Daunton, in assuming that the unreformed electorate were passive raw material who patrons could manipulate at will; instead the possibility should be considered that the situation could be reversed whereby the electorate influenced their patrons.[45] Although full participation in national government and membership of parliament was restricted to a small number of elite landowners, the political system was responsive to the concerns of a much wider propertied and commercial society.[46] This meant that no one who held patronage could take their position for granted; tenants with long leases rather than simply acquiescing would baulk if authority was wielded with a heavy hand. In the event of this happening, tenants would have quit their properties and an estate would have found itself in dire financial straits. Instead Daunton argues patrons had to work with the culture and attitudes of the local electorate, stressing a mutual interdependence rather than imposing deference on lower-class voters.[47] Politics therefore had multi-faceted financial implications; no landowner could risk putting too much pressure on their tenants as this came with a risk, but at the same time failing to return pliant loyal candidates could risk an entire social way of life. Keeping a watching brief on the behaviour and attitude of the electorate in a proprietorial or patronage borough thus formed an essential element of its management. This became even more so when someone mounted a takeover bid.

From 1819 onwards, Lord Darlington attempted to wrest the borough of Milborne Port from the Marquis of Anglesey which resulted in a very expensive housing race. As already seen above, opposition in the form of Henning had persuaded Darlington to purchase eight acres of land so that houses might be built to a rateable standard which would attract voters.[48] Sir William Manners at Ilchester had previously been a victim of

Darlington's borough-mongering and warned that Darlington employed an unscrupulous attorney called Metcalf. He stated that he was 'somehow related to Lady D who was once a streetwalker'. There was a more respectable attorney, but Metcalfe did 'all his dirty work'.[49] Ensor who resided in the borough suggested that Henning acted out of revenge. Henning, a glove manufacturer and Whig (the Marquis of Anglesey was a Tory), had allowed his cows to stray, and consequently they were captured and impounded by Thomas Pitman. Henning was furious, and when he met up with Pitman, he 'boxed his ears' which facilitated a complaint to William Castleman. In response a legal action was brought against Henning who was fined heavily for losing his temper and swore he would seek revenge.[50]

Once posed the threat could not be ignored—this paradigm more than any other illustrates why politics was a financial and economic issue rather than simply being a process which returned MPs to parliament. The estate set out to thwart the challenge by orchestrating the leasing of all Sir William Medleycott's property in Milborne Port. In addition, two plots of land were purchased on which to build, and this it was hoped would ensure the estate stayed ahead in the house building race. By the beginning of 1820, the estate had completed 14 new houses and a further 8 would soon follow suit. These properties were constructed of stone and covered with tiles (rather than thatch). The idea in fabricating buildings of this quality was to prevent some of the extensive and expensive repairs which were annually incurred in the borough. The outlay on each house was expected to be around £100. Although the numbers completed were less than hoped, Castleman felt that this was to Anglesey's advantage as some of the borough houses were unoccupied. Besides these new properties, work was undertaken repairing and altering many of the old houses, for the sole purpose of increasing the number of voters and thus frustrating Darlington's plans. The sums spent were enormous; for example, in 1819 the estate expended some £2121 10s 2d on new houses and £4032 5s 3d in 1820. In this latter year, a further £1260 0s 0d was given to James N. Highmore to pay the workmen in the borough. Besides his £50 salary, Highmore was awarded a further £50 for his extra trouble 'this year'.[51] In order to ensure the estate was not defrauded by the builders, any work carried out had to be inspected and the bills checked under the watchful eye of the foreman Mr. Taylor.[52] For this in 1820 he was paid £152 19s 0d for his work.[53] To further reduce the risk of a takeover bid, those tenants who were unable to vote, alongside those whose loyalty might not be solid or who it was felt could be bribed to vote for Darlington's candidate, were evicted. Anglesey was informed that 'the [number] intended to be removed is 23 including some women and I have supplied nearly all of their places with men' who can 'be depended upon'.[54] Some of the tenants were, after further negotiations, allowed to stay such as Mr. Owen, who, it was considered, 'will become a powerful support to your Lordships Interests'.[55] The monies spent in this small borough over a rough five-year period are staggering, and McKay suggests that the Marquis of Anglesey alone spent more than £15,000.[56] While Darlington according to his agent had spent upwards of £40,000 more than twice that of Anglesey. To add to the problem, Anglesey lacked a commercial presence in the area and those that did exist were Castleman stated 'carried out by our opponents'.[57]

In order to rectify the situation, there was a determination by the estate to try and attract businesses who would bring both employment and additional voters into the borough. In April 1820 he was able to report that 'I have nearly completed the arrangement for establishing Mr Ensor a most respectable young man and man of Property'.[58] Ensor was a glove manufacturer, and importantly for Anglesey's political standing, he would 'bring 3 or 4 respectable journeymen with him on whom reliance can be placed and for whom Houses will be provided'.[59] This plan was almost thwarted when Merest who had previously sat for Ilchester on Darlington's interest was defeated when they had attempted to open the closed borough of Shaftesbury.[60] No wonder he was thought to keep the borough 'in an almost constant state of ferment' and 'endeavoured by every possible means to make voters dissatisfied'.[61] In order to defeat Anglesey, not only had Merest introduced another glove factory, but worryingly he would bring a further 15 workmen from Yeovil to 'occupy new houses'.[62] In an attempt to counteract this move by the opposition, Castleman persuaded Messrs. Thompson who manufactured sails to set up a branch in Milborne Port. He stated that the foreman would immediately take possession of one of the vote houses, and the business would employ 'such of the votes who have become accustomed to the trade and who are now working as Labourers or are employed by our opponents'.[63] There had been an earlier attempt to establish a sail manufactory in 1820 when Mr. Plowman had agreed to take premises at Milborne Port. He had been part of the company at East Coker from whom the Marquis of Anglesey had ordered sails for his yacht 'Esmeralda'. According to the correspondence, Plowman would have needed some additional support, and it was in Castleman's opinion worth the effort as 'he will employ many persons and will become a powerful support to the Cause'.[64] It was hoped that with all of these businesses, Anglesey would continue to use his influence. He had already done so with Ensor when he had persuaded Colonel Thornhill to purchase '400 pair of Gloves for his Regiment'.[65] Running electoral boroughs required more business acumen than political prowess, and this is a factor which is often overlooked. In many respects the process of setting up a range of trades in the borough was expensive, but as seen in Chap. 4 they were of much benefit in 1830 after Swing when these enterprises played a part in raising family standards of living by employing women.

In the end Darlington was not defeated by a scorching election victory but by something as simple as an exchange of property with Winchester College and the Bishop of Hereford.[66] As a result of these talks, Anglesey exchanged land in Dorset for the rectory of Milborne Port through an agreement ratified in a private Act of Parliament obtained on 17 June 1824.[67] At this point Castleman believed that Anglesey controlled 198 votes and Darlington 146 out of a franchised electorate of 344. This gave Anglesey a majority of at least 52.[68] Consequently realising that he could now no longer gain a majority, Darlington sold his property to Lord Anglesey at a price of £5901 which included £2500 for his political influence.[69] There were further complications to this deal as the Marquis of Anglesey did not have the ready cash to buy out Darlington, and thus Castleman organised a loan from Mr. Bankes for some £10,000; this has already been discussed in Chap. 2. To ensure that Anglesey's interest could never again be challenged when Henning's glove factory came up for sale, Castleman wrote:

> It is certainly desirable that your Lordship should be the owner of this property not only with a view to prevent future oppositions from the adverse ownership of it but also for the purpose of retaining the decided superiority you at present have over Sir William Medleycott.[70]

The property failed to sell at auction, and although Feaver was contracted to purchase the building, he could not raise the money to complete the purchase. The risk of waiting for either a fall in price or another purchaser to make a move was a dangerous game to play, and it seemed sensible to pay the asking price of £1650. Anglesey weighed the different options and concluded 'I think it advisable to give the sum now required by Mr Merest notwithstanding always that I should be free from all dispute with Henning's representative & with Feaver'.[71] On weighing up the component elements of the borough, 'a great number of the vote houses' were occupied by the workmen of Ensor, George Feaver, a linen manufacturer, and Thompson in the sail cloth manufactory all of whom all could be relied upon for support. In the new town, however, many of the houses were occupied by the workmen of Wilmington who rented the glove factory now offered for sale. While Castleman believed that Wilmington and his men might be prepared to support Anglesey, he thought those of Feaver (Darlington's agent) would not. He still thought that to be thoroughly safe, any tenants who were uncertain supporters should be removed immediately and replaced with new tenants who had to occupy the houses for six months before they were eligible to vote.[72] This would be time-consuming and come with a resultant cost, but there was a general agreement that there was no other option.

Securing a borough, even a small one, as seen here was expensive. Yet if the Marquis wanted to continue to exert the power that he had previously enjoyed, then a crucial and sudden increase in expenditure was vital. All of the decisions made had a significant financial impact on the estate, as somehow the money had to be found. Often as in the case of the purchase price for Darlington's properties, Castleman organised some form of mortgage or loan. Undoubtedly these had to be paid back and regular sums of interest which became due had to be found on a regular basis. Historians have tended to concentrate on patronage, deference or the emergence of political parties, but these histories omit the detailed financial resources needed even in the smallest of boroughs.[73] In this situation there was great pressure not just to ensure that the properties were tenanted but that they were rented to the right sort of person who could be relied on politically. Besides trying to find the funds needed to take on Darlington, the responsibility of running the borough's business fell to the land agent; this included organising the canvas, keeping a watchful eye on events within Milborne Port and paying for the various aspects of the poll on the occasions when one was held. In this sense the various transactions of the borough fell within Castleman's remit, and these could take a considerable amount of juggling to run smoothly.

Managing the Election Process

It was not the passive nature of the unreformed electorate which fostered and maintained political stability but its vitality, flexibility and not infrequently a healthy injection of cash. The electoral system itself created a framework within which patrons, voters and men across the social spectrum could make the concessions and agreements necessary to maintain electoral and thus political steadfastness. Outside the few seats which were secure, the majority did not assume that all election results were a foregone conclusion. Electoral support had thus to be earned and could only be achieved through hard work, organisation and currying favour. Even when there was a modicum of security, maintaining voter loyalty and consistency was time-consuming, expensive and delicate.[74] At the very least, someone had to be responsible for the interests of the constituency, and with Anglesey being an absentee patron, this fell to his agent. Voters were a 'fickle and demanding lot' who knew how to twist the electoral system to their benefit not only in terms of understanding the value of their votes but also in low poor rates, rent abatements, local offices and the provision of favours. These were all bargaining tools and ones which they were prepared to employ; thus as O'Gorman argues the patron–voter relationship was an 'implied' mutual obligation and not servile dependency.[75] The vote he suggests acted as a form of currency which could be used to purchase an array of wares which might include payments for time and troubles incurred, food and of course alcohol. These payments fell within the understood electoral framework and operated within a given set of values and were not created by the system.[76]

In a modern electoral system, canvassing has two purposes: it serves to identify and mobilise support and allows the candidates to introduce themselves to those who live in the constituency as well as provide an opportunity to advertise party policies. As borough constituencies were relatively small, a prospective candidate could carry out much of the canvas personally. Electors could hardly remain ignorant of either an election or the preferred choice of the patron of the borough when personally solicited by the candidate himself. An electoral procedure such as this allowed the voter greater participation in the process and it was usual for an elector's choice during the canvas to correspond closely to his vote on polling day. That he was able to verbalise his decision in front of the local candidate John Phillips argues aided in the process of politicisation.[77] In both unreformed England and for a long time after the 1832 Great Reform Act, the canvas had a range of other functions, perhaps the most important of which was establishing whether an election was needed. By avoiding the need for a poll, it was possible to dispense with all the financial and organisational demands and thus save considerable expense not just monetary but also the time and effort of local agents. The aim of the initial canvas was, therefore, firstly to assess the mood of the borough/constituency in order to determine whether a poll was in fact needed and secondly to estimate the character of the contest.[78] Defining a contested constituency, simply as one, where votes were recorded on polling day, is misleading. This suggested a degree of limited political activity, whereas the preliminary canvas carried out by the candidates determined the outcome of the election. It might be in the initial stages that there was a contest, and when candidates realised that they could not win, withdrew.[79] Essentially during the canvas, it was necessary to talk to as many voters as possible to ascertain how they might be expected to vote at the poll. The results were then assessed as to the likelihood of returning specific candidates and then one or two would withdraw mitigating the need for an election.[80]

Canvassing then was an important preliminary to an election contest, but O'Gorman suggests that it was more than a mere political event. Like the customary rights discussed in Chap. 4, there was a host of rituals which surrounded this process and not just when an election was called. In a hierarchical society, such as an estate, canvassing was influenced by social and economic factors. It was accepted in this type of community that those who had influence over others on the basis of property, employment, custom, family and personal connections would use it. In county as well as borough elections, elite landowners were thought to have a genuine and justifiable influence over their tenants and dependents.[81] It was essential that those thinking of standing as a candidate attained the support of landlords long before an election was called. For example, in 1841 Mr. Sheridan wrote to the Marquis of Anglesey proposing himself as a potential candidate in any future election. He had heard a rumour that the standing member for the county was intending to retire when parliament was next dissolved. The letter was to register his interest well ahead of any competition. Sheridan stated: 'If you can grant me the aid of your valuable assistance to secure to me this great object of my ambition I shall ever feel most grateful …. I hope if necessary that I may be favoured by your active support'.[82] Although he received Anglesey's backing, he never actually became MP for Dorset. Instead he was returned as member for the borough of Shaftesbury from 1845 to 1852 and then Dorchester until his retirement in 1868. In some areas, where the landed influence was particularly strong, canvassing was in many respects an extension of the estate's management and leadership systems. Ultimately, the landowner had a very powerful call upon the electoral loyalty of his people, and this principle was clearly and universally understood. This meant that a tenant would often refuse to state where his first vote would be cast and often his second until he had received clear instructions from his landlord.[83] The length of time devoted to canvassing varied as to whether it was a county, where the process might take six to ten weeks, or a small borough where the duration might simply be a day or two at most.

Borough politics needed more attention than simply undertaking the canvas when an election was called; this was especially true when there was a challenge to the prevailing patron. As a result, the electorate needed to be tended, cultivated and treated on a continual and regular basis which brought with it an ongoing expense. William Castleman understood the importance of the borough of Milborne Port from the beginning of his agency. Knowing that he would need to keep a close eye on events, to keep expenditure down and to nip any discontent in the bud, he set up a committee of Anglesey's supporters. He stated that they were tasked to meet fortnightly to 'discuss such subjects as arise from time to time in the Boro and to communicate the result to me'.[84] However, things did not progress as hoped, and the petty jealousies that were exhibited within the group caused chaos. As a result, Castleman was forced to spend three days in the borough in the middle of November 1819 to 'set matters right again'. Rather than try and get this group to work in practice it was scrapped, and he determined that as long as Milborne Port continued in its present state 'to go thither every five or six weeks to endeavour to keep matters in the right train'.[85] This was not the only measure put in place to tempt the electorate to remain loyal. In November 1820 it had come to his notice that the friends of Lord Darlington were 'treating' the voters at a private house with free drinks. In trying to vie for votes in this way, there was a worry that some of the electorate had already changed sides.[86] The estate's response was to organise the renovation of the 'long room and Cellar' at Canon Court so that they might provide similar entertainment.[87] Arrangements were made for strong beer to be brewed locally and 'cyder' purchased.[88] Some idea of the quantities of strong beer brewed and purchased for this purpose can be seen in Table 5.2.[89]

On top of the beer and cider, the intention was to buy a hogshead of port and another of white wine and a cask of brandy and rum. Overall, the

Table 5.2 Beer brewed at the Queen's Head Inn and purchased by the estate in 1820–1821

Date	*Amount of beer brewed for the estate*	*£*	*s*	*d*
1820	128 gallons of strong beer to Canon Court	12	6	0
6 March	66 gallons of strong beer to Canon Court	6	12	0
1822				
10 January	Gave away in the market place 30 gallons of strong beer	3	0	0
8 December	262 gallons of strong beer to allotment votes	11	13	0
16 May	66 gallons of strong beer to Canon court	6	12	
		40	3	0

total cost of the original stock, it was suggested, 'will not be much short of £200'.[90] On top of these sums, the accounts for Michaelmas 1820 reveal that Highmore was paid £10 15s 6d to transport the wine and spirits.[91] A further receipt in 1826 detailed the prices the estate expended on other types of alcohol such as 69 gallons of port wine at £52 10s 0d, 59 gallons of suspension Cape Madeira at £23 12s 0d and 10 gallons of best brandy at £13. Altogether with a cask for the brandy, cartage and £3 to Mr. Adams 'for his trouble', the estate spent £92 18s 8d, but there was no charge for the hogshead cask which was customary.[92] Interestingly the bill contained instructions on how to clear the Cape Madeira with egg whites, and if not 'potent' enough, it was suggested that two quarts of brandy should be added.[93] There can be no doubt that the intention was to ensure that Anglesey's tenants were aware of their importance and understood that their landlord appreciated their electoral allegiance which was illustrated by his generous provisions. Fostering loyalty came at a price and continued throughout the election cycle; like elsewhere on the estate, any monetary outlay had to be value for money and targeted where it would have most effect. Local politics, at least here, had economic and financial undertones which are frequently neglected in the historiography. That said, for Castleman, nothing was left to chance.

Arranging get-togethers and dinners for tenants allowed the estate to remain abreast of the tone, nature, happenings and gossip in the borough which in itself rewarded the spending of money on the tenants. Even so Castleman was not above paying for information as the accounts for Michaelmas 1820 reveal. He recorded, 'Paid S Longman for his trouble getting information relative to the Borough' £1 5s 0d and to Robert Buckland 7s 6d for 'endeavouring to obtain information of attempts at bribery by Mr Feaver'.[94] Although women had no political status, E. A. Smith argues that they were effective canvassers and were an effective source of information; this was particularly true of Mrs. Owen, the wife of a local rector.[95] He reported to Anglesey: 'I find Mrs Owen a most zealous friend to our Cause and from her occasional communications with Feaver I get very valuable information from her'.[96] Although there was no monetary payment for the intelligence passed by Mrs. Owen, there were other expectations. Her husband had recently applied for the living at Ryme Intrinseca and there was an inherent perception that Anglesey would use his influence to obtain him the post. Castleman, however, advocated that she played an essential role in observing the opposition and was instrumental in passing the knowledge she obtained to the 'right ear'. Anglesey wanted the best of both worlds and hoped that Owen would obtain the living but remain at Milborne Port.[97]

William Castleman's careful management ensured that Anglesey never lost his patronage, even when challenged. An inferior agent could, as Henry Bankes found, spell disaster at the poll. He wrote to Anglesey (then Lord Uxbridge) in 1806 concerning the collapse of his Dorset campaign. He thanked Uxbridge for his kind offers of support but regretted to inform him that they were completely ineffectual. He stated that 'your Lordship's Steward Mr James, having permitted all your tenants to vote against me, on the first day of the election, without waiting for your instructions'.[98] Bankes reinforced the idea that it was not unusual for the steward to have opposing views to his 'master' and certainly on this occasion 'the influence and power of the former'.[99] This type of juxtaposed ideas meant that chief agents were not always trusted by the candidates; instead some liked to have a friend or relative to take overall charge of their campaigns.[100] At Milborne Port Anglesey left this part of the process to his agent, who by treating the tenants and paying for information was able to control even the unrulier elements of the borough, despite necessary absences to undertake other aspects of estate management. In other words, as already argued in the Introduction, the man who was left to manage an estate mattered, especially when a range of skills was needed, and in the case of politics, he had to be flexible and able to co-ordinate a process that could be chaotic.

Once an election was called, the electoral machinery started to move. Candidates were expected to canvas personally. They were judged not so much on their skill as a politician, but instead were evaluated on traits which included family, place of residence, wealth, opinions and personality.

A potential candidate was also expected to have at least a basic knowledge of the constituency where he intended to stand and its inhabitants. He needed to be a visual force, able to mix with the electorate. To reach the biggest number of people, both public and civic buildings were frequently utilised either to deliver speeches or as meeting spaces. Once the canvas commenced, little significance was given to what the candidate said or did; instead the real crux was simply to be seen and displayed to as many of the electorate as possible.[101] Despite the importance of being present at the right moment, sensibilities of politeness, decorum and respectability had to be taken into account. Essentially this meant that a candidate could only appear the day after nominations had been made. Consequently, time could be short. Providing someone had been managing an interest, the necessary groundwork had already been carried out. Just how brief the canvas might be was evident in a letter from Castleman to one of the candidates in the 1830 election. He wrote on 14 July 1814 that in light of the reports now appearing in the newspapers, the dissolution of parliament could be expected to take place on 'Saturday next'. If that was the case, then the 'writs' would be sent by that night's mail to the sheriff of the different counties. That would allow the notices to be given on Sunday, and, according to the 'Bridport Case in 1784', then the election could take place on 'the Thursday following'. This would therefore leave three days between the day in which the notice was issued and the poll itself; however, if the notice was not given until Monday, then the election could not take place before Friday.[102] The two candidates, Captain Byng and Mr. Bourne, were advised that they should present themselves at Milborne Port the same night as the notice was given. If that was not possible, then they should both be in the borough by twelve or one o'clock the following morning so that they might commence their canvas.[103] Castleman's presence at Milborne Port both during the canvas and any resultant election was essential, and he reassured Anglesey 'I shall proceed to Milborne on the day the dissolution takes place'.[104]

The customary expectations on the day of the poll were very similar to those on audit day. The voters expected to be provided with food and beverages in return for turning up. Besides the refreshments, there would have been charges for music and bell ringing as entertainment during the poll itself. The monies expended could easily mount and reflect the importance of politics as it allowed the patron to influence power both locally and nationally in parliament. The election dinner of 1831 was typical of the type of dinner that the estate provided on these occasions; see Table 5.3.[105]

Table 5.3 Election dinner 1831

73 dinners at 2/6 each	£9 2s 6d
6 dozen Sherry wine	£18
3 dozen port wine	£9
30 mugs punch at 6s each	£9
Dinners for 10 musicians	£1 5s 0d
Beer	£0 12s 0d
Dessert	£0 7s 6d
Pipes and tobacco	£0 5s
Breakage	£1
Messenger to Horsington and candle	£0 2s
Servants	£0 10s
Paid part of Mr. Steel's fare by coach	£0 2s
To Milborne Port	£0 5s
	£49 9s 0d

Once the election was over and hopefully the correct men returned to parliament, the election agent's function changed to one of accountant and financial manager. He had, firstly, to gather any evidence which would be helpful if the result was challenged and secondly arrange the collection, collation and payment of the bills which had been incurred.[106] At this point the focus of management is entirely monetary and in theory should have been a relatively simple exercise, but as seen elsewhere, local tensions and the various personalities within the borough came into play. Even matters which on the surface were apparently simple quickly became more complicated. For example, in January 1819 Castleman reported:

> I enclose all the Milborne Port Election Bills except Mr White's and Mr Fooks's to whom repeated applications have been made for them by both myself and a number of others, Mr F prefers delivering his Bill in person.[107]

As soon as all the receipts had been obtained, they were then sent to the agent-in-chief for approval, and these were then returned for payment. Establishing who was paying for what part of the election could be problematic, and on a previous occasion, Castleman had found himself out of pocket. Consequently, before the approaching election of 1826, he wrote to Anglesey asking, 'exactly what Portion of the costs is to be paid by Lord Graves and Mr Chichester and what by your Lordship'.[108] Understanding how much an agent might charge for his services in staging an election in a small borough is emblematically demonstrated by

Castleman's bill for that which took place in 1831. For the work undertaken between 30 May and 12 July, he charged the estate £93 16s 4d which included £5 5s 0d as a retainer and £31 10s 0d for the journey to Milborne Port and five days canvassing for himself and his son in June. On 11 July a further £17 27s 0d was added for travelling again to the borough to prepare for the poll itself; other items listed are chaise hire, 'writing many letters' previous to the election and afterwards examining the bills of election and their payment.[109] Castleman's time was charged at £3 3s 0d per day and this was on top of his £500 annual salary. According to Smith, complaints against dishonest or inefficient agents can be found in the correspondence of every political man of the period.[110] The rising cost of elections and any disorder were often laid at the door of the agent. Yet, William Castleman seems to have managed to juggle all the problems in the borough, fighting off the challenge by Lord Darlington by organising an exchange of land with Winchester College, finding ways to treat the voters within the clearly defined framework of nineteenth-century canvassing and ensuring that voters who would could be relied upon were those to whom vote houses were let. Despite his hard work in consolidating the borough of Milborne, one short comment suggests that Castleman did not agree with Anglesey's politics. In a letter from June 1841, he commented, 'Your Lordship has alluded to my political sentiments which are well known to you but I trust your Lordship will believe that I shall in no way allow them to influence or interfere with the course which my duty as your Lordship's Agent … will lead me to pursue'.[111] Even after the Great Reform Act of 1832 and the disenfranchisement of Milborne Port, he remained closely in touch with county politics and the representation of Anglesey's interests in the locality.

The Great Reform Act of 1832

Political change came in 1832 with the Great Reform Act and while this volume acknowledges the vast historiography surrounding this Act, it is not intended to review it here in anything other than a cursory manner. The old system had been viewed as corrupt, outdated and in need of modernisation so that it might meet the changing needs of a demographically diverse population. Gash argues that the principle aims of the Bill were to gather the support of the middle classes to the aristocracy. Politically he suggests the Bill had two main aims: firstly, to strengthen the constitution by gaining the support of 'mass public opinion' without which it was felt the gentry would not survive and, secondly, it stopped the middle classes from allying themselves too closely with the lower orders among whom it was acknowledged there existed a general state of disillusionment. The Reform Bill did not so much seek to overhaul the electoral system as to remove those 'defects' and 'abuses' which occasioned most complaint.[112] Under Lord Russell's proposals, 56 boroughs would be disenfranchised of which Milborne Port was one and another 31 would be reduced to just one Member of Parliament. At the same time, 41 towns which had no form of parliamentary representation would be franchised. There were changes at county level too where the plan was to increase the number of men returned to Parliament for 34 out of the 40 counties. For some, such as Macauley, reform was the only way to save England from 'catastrophe'. He believed that failure to do so would be devastating and warned: 'I pray to God that none of those who concur in rejecting it may ever remember their votes with unavailing regret, amidst the wreck of laws, the spoliation of property, and the dissolution of social order'.[113] Historians continue to debate the impact of the Great Reform Act on the size of the electorate. While Phillips and Wetherell argue that the bill both promised and delivered an overall increase in the number of voters by around 50 per cent,[114] others such as Daunton take a different standpoint—he argues that in 1715 approximately 25 per cent of adult males in England and Wales held the vote. In the years leading up to 1831, this fell to 14 per cent and increased under the Reform Act to a mere 18 per cent, still well short of the eighteenth-century electorate.[115]

Elections in unreformed England were time-consuming, and further delays and expenses were often incurred as legal arguments between rival candidates broke out over the qualifications of their or the opposition's voters. So, in an attempt to stop these difficulties, the biggest change between unreformed and reformed elections was the events which happened before the poll took place. There was the introduction of a new annual voter registration which would determine who could or could not vote. Laying out the criteria took up around a third of the Act itself.[116] Before 1832 electors had had to establish their right to vote at the poll itself, and as already seen, this could go on to cause huge problems and petitions sent to parliament which required legal representation and the resultant cost in legal counsel fees. At the core of this issue were the difficulties around establishing who in the borough were £10 householders or in the counties £50 occupiers and who had been in residence long enough to be entitled to vote. By separating the business of claiming the vote from that of casting it, the government sought to remove party rivalry from the process of scrutinising and verifying voters.[117] Instead of the vote just being given at election time and only then in the event of a poll actually taking place, the franchise now had to be acquired annually irrespective of whether an election took place. In an annual procedure lasting almost five months, individual voters had to submit their claim, check any pre-prepared lists and see that their names and addresses had been correctly recorded. When all of this had been done, a one shilling registration fee was paid; to comply with all the regulations, any outstanding local taxes had to be paid in full by a given date, and only then would a name be added to a provisional electoral roll. In an attempt to eliminate men who did not meet the qualifications, any person claiming the right to vote had to be prepared to 'defend' this entitlement against any possible objection in court, often at only three days' notice.[118]

Overall it has been suggested that placing the onus on the individual to enrol increased electoral participation. There was a worry that at least some of those who had acquired the vote in 1832 were either unclear or ignorant of the fact. In June a letter to the agent-in-chief reiterated the above fact stating that 'persons claiming to vote are required to have met with the particulars of their claims on or before the 20th July'.[119] He was concerned that 'many of the Copyholders and others under the Marquis of Anglesey's influence may be ignorant of the fact of their having acquired a title to vote'.[120] If Anglesey wished to continue to exert any form of political influence in the area, then it was essential that those who lived within the estate should register to vote in good time. In the event of Anglesey's acquiescence, the necessary enquiries would take time and would undoubtedly fall outside of the remit of the normal land agent's duties. It would of course be feasible to send 'the best instructions in writing', but he doubted whether such measures would prove satisfactory at the beginning of this new process.[121] In other words it would be far more beneficial to pay Castleman a fee and ensure the job was completed satisfactorily.

The disenfranchisement of Milborne Port had financial consequences not least of which was the decision in 1837 to sell off the borough. Those who had been employed as subagents found themselves unemployed in the wake of the Great Reform Act as no further use could be found for them.[122] Highmore fared a little better and was eventually granted £20 per annum in lieu of his 'long and faithful service as Agent for the Borough'.[123] Highmore still owed the estate large sums of money, and it was hoped that he would use the allowance as a contribution to his outstanding debt. Although there might be individual losses, the estate stood to claw back some of the monies it had spent on a regular basis. Feasts which had been customary such as the annual bread and cheese event for the tenants were to continue as a tradition. Others though came to an end including regular shipments of a London newspaper to the borough. Although Highmore was to continue to receive an annual pension, this was a fall from the 50 pounds he had been paid previously. The expenses of the borough court would be reduced to that of the jury at similar courts, that is around two guineas per year, and the expense of the capital bailiffs would cease. By 1841 Anglesey's influence was waning at county level too, perhaps because it was becoming clear that the estate was likely to be sold off. As a result, tenant loyalty began to falter as it seemed the sale would be sooner rather than later. Worried by this swing, Castleman wrote to Anglesey stating that the *Dorset County Chronicle* had published a list of voters which indicated that the rector and nine tenants at Stalbridge, including some of the most influential tenants, had pledged their support to Mr. Bankes.[124] Deference, it might thus be argued, was freely given when the landowner sought to work for his tenants, but selling the estate broke the established stands of loyalty and the tenants looked to others who would act in their interest.

Conclusion

Politics even in a small borough such as Milborne Port were complicated and affected by the influence of the local landowner and the foibles and idiosyncrasies of the local electorate. While a substantial historiography exists, close textual studies of estate politics provide an added sense of rural communities and the ways in which they worked. Rural relationships were often fragile and fickle. Anglesey and his agent understood the need to manipulate the electorate which essentially meant buying voter loyalty, thus turning politics into a financial and economic issue. Election victory was never a certainty, and the double-vote system meant that tenants and those entitled to vote expected to be canvassed and treated once an election had been called. Voting rights have close links with the working and social relationships of Chaps. 3 and 4, in that a tenant of certain properties expected to have bestowed on them enfranchisement. In many respects the political status of tenants was an accepted customary right and withdrawal was not an option. The Great Reform Act while it disenfranchised the borough there remains an innate sense within the archive that Castleman continued to influence county elections at least until 1841. Although the electorate was small, it was not confined entirely to either the aristocracy or gentry thus creating a sense that 'ordinary' men had the right to reaffirm or change the prevailing government. Social and political change was possible, but as seen here voting against a patron's chosen candidate could result in eviction. If money was to be spent in building and maintaining properties in the borough, then at least the tenant should be one that could be relied on to vote in Anglesey's interest. Petitions it is argued allowed both men and women who had no political voice a chance to air their opinions and an expectation that they would be listened to and the issues debated. Ultimately, any petitions that came from the electorate and presented to parliament would require Castleman to provide an opinion, and so with the anti-Catholic petition, he attempted to distance himself from its compilation. The early nineteenth century, it has been argued, witnessed an expanding interest in political affairs that extended beyond the borough and county borders. The mere fact that the estate paid for a London newspaper to be available locally, possibly in the King's Head, suggests a growing awareness of national and regional affairs.[125]

To fight an election, even when there was no contest, cost considerable sums of money and could take the land agent away from his main task of managing the estate. In the event a result was challenged, there would be additional and of considerable legal fees, and any enquiry undertaken by a Select Committee would have added to this financial burden. Elections and maintaining a borough did not come cheap. When faced with Darlington's takeover attempt, the estate had to move quickly and in the end was left with no other options than to rent Medleycott's premises which cost around £400 per annum. This added to the fiscal expense of the election process. Furthermore, Castleman was forced to enter the rental payments of tenants in these properties monthly thus taking up considerably more of his time than any of the other tenants. After the Great Reform Act, the borough which had aided in diversifying and extending Anglesey's patronage lost its importance and was sold off. There was nothing particularly unusual here; as already seen in the Introduction, the estate had regularly sold off areas that became a financial burden.

A study of the borough of Milborne Port reveals a remarkably efficient network of electioneering created by the agent and established a prism in which was played out many aspects of local life. At the apex of these local links sat William Castleman, balancing the finances and organising events like the canvas in much the same way as collecting the rent. The election process in many ways mirrors the management of the estate itself, including the way in which decisions made were underpinned with a financial consideration. Monies had to be found to fight off any opposition; tenants and other voters managed so that they not only understood for whom they should vote but that these intentions were reflected on polling day. Castleman's skills in handling money were invaluable, and it was easy for him to adapt his daily working practices to running and organising the electoral process. Nineteenth-century elections often elucidated and 'propped up' the existing structure of local society. They are as much a part of the financial history of this estate as the day-to-day economics of collecting the rents or letting farms. Anglesey intended to bolster his influence through his patronage within the area, and somehow Castleman as in all else had to find the money to fulfil his employer's ambitions.

Notes

1. F. O'Gorman (1989) *Voters, Patrons, and Parties: The Unreformed Electoral System of Hanoverian England 1734–1832* (Oxford: Clarendon Press), p. 6.
2. See O'Gorman *Voters, Patrons, and Parties*; D. C. Moore (1976) *The Politics of Deference: A Study of the Mid-Nineteenth Century English Political System* (Hassocks: Harvester Press).
3. See for example, J. R. Fisher (1981) 'The Limits of Deference: Agricultural Communities in a Mid-Nineteenth Century Election Campaign', *Journal of British Studies*, 21:1, pp. 90–105.
4. G. E. Mingay (1963) *English Landed Society in the Eighteenth Century* (London: Routledge), pp. 206 and 286.
5. Fisher, 'The Limits of Deference', p. 91.
6. D. Hainsworth (1992) *Stewards, Lords and People: The Estate Steward and His World in Later Stuart England* (Cambridge: Cambridge University Press), p. 142.
7. J. A. Phillips (1979) 'The Structure of Electoral Politics in Unreformed England', *Journal of British Studies.* 19:1, p. 77.
8. J. A. Phillips (1982) *Electoral Behaviour in Unreformed England: Plumpers, Splitters and Straights* (Princeton, New Jersey: Princeton University Press), p. 20.
9. N. Gash (1963) *Politics in the Age of Peel: A Study in the Technique of Parliamentary Representation* (London: Longmans Green), p. 127.

10. Ibid.
11. Hainsworth, *Stewards, Lords and People*, p. 140.
12. E. A. Smith (1969) 'The Election Agent in English Politics, 1734–1832' *The English Historical Review*, 84:330, pp. 12–13.
13. Ibid.
14. T. C. Hansard (1812) *The Parliamentary Debates From the Year 1803 To The Present Time, Vol XIV* (London), p. 665.
15. This was an essential denominator of franchise rights in scot and lot boroughs such as Milborne Port.
16. O'Gorman, *Voters, Patrons, and Parties*, p. 241.
17. Ibid., p. 27.
18. Ibid.
19. See, O'Gorman, *Voters, Patrons, and Parties*, particularly Chapter 2, 'The Structure of Local Politics'.
20. See, U. Corbett and E. R. Daniell (1821) *Reports of Cases of Controverted Elections in the Sixth Parliament of the United Kingdom* (London: J. &W. T. Clarke), pp. 204–228.
21. Ibid., p. 205.
22. DHC, D/ANG/B5/23, 27 October 1818.
23. https://www.historyofparliamentonline.org/volume/1790-1820/constituencies/milborne-port accessed 23 September 2018.
24. S. G. McKay (1986) *Milborne Port in Somerset* (Milborne Port: Remous Ltd), p. 133.
25. DHC, D/ANG/B5/23, 27 October 1818.
26. Corbett and Daniell, *Reports of Cases of Controverted Elections*, p. 206.
27. Ibid., pp. 204–228.
28. This was the London home of the Marquis of Anglesey and presided over by the agent-in-chief Mr. John Sanderson.
29. DHC, D/ANG/B5/25, 20 April 1819.
30. D. Roberts (1979) *Paternalism in Early Victorian Britain* (London: Croom Helm), pp. 4–5.
31. O'Gorman *Voters, Patrons, and Parties*, p. 286.
32. Ibid.
33. *The Sherborne Mercury*, 5 July 1918.
34. Ibid.
35. O'Gorman (1989) *Voters, Patrons, and Parties*, p. 286.
36. Ibid., p. 287.
37. T, Jenkins, (2009) 'Milborne Port' in D. R. Fisher, (ed.), *The History of Parliament: The House of Commons 1820–1832* accessed via www.historyofparliamentonline.org
38. D/ANG/B5/36, 23 Sept. 1825.
39. Ibid.

40. DHC, D/ANG/B5/41 Letter to N Highmore from William Castleman 19 January 1829.
41. See, J. A. Phillips (1980) 'Popular Politics in Unreformed England', *The Journal of Modern History*, 54:4 (December), p. 604.
42. F. M. L. Thompson (1963) *English Landed Society in the Nineteenth Century* (London: Routledge & Keegan Paul), p. 204.
43. Ibid.
44. Ibid.
45. M. J. Daunton (1995) *Progress and Poverty: An Economic and Social History of Britain 1700–1850* (Oxford: Oxford University Press), pp. 480–481.
46. Ibid.
47. Ibid.
48. Jenkins, 'Milborne Port'.
49. DHC, D/ANG/B5/28. This letter from Manners appears in the records for 1820 but was probably written the previous year.
50. Jenkins, 'Milborne Port'.
51. DHC, D/ANG/B4/1/32 Accounts to Michaelmas 1819 and D/ANG/B4/1/34 Accounts to Michaelmas 1820.
52. DHC, D/ANG/B5/26, 5 January 1820.
53. DHC, D/ANG/B4/34.
54. DHC, D/ANG/B5/25, 23 June 1819.
55. Ibid.
56. Jenkins, 'Milborne Port'.
57. DHC, D/ANG/B5/26, 13 April 1820.
58. Ibid.
59. Ibid.
60. Jenkins, 'Milborne Port'.
61. DHC, D/ANG/B5/32, 5 April 1823 and 19 September 1823.
62. Ibid.
63. DHC, D/ANG/B5/32, 19 September 1823.
64. DHC, D/ANG/B5/26, 14 August 1820.
65. Ibid.
66. Jenkins, ('Milborne Port').
67. See, Jenkins, 'Milborne Port' and 5 Geo. IV, c. 25.
68. DHC, D/ANG/B5/33, June/July 1824.
69. DHC, D/ANG/B5/36, 31 May 1825 and Jenkins, 'Milborne Port'.
70. DHC, D/ANG/B5/36, 26 October 1825.
71. Ibid.
72. Ibid.
73. See for example: O'Gorman, *Voters, Patrons, and Parties*; Roberts, *Paternalism in Early Victorian Britain* and Moore, *The Politics of Deference*.

74. See, F. O'Gorman (Jan., 1986) 'The Unreformed Electorate of Hanoverian England: The Mid-Eighteenth Century to the Reform Act of 1832', *Social History*, 11:1, pp. 33–52.
75. Ibid., p. 48.
76. Ibid.
77. Phillips, *Electoral Behaviour in Unreformed England*, p. 107.
78. Gorman, *Voters, Patrons, and Parties*, pp. 90–91.
79. R. Worthington Smith (Jun., 1969) 'Political Organisation and Canvassing: Yorkshire Elections before the Reform Bill', *The American Historical Review*, 74:5, p. 1539.
80. Phillips, *Electoral Behaviour in Unreformed England*, p. 72.
81. O'Gorman, *Voters, Patrons, and Parties*, p. 95.
82. DHC, D/ANG/B5/56 Letter from Mr. Sheridan.
83. Gorman, *Voters, Patrons, and Parties*, pp. 95–96.
84. DHC, D/ANG/B5/26, 30 November 1819.
85. Ibid.
86. DHC, D/ANG/B5/26, 20 November 1820.
87. Canon Court was a farm in the borough rented by one of the Highmores.
88. DHC, D/ANG/B5/26 20 November 1820.
89. DHC, D/ANG/B4/45 Bill from the Queen's Head Inn.
90. DHC, D/ANG/B5/26 20 November 1820.
91. DHC, D/ANG/B4/1/34. Accounts for 1820.
92. DHC, D/ANG/B4/45 Although dated 1826, this receipt is filed with the vouchers for 1820.
93. Ibid.
94. DHC, D/ANG/B4/1/34 Rental Accounts for 1820.
95. See Smith, 'The Election Agent in English Politics', p. 15; and DHC, D/ANG/B5/31, 10 July 1822.
96. DHC, D/ANG/B5/31, 10 July 1822.
97. Ibid.
98. O'Gorman, *Voters, Patrons, and Parties*, pp. 80–81.
99. Ibid.
100. O'Gorman, *Voters, Patrons, and Parties*, p. 81 and Smith, 'The Election Agent in English Politics', p. 15.
101. O'Gorman, *Voters, Patrons, and Parties*, p. 81.
102. DHC, D/ANG/B5/42, 14 July 1830.
103. Ibid.
104. Ibid.
105. DHC, D/ANG/B4/54Estate Vouchers for 1831.
106. Hainsworth, *Stewards, Lords and People*, p. 157.
107. DHC, D/ANG/B5/25 Letter to Mr. Lowe from William Castleman January 1819.

108. DHC, D/ANG/B5/37, 24 May 1826.
109. DHC, D/ANG/B4/54 this bill was charged to the account to Lady Day 1831.
110. See, Smith, 'The Election Agent in English Politics', pp. 27–28.
111. DHC, D/ANG/B5/56, 4 June 1841.
112. N. Gash (1979) *Aristocracy and People: Britain 1851–1865* (London: Edward Arnold), p. 147.
113. J. A. Phillips and C. Wetherell (Dec. 1991) 'The Great Reform Bill of 1832 and the Rise of Partisanship', *The Journal of Modern History*, 63:4, p. 622.
114. Ibid., pp. 413–414.
115. Daunton, *Progress and Poverty*, p. 482.
116. P. Salmon (2003) 'Electoral Reform and the Political Modernization of England, 1832–1841', *Parliaments, Estates and Representation*, 23:1, p. 53.
117. Ibid.
118. Ibid., pp. 53–54.
119. DHC, D/ANG/B5/44, 13 June 1832.
120. Ibid.
121. Ibid.
122. See for example, DHC, D/ANG/B5/44, 12 June 1832.
123. DHC, D/ANG/B5/44, 27 September 1832.
124. DHC, D/ANG/B5/44, 12 June 1832.
125. Both elections and political meetings held in the King's Head appear in the Anglesey/Castleman archive.

CHAPTER 6

Social Control: Church, Charity and Education

Overview

There is an overriding assumption that social control in nineteenth-century England was not simply about rule through the existing legal systems but was instead a product of a range of interactions with a variety of social institutions. These ranged from religion to family life and incorporated leisure, recreation, charity, philanthropy, social work and poor relief.[1] The idea of exerting social control does not, according to Tony Donajgrodzki, commit the social historian to 'a species of a crude reductionism' which doubts the humanity of the humanitarian neither does it see clergymen, social workers and educators as the policers of society. To do this would diminish a sense of the complexities of social relationships and its associated historical processes.[2] There are two different but often interlinked concepts of the poor in the nineteenth century according to Donajgrodzki. The first saw the poor as an ongoing and chronic problem, while the second related poverty to specific social and economic contexts whereby the issue becomes an acute problem. Those in the first group often tried to exert a 'moralising' influence on those aspects which were perceived as vices such as hedonism, improvidence, cruelty, licentiousness or a lack of religious belief. These ideas were not new and campaigns to inspire a 'moral' life-style dated back to at least the eighteenth century. In cities which were often classed as places of disorder and in urban areas, the masses were seen as problematic and appeals were often

C. Beardmore, *Financing the Landed Estate*, Palgrave Studies in the History of Finance, https://doi.org/10.1007/978-3-030-14552-1_6

made to establish some form of 'personal influence' over the lives of the poor.[3] Dennis Mills suggests that in rural societies social control on the part of the gentry, clergy, land agents and other allies was partly achieved by the segregation of the more unruly elements from the remainder of the population.[4] Social control as argued in the Introduction was important for estates with their diverse societal mix. Separation of the different groups is not a solution on rural estates because agricultural labourers were an essential part of the work force. Landowners often took a multi-pronged approach to the problem in order to attempt to maintain some degree of social control. It was especially difficult to exert pressure over those with whom they had in effect little financial influence and so other means had to be found.

There was a strong belief that social order was linked to the church, education and charity. The church provided moral instruction and sermons could reinforce stereotypical ideals as they justified and explained the existence of poverty and inequality in society.[5] Many of the clergy became involved with mediating the needs of the poor; this was done through their work as magistrates, members of poor law boards and administrators of charity. Alongside the church, education was another factor which was deemed important in bringing moral education to the poor. There was an ongoing debate during the nineteenth century as to whether the state or church should control education, and this will be taken up again later. For landowners, schools like churches were an outward and visual symbol of the control they exerted locally. The land agent was often called upon to manage his employer's charitable impulses by either pointing out those who were most in need or overseeing the requests that came from local ministers or others. He needed to ensure that annual distributions were made and recorded, though the scale of relief offered, and its frequency would be in the hands of the landlord.[6] All agents witnessed a wide variety of social problems. Inevitable control of this section of the population rested on ensuring enough monies were spent and that the estate was not overwhelmed by requests. With their extensive managerial skills, it is hardly surprising that many landowners relied on their land agents to manage their charitable expenditure. The local clergy came most regularly into contact with the poor, and as a group they fully understood that the land agent had at his fingertips sufficient cash to extend and repair their churches, to build or support day and Sunday schools and to make one-off payments when poverty became overwhelming.

The land agent on behalf of his employer had therefore to negotiate two distinct problems. In many respects the first which necessitated maintaining social and political control of the tenantry was a relatively simple process. At the core of these relationships was a symbiotic framework between landowner and tenant that laid out the basics of all relationships as seen in the Introduction and other chapters of this volume. Part of this included financial support when necessary and an understanding from the tenants that political loyalty was important. Ultimately the estate could rid itself of any that did not conform, or a lease could be broken and the farm quit at either Michaelmas or Lady Day. Controlling the lower strata of the rural community created significant worries which were exacerbated through the fear generated by the Swing Riots. Although historians in the past have tended to see these riots as rather minor and inconsequential, there was as seen in Chap. 4 a general fear that they could develop into something more serious.[7] F. M. L. Thompson argues that on the one hand landowners used 'analogous coercive' power combined with fear to control, and this ensured that agricultural labours and other minority figures within the rural community harboured a dislike, hatred and resentment to any in positions of authority.[8] Yet during the Swing Riots while physical violence was threatened, there was relatively little personal violence and in Dorset the status quo was quickly restored. On the other hand, rural social relationships were not so much one of conflict contained through compulsion and intimidation but existed instead as an awkward independence kept in check by social leadership, conditioning and paternalism. In estate terms this often resulted in using the full process of the law to identify and prosecute specific ringleaders of events which threatened social stability.[9] Although the underlying sentiment remains one of conflict, in this second scenario social control relies on continual mediation, deference and where possible the maintenance of social discipline. In many respects this often creates a somewhat biased view as it is only when things moved out of kilter that they attracted enough attention to elicit the opinion of either the Marquis of Anglesey or his land agent.

In effect neither landowner nor agent could neglect the agricultural labourer and the other poorer elements of the estate. As already seen in Chap. 4, if customary rights were at risk the entire population of an area might riot and so maintaining at least a modicum control of the labouring poor was essential. Like everything else within the estate, there was a financial cost, and this underpinned any decision as to how and where money might be spent. The sums involved were often small but nonetheless it had to be cost-effective and bring results. For example, consideration had to be given as to whether the monies spent should demonstrate the rewards of good behaviour as the estate did with the cottages built in Stalbridge. These were rented to the better tenants of the town after Swing or it had to decide whether to withhold payments to punish those who deliberately broke the unspoken rules of estate life. In exploring social control within the landed estate, this chapter takes a threefold approach. It will firstly explore visual structures in the form of church expansion and repairs. Secondly, it will examine the way in which the estate sought to share the burden of poor relief through making payments for coal, bread, clothes and one-off payments to the poor. Finally, it will investigate education within the confines of the estate villages and argue that the monies spent here took a long-term approach to improving behaviour and exerting social control through the education of the children. As always, the solution was to take a varied approach and to adapt this as necessary. Despite the meagreness of the sums expended, they were continual and give some indication to the importance that was placed on maintaining control of the lower echelons of society.

Church Expansion

The French Revolution had helped to convince both clergymen and politicians that the Church needed strengthening to preserve the social fabric of society. Legislation was passed which sought to curb the non-residence of the clergy, augment poor livings and encourage church building. The parish was the centre of these reforming initiatives, and an assumption existed that parish clergy were one of the most, if not the most, important figures in the fight against immorality and infidelity. With the rise in population, a programme of church building was essential if all parishioners were to attend public worship and later both Sunday and National Schools would be organised on these parochial lines.[10] The clergyman's life was one of a 'model shepherd' which should inspire the 'emulation' of the rich who in turn should motivate those beneath them.[11] One way this could be achieved was for the estate to take part in church expansion and repairs as the building itself was an outwardly obvious symbol of social hierarchy and control. Spending monies on this area ensured that churches remained at the centre of communities and were part of projecting the message of industriousness, soberness, obedience and subordination.[12] Chris Brooks argues that the effectiveness of the system relied on the residence of the squire or principal landowner, it was not enough to just own the land but if he was to coerce he needed to live there too.[13] The theme of absentee landowners already discussed in the Introduction argues that absenteeism was not as significant as many historians have assumed and a good land agent acting in loco parentis could be just as effective. While Brooks argues that absenteeism was bad for the rural church, parish and clerics nothing within this archive suggests this to be the case. The local clergy would send letters to the land agent with a variety of requests and these were acted upon or not accordingly, that said aid was often provided because of the inherent sense that the clergy formed an important element in helping to maintain control.

Landowners saw the restoration and rebuilding of parish churches in two ways. The first was to encompass repairs within the general matter of estate improvements which ensured their upkeep. Second, churches articulated the stability of the agrarian status quo and thus functioned as part of the mechanisms of social management. They were a visible entity and sat in the landscape as a prominent symbol of the state, law, the power of aristocracy and estate ownership. These ideas are apparent from the onset of William Castleman's agency. In December 1815 he wrote to the Marquis of Anglesey regarding Gussage Church. In this case the lead of the roof was in such a poor condition that it had been removed by the churchwardens. The expense of having a new roof cast had proved much more expensive than anticipated and beyond the normal annual average of repairs. Although essentially outside the usual scope of allowances made in the past, it was argued that on this occasion an exception should be made. In other local cases where the same situation had arisen, the landowner had made a personal contribution to help cover the cost.[14] By supporting this extraordinary expenditure, the estate recognised the role of the church and its clergy within the social and fiscal processes of the estate. The sense that landowners should be seen to be wealthy is an inherent principle here, a dilapidated church gave out the wrong set of symbols.

The plan for the enlargement of the church at Milborne Port was more controversial and appeared to be reliant on a substantial subscription from Anglesey. Castleman would not have recommended the scheme, but by the time he became aware of the project, planning was already in an advanced stage and had received the sanction of the Bishop of Hereford and Winchester College. Mr. Owen the curate was at the centre of the scheme and, as soon as he had submitted the papers, enquired of Anglesey how much he and the two Members of Parliament would be prepared to contribute. Rather than making any suggestions as to suitable amounts, an enquiry was initiated to find how others thought and what they might be prepared to spend. It was discovered that Sir William Medleycott who was another substantial property owner at Milborne Port was allegedly inclined to evade the subscription altogether.[15] Mr. Sanderson the agent-in-chief complained that the papers which had been furnished on the subject did not give him enough information to guide either Anglesey or the members' judgement. There was no estimate of the total expense and no subscription listed other than that of the Bishop of Hereford. Sanderson argued that Medleycott as resident parishioner and chief landowner in the area ought to be taking the lead rather than evading it.[16] Castleman suggested that the only hope of avoiding payment lay with Owen's idea of raising the entire monies without mortgaging the church. If unsuccessful Owen would abandon the plan. Two interviews with Medleycott in early May revealed that he was willing to donate £10. As the entire cost of the aisle was expected to be in the region of £630, it left Owen disappointed and far short of the total. In the end it was ascertained that Owen thought 'a handsome subscription' would amount to £50 from Anglesey and £25 each from the two MPs. Castleman determined that if Anglesey was to agree to Owen's request, he should only pay when the entire sum had been raised and the suspicion existed 'that that time will never come'.[17] In many ways this solution was the practical land agent and businessman at work, it sought to limit fiscal spending while continuing to negotiate the diverse social relationships within the rural community without creating unnecessary antipathy. In reality and unsurprisingly, the state of affairs was far more complex.

Mr. Owen, as already seen in Chap. 5, had applied for the incumbency at Ryme Intrinseca, and this seemed to present the perfect solution. He had been promised the parish by the chancellor and it was suggested that Anglesey follow up the post through the official channels. Owen would then be required to live on the benefice with his interests tied up in his new parish.[18] Unfortunately, the King too wanted the living and so the proposal fell through and this left Owen in situ. There was, however, a complication to the situation because as seen in Chap. 5, Mrs. Owen, his wife, was an ardent supporter of Anglesey in borough politics and provided valuable information regarding the opposition. The snippets of intelligence she offered were particularly useful considering Lord Darlington's attempt to take over patronage of the borough. In practice this case illustrates the way in which financial decision-making was often complex and could have huge implications far beyond simply extending the church. Alienating Mrs. Owen, by offending her husband, was not an option, and any resolution was a delicate matter of balancing benefits against expenditure. The decision therefore to wait and do nothing seemed the best outcome, especially as Owen faced a monumental task. No-one had taken into account the dogged determination of this curate, and by February 1823 he had managed to raise all of the monies for his church extension. This meant that Anglesey now had no option but to pay his promised subscription.[19] Given that help had already been given to Gussage Church, the question must be asked as to why there was such opposition to Owen's proposal. In essence the objections came down to simply not wanting to spend extra money at the level of the sums requested. While the amount seems relatively small at £50, this would have, as will be seen later, supported the school at Hanley for more than two years. There was no dispute over the increase of population in the town or that the church was too small to hold them all comfortably. The objections arose solely from committing Anglesey to any unnecessary expense. Already aware of Anglesey's not insignificant financial problems, attempts were made to spare him from spending anything beyond that which was essential. Inherently understanding that Mrs. Owen could not be isolated during the rather delicate political situation was a necessity, and thus the money had been promised but in the hope that it would never be called down. It had been subject to seemingly unsurmountable criteria which when breached meant the promised donation had to be paid.

Other churches were not subject to such conditions and in 1834 the rector at Coombe Church approached the estate. With his parishioners he had been enlarging the church with voluntary subscriptions. Altogether around £320 was needed but they were short by approximately £80. The Rector had personally given £50 and seemed to expect a large subscription from Anglesey; Castleman stated 'I told him I thought he would be disappointed'. His reasoning was that Anglesey only had one farm in the parish rented by Stay at £440 per annum. In other words, there was little if any benefit to the estate in terms of either controlling its population or extending its visible presence within the landscape. Anglesey, however, decided that a smaller donation of £15 was a prudent move.[20] The church at Charlton Horethorne was different again, and the estate's involvement fell more into the more usual schedule of repairs. Consequently, in 1846 after the audit Edward Castleman went to inspect the chancel as the churchwarden had written to say the building needed immediate attention. He reported that the southern wall had within the last three months fallen out, which he thought had been caused by the pressure of the roof which appeared rotten. He advocated that as soon as the weather permitted it would have to be repaired, not least because it put at risk the lives of the estate tenants when attending services. Overall the conservation work was not expected to cost more than £50 and was more likely to be much less in the region of £15 or £20.[21] The church within the landscape was a symbol of both the state and estate's power, and ultimately the reputation of Anglesey was at stake because if he failed to repair a building such as the church at Charlton Horethorne, what could the tenants expect in their time of need? Failure to act at Charlton Horethorne was, therefore, not an option for the Marquis of Anglesey. Deciding which church buildings to repair or expand were as much part of the complex relationships within this estate as customary rights and other financial expectations. The clergy expected as part of their ongoing relationship with their landowner a return on the investment they put into managing local communities through the maintenance and enlarging of their churches. As a group these were the people most likely to understand the needs of the poor, and thus there was a value to be gained from this type of extra spending. In general, these judgements were made at the remit of the land agent. As the clergy played an important role in dispensing much of the charitable funds donated by Anglesey as well as running the schools to which he regularly subscribed, they were influential men who were used by the estate to promote Anglesey's largesse.

Charity

Estates and the land agents/stewards who managed them witnessed a diverse range of social processes and social change. A not insignificant part of their remit was to report on all aspects of local life and as such it is hardly surprising that their correspondence acts as a window into the rural community.[22] Part of an agent's duties often entailed him overseeing his employer's charitable impulses. His unique viewpoint on the rural community ensured that those who were most in need could be reached. Although the Old Poor Law enabled people to apply for relief from their parish of settlement, the amount offered varied enormously and thus land agents often found themselves as mediators who supervised the flow of charity, patronage and other forms of assistance. Sometimes payments were made to individuals in the form of pensions, but more commonly as will be seen below disbursements were made to responsible members of the community to dole out as they saw fit. Stephen King and Alannah Tomkins argue that this along with other coping strategies formed sporadic, intermittent and frequently inadequate tactics which were essential for the 'material survival' of the poor.[23] The south and east of England according to Samantha Williams faced an ever-growing poverty problem between 1780 and 1834. Real wages either fell or were stagnant, at a time when the fragile economic climate ensured that many rural industries failed.[24] The silk industry, for example, in the south had been in decline since the start of the Napoleonic Wars when supplies from Turkey had been cut off.[25] In combination with low wages, the poor in the south needed to find a range of ways in which to survive, and the estate with its one-off payments fell into the economy of makeshifts. Charity thus had an important role to play in maintaining social control.

Rural philanthropy according to Anne Digby consisted of two main elements, first, endowed charity which was generally the product of past generosity and appeared in the form of bequests, voluntary charity and contemporary benevolence. The commonest form of this type of charity came in the form of doles. Despite the charity commissioner's attempts to tunnel these monies towards educational purposes, payments in the shape of coal, clothing, blankets, bread, meat and money continued. There was a common perception that these one-off payments pauperised in the same way as outdoor relief and did not necessarily reach those who needed it most. The second type was voluntary charity or private benevolence and should be viewed through a different lens as it was supposed to elevate the moral character of the recipient, to increase his self-respect and therefore to help a man to achieve the goal of self-help which would have led to stability and sustainability. Charitable donations were allegedly an exercise in moral discipline, whereby the landowner chose who was to receive the money and the amounts to be given. This was not a passive paying of the poor rate but could instead act as a clear form of social control.[26] This was essentially a more personal type of charity which revealed that those in authority were not immune to social sensitivity.

While not all land agents found themselves having to manage large and long-standing benevolences, most dealt daily with a whole host of problems created by poverty. Land agents could certainly be approached and asked to intercede with their employer on behalf of tenants or tradesmen particularly with petitions. As we have seen throughout this volume, promoting harmony amongst the tenants was essential for the well-being of the estate which in its entirety stretched way beyond merely lands, buildings, forests and deer parks. Essentially as detailed in the Introduction, an estate was the sum of its people and if these were not nurtured and sustained, they could easily become a burden on the poor rates themselves. The letters that agents wrote to their employers are one of the best sources for examining the year-on-year incidence of economic downturns, stagnation of trade or the rise in price of vital food stuffs. The way in which the estate sought to manage those who ended up in financial difficulty or the poorer elements of its inhabitants are hidden mainly within the estate vouchers and occasionally the accounts. They are overall the least visible group in the archive and yet perhaps the neediest.

The local clergy played an important role both in informing the estate when those in their parishes reached desperation levels. If they were able to persuade Anglesey to contribute to a given scheme, they then played an important role in distributing the monies received. An emblematic illustration of the ways in which the clergy might influence the local community was revealed in a letter from Bernard Husey-Hunt in 1844. Although he was writing to try and secure some form of annuity for the Reverend Peter John Hatherston's widow and children, it reveals the amount of work a local vicar might carry out for the benefit of the local population. Hatherston's living had been purchased by his mother for £2500 in 1839 and he was inducted in 1840. The parish at the time was described as being in a state of 'moral and religious destitution', and the vicarage classed as a ruin. At this point there was no village school and clothing, coal funds and benefit societies were unknown. Husey-Hunt claimed that during Hatherston's short incumbency, a suitable house had been erected of which the cost exceeded £1000 and for which Anglesey had sanctioned a loan of £777 16s 0d from the commissioners of Queen Anne's Bounty. A clothing, coal and benefit society were all secured for the poor and a daily school established and maintained by Mr. Hatherston at his own individual expense. As the now empty parish fell within the remit of Anglesey to give to a man of his choice, Husey-Hunt hoped he would pick someone else who understood the needs of the local community and who would continue to exert a moral influence on the locality.[27]

The importance of the clergy in the charitable networks established by the estate is demonstrated by the following letters. In 1831 Mr. Glossop wrote two letters to Anglesey. The first stated 'the season of the year having arrived when the wants of the Poor call imperatively on the landed Proprietors for assistance', and he now asked that Anglesey would kindly send a few pounds in aid, particularly for coal. Last year's contribution he added had managed to benefit 148 families with '1cwt pr week for 8d' which was less than half the normal retail price.[28] Fires kept the cottages dry, providing fuel was perceived as a sure means of averting sickness.[29] The second letter thanked Anglesey for the order of three pounds which had been sent towards supplying the poor at Henstridge with coals. He complained, however, that in the past his Lordship had previously contributed five pounds, the same amount as the Bishop of Ely, and more scathingly 'his Lordship being Lord of the Manor leads our expectations from him rather higher'.[30] In other words complaints would arise if the local landowner was not generous enough or failed to meet his perceived obligations. At Bradford Abbas in the same year, the Reverend Grant wrote to thank the estate for its annual subscription and hoped that this year the winter would not be so severe. He was concerned because the previous year his provision of fuel had fallen far short of what was needed. Contrary to Glossop's thoughts on keeping the house dry, Grant believed it might be more judicious to provide blankets. The theory behind this idea was that the poorest of inhabitants could not afford more than 100 weight of coal even when the price was much reduced and this was insufficient to get through the cold period of the year.[31] In December 1844 Henry Taylor wrote to thank Anglesey for his cheque of five pounds which had been sent for the relief of the poor sick labouring families in Stalbridge. Alongside this contribution Mr. Powys had also given a similar amount and expended a considerable sum in providing comfortable clothing and other necessities. In 1844 Henry Taylor at Stalbridge had written to the estate, to thank it for its annual subscription but also to ask for more practical help. He reported that 14 able-bodied men with families had been waiting at his door that morning. They were in a starving condition and complained that they had no work. Taylor was obliged to 'buy bread for them to take home for their families'. In the past William Castleman (who had died earlier in the year) had been in the habit of finding ditching and draining work in the bottom lands of the parish during the winter months. He argued that if this could be done again, it would at least employ some of them for the remainder of the winter.[32] The poor were still suffering in 1847 when Mr. Powys wrote to Edward Castleman to thank him for Anglesey's £10 subscription towards 'the relief of the poor of this place'. He stated this donation 'will serve to mitigate the suffering still pressing heavily upon very many among us'.[33] The extent to which the clergy distributed relief is evident here when Powys states 'the committee have sold at reduced rates to those in need of assistance, 436 loaves of bread, 24¼ buckets of barley, 5½ buckets of wheat at a loss of about £7'.[34] A further 20 pounds were given to the parish of Hanley in the same year on account of the high price of provisions.[35] While this latter sum might seem high, Hanley had a reputation for being 'riotous'; it was the worst hit area during the Swing Riots and the estate would have been keen to quell any problems before they had the chance to fester. In order to get the estate to part with as much money as possible in terms of subscriptions, it was not unusual to emphasise how the money had been spent and why it was so important to the poor.

There was an element of status in subscribing to the different societies and charitable funds to be gained and a landowner's benevolence was noted. Failing to provide was seen as being derogatory to the health of the rural community and could elucidate comments from other landowners. A letter from Lord Portman's agent in December 1838, for example, described the situation at Gussage where he had noted while collecting the rents for the allotments that many of the cottages were 'destitute of fuel'. In an attempt to relieve their plight, he had promised to attempt to establish a fuel fund for them. Lord Portman had promised to give five pounds and his tenants one pound each. He hoped that William Castleman could be persuaded to do the same especially as 'the people are very poor and have no means of picking any up'. There was another motive behind this idea, as when they were unable to afford fuel and driven to despair the poor would break up the fences and thus cost the landowners considerably more in replacements. There is a sense of annoyance in this letter too; Portman's agent suggested that Anglesey needed two or three more cottages on his estate as the only one he had in Gussage was lived in by two 'out parishioners'. This meant that in order to find room for those who had been removed, Lord Portman's cottages were overcrowded 'in a very indecent manner' with people who in fact worked for Anglesey's tenants. Portman's agent begged that the matter be given some serious thought because if 'you were to see the state in which they are living together, you would see the necessity of something being done'.[36] Before acting on the suggestions made and in order to assess the scale of the problem, an enquiry was instigated and when complete a report would be sent to Anglesey with its findings. This approach as we have seen throughout this volume was typical. No monies were committed or promised without an innate understanding of the facts and what might be achieved should a subscription be agreed. More importantly, Castleman was more than willing to withdraw payments when they no longer had an effect or as a means of gaining specific information. For example, in 1842 there had been significant damage caused by persons unknown to the saplings and bushes at Stalbridge Park. Notice was given that 'unless some of the Offenders are discovered & punished forthwith that his Lordships Annual Donation to the Coal fund in Parish will in future be wholly withdrawn'.[37]

Charity on occasions did not necessarily rely on money but instead depended on the time and skills of the estate to sort out a given problem. In early 1845 a malignant fever had broken out in the Stalbridge area, and Edward Castleman noted that 'No parishes but the poorest have been attacked'. He believed that the spread of the fever could be found in the lack of employment and insufficient support given to the labourer. This was of course balanced alongside the not insignificant 'very dirty habits of the Poor themselves and the neglect of the Waywardens in allowing heaps of dirt and filth to accumulate in very many of the back Lanes where the poorest of the Inhabitants reside'.[38] 'The mortality of those who contracted the disease was high with around 25 per cent of those infected dying'.[39] Consequently, the Waywardens were instructed to give notice to the offending parties to clean the area within 24 hours, and if this was not accomplished, the estate ordered they were to personally undertake the task. In order to prevent a repeat, anyone in the future who transgressed in this manner was to be summoned before the magistrates and prosecuted.[40]

The estate understanding that poverty was a factor in this situation set about using their resources to try and rectify the problems. Efforts were made to find winter work for those unemployed. In the course of his investigation into the problems, Edward Castleman had discovered that a number of men were about to sign on the following day at Sturminster Newton Union. Rather than risk adding pressure to the poor rate and as detailed in the Introduction, the estate sought to share the burden of relief. Consequently, these men were set to work widening the road in Stalbridge which the Waywardens had been seeking to implement for some time. Monies that had been set aside for the cleansing of one of the water carriers had not been fully spent, and it was suggested that this spare cash could be used to clean out Bibbern Brook and the main sewer thus opened. It was estimated that this would create enough work for three weeks, by which time the farmers would have begun preparing the land for their spring crops and the labourers would be back in employment. At the same time, an order was made to move the position of the privy from the gardens of the cottage, as it was thought this was the most likely source of the infection.

The local surgeon Mr. Fooks had reported 'that he could hardly remain in the House where the Fever first broke out for the smell which arose from it'.[41] While the estate made no specific payments in this case, it employed a number of men short term at its own expense and used its expertise to better the living conditions of the poorer section of the town. It was hoped that the changes made would prevent a recurrence of the fever.

The Marquis of Anglesey was renowned for his benevolence, and the correspondence, vouchers and accounts reveal the extent to which he donated extra payments towards the poor within the estate. While these were frequently paid by the land agent to local clergymen, the estate stipulated how the sums were to be used but no accounts seem to have been furnished by the recipients. Charity did not just come in one-off payments, but as seen both here and elsewhere in this volume, the estate frequently paid the labourers during difficult economic periods. By acting in this manner, the estate was sharing with the tenants not just the risks of farming but that of supporting the lower elements of the rural community. The Swing Riots, which were discussed in great detail in Chap. 4, were indicative of the damage that could be caused when poverty, under- and unemployment and local tensions became uncontrollable. The largest part of the monies spent annually by the estate on the lower elements of the estate society was on education, because it was here that they could exert the greatest pressure on social control and behaviour. This was designed as a long-term investment, and one where its affects would be passed down to the next generation. Education in the early nineteenth century was a very mixed bag, and the estate contributed to a wide variety of establishments.

Education

During the nineteenth century, there was a sense that social order in Britain was threatened by the processes of urbanisation and industrialisation. At the same time, those who had power, authority and influence sought to maintain the status quo while maintaining the 'peaceful and preferably contented' subordination of those less well off or lower down the social scale.[42] Social historians have explored a range of the mechanisms used by the elite power groups to socially control, condition and manipulate the propertyless masses into accepting the forms and functions of behaviour necessary to sustain social order within an industrial society.[43] Research has in the main concentrated on urban areas, but the same ideas of social control working to underpin a bourgeois and capitalist society are also prevalent within rural communities. The term social control is generally used by historians in the context of inter-class relations whereby a group or class seek to impose its own ideas of suitable habits and attitudes upon another group. Phillip McCann argues that the provision of schools 'from above' was mainly concerned with transmitting suitable skills, values and norms. Overall, they reflected society's need to guide, restrain or control its members and particularly the young.[44] F. M. L. Thompson argues that the exercise of social control in one generation meant the imposition by middle-class philanthropists and educators on the children of the poor ideas of submission, deference, orderliness, punctuality, respect for property and other desirable elements of social stability. Children thus indoctrinated would pass on these 'norms' to their offspring and would themselves become part of the socialisation process; in other words, it would become self-perpetuating.[45]

Given the obvious benefits of education in maintaining the status quo, a small number of reformers at the beginning of the nineteenth century had begun to suggest that education should be universal. In 1807 the radical MP Samuel Whitbread unsuccessfully presented to parliament a bill which would have provided 2 years of free elementary education to children between 7 and 14. Those who could not afford the usual one or two pence a week would be funded from the rates. Opposition came from many and included the Archbishop of Canterbury who stated that the scheme was 'likely to subvert the first principles of education … which had hitherto been … under the control and auspices' of the Church of England.[46] Other critics including Mr. Pole-Carew MP objected to the bill on the grounds that it would be too expensive. He estimated the project would need the landed interest to subscribe in the region of two million pounds. Others believed teaching the labouring classes reading, writing and arithmetic instead of reducing the number of existing social problems would have the opposite effect and encourage further sedition and growth in the size of the population. With the failure of Whitbread's bill, the cost of even the most basic of education was left to the clergy and gentry. Despite the collapse of free schooling for all, education was gaining traction even for the children of the labouring poor. This was emphasised in 1869 by the contemporary writer Robert Brown who argued that success in 'any department of business' was reliant on the 'character' of those employed and agriculture was no different. Brown continued that when 'inferior' workmen were employed, performance was indifferent, and productivity affected.[47] He accused farmers of looking for ploughman in terms of their outward bulk and quality of muscle rather than through their intelligence and general ability, much the same way as they looked for a horse. The observant farmer, however, realised that intelligent, active and skilful men even if small-bodied made much better ploughmen and farmworkers in general.[48] Farmers often feared that men who were better educated would be less obedient to their employers, but Brown advocated that this was nonsense. In fact, he suggests the opposite was true and education made men more useful, in as much as it made them more reasonable and better able to understand all aspects of business.[49] Brown stressed that landed proprietors should ensure that the children of every man employed was educated, as this would make them more useful to their future employers.[50] Undoubtedly, as will be seen, the Marquis of Anglesey endorsed the idea that education could aid in achieving societal stability. He appreciated and condoned the notion that teaching children ideas of piety, virtue, honesty, veracity and sobriety might have an impact on their parents. Despite a wealth of information hidden in estate records, relatively little research has been undertaken into the influence of estate management on rural education or even the attitude of landowners to this aspect of rural life.[51] Yet it formed a fundamental principle of social control and needed considerable financial acumen on the part of the landowner and agent as to the placement of schools and what they might achieve.

Educational facilities on the Marquis of Anglesey's Dorset and Somerset estate were varied and did not simply concentrate on the more traditional forms, Anglesey and Castleman were open to aiding the formation and support of traditional institutions as well as those that would provide children with a trade and employability skills. Schools of this latter sort would aid in keeping people employed in the future and more importantly off the poor rate. The estate had been approached by one Mr. Bourne who wished to establish a flax school at Stalbridge. His premise was to teach the boys under his care a craft which would in turn reduce any future burden on the poor rate. Importantly it would keep the boys occupied at a time in their lives when they were most likely to find mischief. Getting the scheme up and running demonstrated the way that the estate might work with outside agencies, in this case, parish officials especially in the sharing of expenses. At a meeting of the vestry held on 21 October 1823, it was agreed that the parish of Stalbridge would provide Bourne with 15 healthy boys suitable in age and strength for his purposes. An allowance of £1 17s 6d per week was to be paid from the rates for the first 12 months. Bourne agreed to provide the boys with board, lodging and a suitable education for a five-year period. Once the parish's initial contribution came to an end, the responsibility for clothing the boys was to pass to Bourne. At the end of the five years, he guaranteed that the boys would leave as well clothed as when they arrived. It was, however, not simply a case of giving Bourne the money, and in the latter stages of this agreement, the parish intended to claw back their initial investment, and consequently, Bourne consented:

> To pay the parish one shilling a week for each boy for the fourth year and one shilling and three pence a week for the fifth year in order that [some recompense] might finally result to the parish from this arrangement.[52]

Bourne also needed the help of the estate if this scheme was to work. The estate, in return, wanted a clause written into the vestry agreement that in the event of a scarcity of labour arising within the parish, Bourne would accommodate 'any respectable farmer' with the labour of three boys on 'fair and reasonable terms'.[53] While the estate realised that this could be a useful way of educating a number of young boys with a trade, there is still a sense that this was a financial decision from which the estate could benefit in a number of ways. In fitting with the idea that religion and education were intrinsically linked, Bourne agreed the boys would be 'trained in the paths of virtue and instructed in the Principles of Christian religion'. There was no emphasis placed on which denominational church they were to attend as he agreed 'the boys shall attend regularly such place of worship as their parents or Guardians may prefer'.[54]

The scheme was not perfect and Castleman had some misgivings and wrote to Anglesey, 'I am no friend to the establishments of Manufactories in Agricultural districts'.[55] This might seem a strange comment given the industries established at Milborne Port in Chap. 5. It should be noted that these were founded for the express purpose of forging political stability and not for estate profit neither where they an attempt to prevent people both now and in the future from claiming relief. Furthermore, they were positioned in a town, whereas this establishment was to be within the confines of Stalbridge Park in a more rural setting. Rather than being a manufactory, the boys were to be involved in 'spade husbandry' and educated in the processes of cultivation as well as the manufacturing aspect of flax production, thus fitting within conceived rural occupations. In many respects this was a cost-effective way of ensuring the next generation of tenant farmers had up-to-date skills and knowledge and as such there was an inherent future benefit within the scheme for the estate. In the initial stages, Bourne received cash from the vestry rather than the estate, instead it granted Bourne the use of any part of the house, park, garden or materials at Stalbridge manor that the tenant did not want or could not use. He and the boys were granted free range over the house until such time as Anglesey wished for it to be returned and allowed to use 'such parts of their Arable lands as Mr Castleman may approve to grow flax'.[56] The estate intended, however, to protect its interest and ensured that Bourne agreed where possible to prevent any damage to the property by those under his care and likewise not to conspire with others intent on causing destruction to the premises.

Theoretically this was a good plan and it was not just the vestry and estate who thought it might work. Bourne managed to convince Lord Digby and other notable men in the neighbourhood to invest.[57] By November 1830, however, disillusionment had set in. Although Bourne's ideas had been visionary in practice, they had proved unworkable.[58] Furthermore the estate alleged that he had 'violated his engagements … by receiving Apprentices from Neighbouring parishes' and who were then under the Settlement rules of the Old Poor Law able to claim residence at Stalbridge. Anglesey's tenants insisted Bourne be removed immediately from the parish and the flax school closed. Hardly surprising, they were now responsible for a set of boys who came from elsewhere. A furious Bourne started a campaign against Castleman by publishing a number of anonymous letters protesting against the land agent's behaviour. Retaliation came in the form of denouncing Bourne as a 'convicted Libeller' and a statement was made that he had been removed before a heavy and unnecessary burden had been placed on the poor rate. A letter reassured Anglesey that his agent was not against such far-sighted or imaginative ideas but that he would not sanction the type of scheme currently in operation, as it was the preserve of a 'needed and visionary adventurer'.[59] This example emblematically demonstrates the estate's financial considerations in the decision-making process. In both the setting up of the scheme and its closure, the estate was seeking to reduce its financial burden. By taking up this unusual idea, the estate sought to balance out its share of the maintenance of the poor and to prevent a future generation from relying on poor relief. Ultimately it aimed to lower the fiscal burden of the tenants through an eventual lowering of the poor rate. The land agent's business acumen was evident even here as he assured the estate would benefit from the scheme's success yet continued to maintain enough power over the venture to bring it to swift end if necessary. In effect this is exactly what happened when matters began to unravel. This was the most outlandish of the estate's approach to education which in general were much more conventional.

There is a significant historiography around Sunday schools which argues that these educational establishments played an important role in forging social control through education. This was particularly true for elementary schooling before 1870 which was in general provided by the church. Anne Digby and Peter Searby, however, suggest that these motives have been overestimated and yet here on this estate it was certainly part of the rationale for providing funds to schools. They contend that the idea of 'warring sects' fighting for the control of children's behaviour, morals and general outlook is yet another myth which surrounds educational practices during this period.[60] To a certain extent as will be seen with the school at Bradford Abbas, this was indeed the case. Keith Snell on the other hand argues that Sunday schools were instrumental in the promotion of orderliness, punctuality and sobriety and social discipline.[61] The morals taught in Sunday schools were not new and had long been the staple of education for children. Teachers were advised that children should be encouraged to discover an 'instant, constant and cheerful obedience'.[62] The children received a basic religious education alongside more secular skills such as reading and occasionally writing. Writing was sometimes seen as a 'secular art' and therefore an abuse of the Sabbath. Learning scriptures was for the spiritual good of the child, but writing was an aptitude that the poor could use to gain worldly advantage and from which no good could come.[63] Snell suggests amongst others that before the 1870 Education Act, Sunday schools were the prominent force for promoting literacy.[64] Certainly the estate thought this type of establishment was worth promoting and the vouchers and accounts contain examples in every year of payments made. For example, regular donations to the Sunday school at Bradford Abbas £3 3s 0d, at Handley £6 6s 0d and that at Stalbridge £20. Given the importance of Milborne Port as a political borough, there is surprisingly little within the archive relating to educational establishments in the locality. *The Digest of Parochial Returns* states that there were 5-day schools which were attended by about 100 children and two Sunday schools which taught approximately 70 children.[65] It appears that Anglesey contributed towards the Sunday school from the moment he inherited giving £2 2s 0d per annum but not to other establishments in the borough.[66] Other church schools were better supported.

The local clergy's attitude towards tutelage is nowhere clearer than in a letter in July 1814 from Dr. Hughes at Hanley who asked the estate to help support a school in the area. Like elsewhere the land agent wanted to establish exactly what the estate might be contributing to. He therefore suggested to Anglesey that he should set out to discover whether the school was a Sunday school or one established on Dr. Bells or the Lancaster plan as the expenses incurred by each would be markedly different.[67] As Hanley was 'one of the most disorderly parishes in whole District of the Chase',[68] 'the support of a school there appeared extremely desirable'.[69] Historians have suggested that farmers were vehemently opposed to and mistrustful of any form of education and were thus almost certainly disinclined to offer their support.[70] Yet Castleman did not believe that he would have any problems 'in prevailing upon the Tenants to subscribe something towards the Expenses'.[71] The enquiries undertaken at Hanley provided confusing results. At first it appeared there was no established school, and instead Hughes had taught at his own expense some 20 to 30 children. Hughes had advocated the foundation of a school on the lines of Dr. Bell's plan which 'would unquestionably be the best'. The main opposition to this idea was the cost, which Hughes estimated, would require an annual fund of between £60 and £70 and the farmers were unlikely to be persuaded to subscribe to this extent. In reality Anglesey would then be expected to make up the shortfall on a regular basis.[72] It was quickly ascertained, however, that the existing school at Hanley was in fact a Sunday school and therefore a contribution of just four or five guineas a year would be more than sufficient.[73] By 1821 this school was now based on 'Dr. Bell's system' and the estate had increased its annual payment to six guineas a year towards its upkeep.

The estate supported a variety of educational establishments at Stalbridge. The vouchers record payments made by the local populace towards Harriet Mead-Habersham's school. All are headed 'To H Habersham Education of Children on Charity in Reading &c' and all the subscriptions stipulate for one girl.[74] The estate also contributed £5 per annum to Habersham's salary. Despite the perceived concept by modern historians that farmers would not contribute to educational establishments as discussed above, Harriet Habersham's school relied on subscriptions. The names that run throughout the vouchers for this school are also included in the correspondence and rental accounts of the estate. This suggests that at least where the poor were concerned, tenants were prepared to pay for the girls to gain some form of education which would hopefully allow them to obtain useful employment in the future. Competition towards this charity came from the National Society which the parochial returns for 1818 described as a 'school on Dr Bell's plan' supported by voluntary subscriptions. It recorded that 74 boys and 30 girls attended the school and deemed that the 'poorer classes [in this parish] have sufficient means of educating their children'.[75] Although Harriet Habersham continued for some time, in 1832 it was concluded that in light of the National School's contribution to education in the town and to which Anglesey was a liberal supporter, her salary should cease. Despite the on-going support it had received the evidence suggested that no child appeared to have attended Habersham's for some time.[76] Anglesey and the agent-in-chief whose role was discussed in Chap. 2 agreed to this proposal providing that it could be emphatically proved that this could be done 'unattended by any hardship or injustice towards the School mistress and a satisfactory assurance that the exercise of her functions have ceased'.[77]

The success of the National School at Stalbridge led the Reverend Luke in 1831 to propose the construction of a new school house, but the society turned down his request. In time-honoured fashion when things did not go to plan, Luke applied to the estate for help in building the suggested property on a plot of land at Drews Lane. He managed to raise most of the required monies and by 1832 had some £74 11s 0d in hand, but this still fell short of that needed. A request was sent to the Marquis of Anglesey suggesting that as the payment to Harriet Habersham had ceased perhaps, he would consider giving the equivalent of one year of her salary towards discharging the deficiency. This was by no means the only National School which requested help. In 1844 the parish at Kington had solicited the aid of the various landowners within the parish to assist in the founding and building of a National School. On this occasion Anglesey had given 15 pounds towards the project and the promise of an annuity of 3 guineas per annum once the works were completed. Dugdale was prevented from bringing the idea to fruition until 1854 when he managed to procure £150 from the 'Committee of Council' and £20 from the National Charity in addition to the subscriptions from the Duke of Rutland as 'Patron of the Living' and various other friends. In consequence of his tenacity, the school room was now complete. In all it had cost £330 and was suitable in size for the education of 80 children. It would be a mixed school under a schoolmaster who had been training for the purpose at the Institution of the National Charity in Westminster. Although the funds raised had not allowed for the building of a residence for the master, it had been constructed anyway as an appendage to the school room. The architect Mr. Turner had given his service gratis, and in order to commission the said house, Dugdale hoped to gain a further grant from the committee. Unfortunately for Dugdale, the 1st Marquis of Anglesey who had made all the promises had subsequently died and he was now writing to ascertain whether the new Marquis would be kind enough to take up where his father had left off.[78] Although the local clergy and in particular the Reverends Grant, Luke and Dugdale exhibited great enthusiasm in educating the children within their parishes, they were always reliant on some form of assistance from the estate.

Perhaps the most unusual educational establishment was the charity school at Bradford Abbas which the Reverend Grant described as being of a 'peculiar and somewhat anomalous nature of the Charity Schools of this Parish'. It appeared around 1740 that Mr. Preston the then Vicar had left on trust to his successor certain lands (18 acres) in the parish of Compton for the support of a charity school. The church was initially run by the Church of England and known locally as Preston's Charity.[79] Owing to the inability of the Reverend West to attract a schoolmaster, two parishioners Messrs. Reid and West had decided to establish a school of their own. They invested £220 of their own cash and raised a further £50 through the trustees. According to Grant all those involved were dissenters from the Anglican Church. Despite this in 1794 the Earl of Uxbridge granted a lease of a cottage and premises on the lives of two of the trustees, namely, Thomas Thompson and Mark Fooks, for a school and dwelling house for the master. Mr. Thompson was a trustee of both Preston's and Reid and West's schools. Around 1800 both charities were united (although the funds were kept separately) under the master John Custard.[80]

In 1835 the original school had been destroyed by fire. It was decided that once rebuilt, the two groups which had worked together as one operation for such a considerable period should take the appropriate steps to strengthen this union. To try and bring this, about an inquiry into the lease was undertaken and it was discovered that only one life remained on the lease. Castleman was thus approached to make a fresh application to the Marquis of Anglesey for the creation of a new lease without fine and vested in the name of joint trustees. In order to begin the process, Grant and Pretor on behalf of Prestons and Fooks and Harman on behalf of Reid and Wests met Castleman in October 1835. As well as the buildings already included in the previous agreement, they requested that three small tenements held by Richard Rideout be included within the lease. It was understood that the estate would have to pay a price as these additional buildings were still held for two lives. Grant saw the benefits of annexation of these extra properties as twofold. Firstly, the school would now be detached from other structures, thus making it more secure. Secondly and perhaps more importantly, it would give the school a 60-foot frontage which would have 'such an external character; as would give it a certain respectability in the eyes of the people and to have an influence however small on their character'.[81] There was an innate sense that size meant status and by linking church and education within one space, it might just be a powerful enough presence to exert some pressure on the morals and behaviour of the local population. In order to bring about these changes, the parties needed the support of the land agent who would then mediate on their behalf.

While the Marquis of Anglesey had ultimate control, the decisions made often came down to his land agent. On this occasion having weighed the evidence he then wrote a report to Anglesey that stated, 'I believe this school (for reading and writing) has been much improved by the attention of Mr Grant since he was appointed vicar'.[82] Having thus provided Anglesey with the present and possible values of the property, he believed the success of the application rested in reality on whether his 'Lordship' favoured the instruction of an 'agricultural population in writing'. In the past this had not been the case and financial support for educational establishments of this kind had not been given. On a more positive note, an endowment from the estate would probably attract more efficient schoolmasters who might in the future be encouraged to undertake its management.[83] Despite all the hard work to try and sort the situation, at the last minute in 1835 Fook's brother, a co-trustee, withdrew his support for the plan and refused to consent to the arrangement. Consequently, the unification of the two trusts fell through. Grant still tried to push through his ideas and met with His Majesty's commissioner, but Fook could not be persuaded to change his mind and the matter was left to rest.

The premises were rebuilt under the watchful eye of the schoolmaster John Custard. On his death Mr. Thorne was appointed as schoolmaster for both charities. By 1845 the number of trustees of Reid and West's charity had been reduced to two and they were both now willing to revise the situation and forge ahead with unification. They aimed to affect the plan which had first been devised some ten years previous, with the Marquis of Anglesey providing a fresh lease on the same terms as before, free of fine and vestry and in the names of the trustees of both charities.

Grant aimed 'to prevent any future collision between the [two] trusts from which the parish could suffer'.[84] One of the main provisions of the new joint charitable school was a distinct and clear understanding that the schoolmaster must always be a member of the Church of England. Thompson, one of the trustees for Reid and West, indicated that he thought this a suitable and proper condition especially as the founder of Preston's had stated in his will 'that the boys should be brought up in the doctrine and principles of the Church of England'. On the other hand, there was no such clause in the initial set up of Reid and West. From around 1800 onwards, these charity schools had shared not only the same building but the same teacher. They reflect the assumption that different denominations did not compete for 'hearts and minds' but instead worked together to instruct the children in order to improve morals, cleanliness and industriousness. The way in which church and estate worked together reflects the power that both sought to exert over the population in order to enforce a modicum of social control. In many respects the clergy on the estate understood that this could be best achieved with Anglesey's support. On the ground there was far less animosity between the different religious groups than the historiography suggests and at least at Bradford Abbas a shared sense that together they might improve the behaviour and morals of the local population.

Other schools were given small contributions towards construction costs, although arriving at a decision was not always easy. In 1844, Castleman was approached by Mr. Fox at Templecombe, who requested a significant contribution to the £370 needed for the building of a school room and house. He complained that at present the girls on a Sunday had to assemble in the public house and the boys are 'most inconveniently instructed in the church'.[85] This was not unusual, and many villages remained without school buildings by the time of Victoria's accession.[86] Altogether some £283 had been raised leaving a considerable shortfall; it seemed that these sums were excessive for a small agricultural parish, and thus it was recommended that Anglesey should decline to subscribe.[87] Despite his land agent's opposition to the scheme, Anglesey agreed to subscribe £15 and a similar sum was given to the proposed school at Kington Magna. This too had been problematic and Castleman had refused to forward details of the scheme until he was satisfied with the extent and expense of the building. Once again, the plans submitted by Rector Dugdale were too grand, but aware of the necessity of keeping the estate onside, Dugdale produced a new scheme which was much reduced.

Dugdale had managed to raise a grant from the Privy Council of between £60 and £70 and around £32 from the Diocesan Board, leaving £103 to be found from local landowners and inhabitants. As Anglesey owned around 20 per cent of the parish, Dugdale waited until he had received his subscription before he asked the others as this would set the precedent.

The assistance offered had to be value for money and put to use in an area where it might be most influential, consequently not every request was met with patronage and sponsorship. Neither was the estate prepared to stand the entire cost of a project. The following example illustrates why the estate might not go forward with an application. Messrs. Boucher and Powys sought extra funding for their school at Thornhill, and Mr. Powys made an approach to the Marquis of Anglesey. Taking up the entreaty, Castleman wrote to the agent-in-chief warning him and apprising Anglesey of the situation should they be approached directly. Of the school he stated 'it is a very neat and ornamental Building near the entrance to the Thornhill's estate'. Despite this he suggested that its situation with the respect to the local population was of little or no use to the school. There was also the simple matter that Castleman had never been consulted on the matter. He stated that he would have told Powys that for the aforementioned reasons he would be unable to recommend the venture to Anglesey, stating 'It is more distant from Weston, where there is a considerable Population, than the National School in Stalbridge'.[88] Boucher had not been impressed by the negative response to the application; he complained that most of the population living near to the proposed school all belonged to the estate. Anglesey, however, could not be persuaded to change his mind. Overall this was assessed as being a nonfinancially viable proposition and would have little impact on the local population and was essentially a waste of money.

Education was undoubtedly important but expensive especially in terms of building new schools. Even though Stalbridge was the most profitable part of the estate, it declined to support another school there in 1826, partly because as seen above Anglesey was already subscribing quite heavily in the parish. That said he was not against the new school in principle because 'Anything that can tend to improve the Morals and Conduct of the rising generation in Stalbridge must be highly desirable and I have no doubt but the Institution recommended by Mr Bradford would have that Tendency'.[89] While his objections here were of a pecuniary nature, the estate was already spending more than £50 per annum in the town in various guises. Less compassion was exhibited when Mr. Mason the curate at

Hanley wrote to request Anglesey's subscription of £6 towards the running of his charity school in 1834. Castleman wrote to the agent-in-chief 'This is the person who has lately been making an Encroachment on a part of Lord Anglesey's property'. He stated that 'there is scarcely a person in the place that is not openly or covertly … lying in opposition to Ld Anglesey's Interest'.[90] There was thus considerable reluctance to make the payment. This plan, however, was thwarted by John Sanderson the then agent-in-chief who would not allow the withholding of a charitable subscription given in 'Lord Anglesey's name' to the school unless it could be proven that the school was actually instructing the children 'in the vicious causes of many of the Inhabitants of the place'.[91]

The main thrust of the historiography for education has concentrated on two main areas, namely, the battle between the Anglican Church and non-Conformists group and education in urban areas as a means of social control. While there is a body of research which explores the rural school, this has tended to concentrate on the period from the mid-nineteenth century onwards.[92] There is a gap in the historiography, therefore, in the way that estates used education as a means of trying to instil better behaviour and morals among the lower echelons of the agrarian community. This over the long term would produce industrious people who would not be reliant on poor relief to survive. By subscribing to schools and school buildings, the spaces become part of the power and status of the estate, financial contributions were often essential to ensure that the myriad of schools discussed here were able to function in any shape or form. Much more could have been spent, but power and image had to be balanced against impact.

Conclusion

Finding the means to exert some form of control over those who did not fall within the remit of the landlord/tenant relationship was often difficult. Tenant farmers received and expected a range of customary social and working rights which have been explored in detail in Chaps. 3 and 4 and a role in the election process which is the subject of Chap. 5. The Swing Riots were a wake-up call as to what might happen when grinding poverty, under- and unemployment alongside local tensions became untenable. For all the monies spent, the estate expected at least some form of result, whether through improved behaviour, amended morals or an extension of its power and status. That said there was a general consensus that landowners should not allow the lower members of society to fall into total abject poverty. As seen with Lord Portman's agent when he felt that Anglesey had let the standard of living of his labourers fall too far, he was prepared to take a stance. This did not bode well for the social standing of Anglesey within the community. Overall the estate used three means of extending its power and impact on working people: the building and enlargement of churches, which set the position of both state and landowner clearly within the visual landscape, the doling out of charitable payments to the poor for a myriad of reasons and the use of education to improve behaviour and hopefully to create the next generation of well-behaved and moral workers.

F. M. L. Thompson argues that there were many individual landowners whose sense of duty and responsibility led them to minister to both the moral and material welfare of what they thought of as 'their people'.[93] This was a type of pastoral care of their flock which would mould them into a group who knew their place, kept it and did not question the social order of society. Thompson suggests that the silent majority of landowners were neither sufficiently active, imaginative, responsible nor assertive enough to try and influence the rural community in any systematic way. Instead for most they were solely concerned with ideas and actions that would protect their own interests, keeping up appearances and were generally indifferent to the wider issues of the social order in the countryside and the means by which it should be maintained.[94] In general Thompson claimed that they did not regard it as their business to make any special contribution. While there were pecuniary issues to be considered and monies had to be spent with a specific purpose in mind together, they exhibited a keen interest in using effective measures to influence all layers within the rural community. The monies spent, for example, on repairing and enlarging churches took a multi-faceted approach. Outwardly repairing a dilapidated church was part of the restoration of the fabric of the estate, a well-maintained and suitable church to serve the community was important and re-enforced the status of both state and local landowner. Importantly the clergy played a role not just in church life but also in administration of the estate's charitable payments, in providing vital political gossip and in establishing, running and organising a wide range of educational provisions. Consequently, the estate might be persuaded and indeed did spend money on church projects which it had hoped to avoid. The knock-on effect of refusing would have caused enormous repercussions on more than one aspect of maintaining social control including the distribution of its own charitable payments.

This chapter has explored charity in its broadest context, not through the organised efforts of the vestry or parish but instead through the ways in which the estate sought to relieve the deepest levels of poverty. It did this through single one-off payments, many were made annually but could be topped up where necessary. There is a sense within the archival documents that the estate felt duty bound to take up some of the burden of poor relief and to ensure that the tenants were not saddled with the full cost through the poor rates. Consequently, the working partnership which is the subject of Chap. 3 extended far beyond the borders of agriculture. The financial obligations of the landowner to the tenant are part of a much greater whole within the agrarian. Each section of the fiscal panorama interlinks into a complex set of relationships which are inseparable from one another, and all the decisions made are financially underpinned by the next. Social responsibility extended to promoting healthier living conditions and was evident in the way that the estate sought to prevent the spread of a 'malignant' fever in Stalbridge. Here the money was spent on moving the privies and putting some of those who were unemployed back to work, albeit temporarily, until the spring seasonal work commenced. While the estate fought poverty in all its guises, it hoped that better education might provide the best way to create a local population which would have improved morals, attitudes and behaviour.

The estate was not averse to a range of educational schemes. The charity school at Bradford challenges ideas that there was a battle between the Church of England and other dissenting groups at least in this locality. The support of Habersham's school at Stalbridge by the tenants likewise suggests that the idea of farmers refusing to support the education of the labourers' children needs to be reassessed. Bourne's flax school was on paper an inspired idea, to provide poor boys recommended by the parish some manufacturing experience from the growth of the crop to the finished project. The aim was to ensure that they did not fall back on the parish at a later stage. Its failure was not the result of the idea but more the character of Bourne himself. The estate as seen above spent annual sums on schools, and there are references throughout to the hope that this would quell the riotous nature of some of the estate villages. Education was perhaps the single most important method of improving the attitudes of the lower orders, but without being reinforced by a visual church presence and averting abject poverty where possible, the monies spent on schools would have had little impact. Social control of the estate relied as much on a fiscal policy as everywhere else, and in similar vein it is not an isolated procedure but was instead part of an integrated estate system which was closely interlinked to working, social and political relationships. All these affiliations are commonly linked through a common pecuniary practice whereby Anglesey and Castleman understood that spending money was at the core of all decision-making. While the sums expended in the activities which are the subject of this chapter might be relatively small, they were as important as the accrual of large arrears, the provision of customary rights and the ability to grant rent abatements.

Notes

1. A. P. Donajgrodzki (1977) 'Introduction' in A. P. Donajgrodzki, (ed), *Social Control in Nineteenth Century Britain* (London: Croom Helm), p. 9.
2. Ibid.
3. Ibid.
4. D. Mills (1980) *Lord and Peasant in Nineteenth-Century Britain* (London: Croom Helm), p. 181.
5. Donajgrodzki, 'Introduction', p. 17.
6. D. Hainsworth (1992) *Stewards, Lords and People: The Estate Steward and His World in Later Stuart England* (Cambridge: Cambridge University Press), p. 167.
7. See Castleman's letter in Chap. 4.
8. See F. M. L. Thompson, (1981) 'Landowners and the Rural Community' in G. E. Mingay, (ed.), *The Victorian Countryside, Vol. II* (London: Routledge & Kegan Paul).
9. This was certainly the case with timber shrouders and stealers as seen in Chap. 4.
10. J. Walsh & S. Taylor (1993) 'The Church and Anglicanism' in J. Walsh, C. Haydon and S. Taylor (eds) *The Church of England c.1689–c.1833* (Cambridge: Cambridge University Press), p. 20.
11. D. Roberts (1979) *Paternalism in Early Victorian England* (London: Croom Helm), p. 152.
12. Ibid.
13. C. Brooks (1995) 'Building the Rural Church: Money, Power and the Country Parish', in C. Brooks & A. Saint, *The Victorian Church: Architecture and Society* (Manchester: Manchester University Press), p. 55.
14. DHC, D/ANG/B5/16, 26 December 1814.

15. See C. A. Beardmore (2016) 'The Rural Estate through the Eyes of the Land Agent: A Community in Microcosm *c.*1812–1844' *Family and Community History* 19:1, p. 26 and DHC, D/ANG/B5/31, 18 April 1822.
16. DHC, D/ANG/B5/31, 25 April 1822, Letter from John Sanderson.
17. Ibid, 11 May 1822.
18. Ibid., 18 May 1822.
19. DHC, D/ANG/B5/32, 23 February 1823.
20. DHC, D/ANG/B5/46. 11 November 1834.
21. DHC, D/ANG/B5/66, 15 April 1846.
22. Hainsworth, *Stewards, Lords and People*, p. 159.
23. A. Tomkins and S. King (2003) *Poor in England: An Economy of Makeshifts* (Manchester: Manchester University Press).
24. S. Williams, 'Poor Relief, Labourers' Households and Living Standards in Rural England c. 1770–1834: A Bedfordshire Case Study', *Economic History Review*, 58:3 (August, 2005), p. 485.
25. I. Jones (1993) *The Stalbridge Inheritance 1780–1854* (Dorchester: Friary Press), p. 13.
26. A. Digby (1981) 'The Rural Poor', in G. E. Mingay (ed.), *The Victorian Countryside, Vol. II* (London: Routledge & Kegan Paul), p. 594.
27. DHC, D/ANG/B5/61, 16 November 1844.
28. cwt is the abbreviation for a hundredweight.
29. DHC, D/ANG/B4/54.
30. Ibid.
31. DHC, D/ANG/B4/53.
32. DHC, D/ANG/B4/67, 15 December 1844.
33. DHC, D/ANG/B4/69, 10 January 1847.
34. Ibid.
35. DHC, D/ANG/B4/69.
36. DHC, D/ANG/B5/54, Letter from Lord Portman's steward 11 December 1838.
37. DHC, D/ANG/B5/59, 25 January 1842.
38. DHC, D/ANG/B5/63, 14 February 1845.
39. Ibid.
40. DHC, D/ANG/B5/63, 14 February 1845.
41. DHC, D/ANG/B5/63 Letter from Edward Castleman to Thomas Beer agent-in-chief.
42. F. M. L. Thompson (May, 1981) 'Social Control in Victorian Britain', *The Economic History Review* 34:2, 189.
43. Ibid.
44. P. McCann (1977) 'Introduction', in P. McCann, (ed), *Popular Education and Socialization in the Nineteenth Century* (London: Methuen & Co), pp. x–xii.

45. Thompson, 'Social Control in Victorian Britain', p. 191.
46. Quoted in P. Horn (1978) *Education in Rural England* (London: Gill and Macmillan), p. 34.
47. R. E. Brown (1869) *The Book of the Landed Estate* (Edinburgh and London: William Blackwood and Sons), p. 287.
48. Ibid.
49. Ibid., p. 288.
50. Ibid., pp. 288–289.
51. A notable exception is G. Monks (2016) 'The Duke of Portland and his Agent; The Education Act of 1870' *Family and Community History,* 19:2, pp. 95–105.
52. DHC, D/ANG/B5/32, 14 November 1823.
53. Ibid., 21 October 1823.
54. Ibid.
55. Ibid., 14 November 1823.
56. Ibid.
57. DHC, D/ANG/B5/42, 20 November 1830.
58. Ibid.
59. Ibid.
60. A. Digby and P. Searby (1981) *Children, School and Society in Nineteenth-Century England* (London & Basingstoke: The Macmillan Press), p. 14.
61. K. D. M. Snell (August 1999) 'The Sunday School Movement in England and Wales: Child Labour, Denominational Control and Working Class Culture', *Past and Present*, 164, pp. 129–130.
62. See T. R. Tholfsen (Spring 1980) 'Moral Education in the Victorian Sunday School', *History of Education Quarterly*, 20:1.
63. E. P. Thompson (1963), *The Making of the English Working Class* (Harmondsworth: Penguin), p. 138.
64. Snell, 'The Sunday School Movement in England and Wales', pp. 129–130.
65. *A Digest of Parochial Returns Made to Select Committees Appointed to Inquire into the Education of the Poor: Session 1818 Vol I.*
66. S. G. Mackay (1986) *Milborne Port in Somerset* (Milborne Port: Remous Ltd), p. 75.
67. In many ways the two plans were synonymous. Dr. Bell an Anglican clergyman with the East India Company had first set up the scheme in India and is sometimes referred to as the Madras system. In England the first school to use this method had been set up in London about 1801 by the Quaker Joseph Lancaster. In 1811 the Church of England had formed the 'National Society for Promoting Education of the Poor in the Principles of the Established Church'. More commonly known as the National Society. See Horn, *Education in Rural England*, p. 34.

68. This is Cranborne Chase nearly always shortened to Chase in the Anglesey archive.
69. DHC, D/ANG/B5/15, 1 July 1914.
70. J. H. Porter (1989) 'The Development of Rural Society: Social Institutions' in J. Thirsk (ed). *The Agrarian History of England and Wales 1750–1850, Vol. VI* (Cambridge: Cambridge University Press), p. 902.
71. DHC, D/ANG/B5/15, 1 July 1814.
72. DHC, D/ANG/B5/14, 18 August 1814.
73. Ibid., 13 August 1814.
74. DHC, D/ANG/B4/45, Vouchers for 1830.
75. *A Digest of Parochial Returns Made to Select Committees Appointed to Inquire into the Education of the Poor: Session 1818 Vol I.*
76. DHC, D/ANG/B4/44, 20 October 1832.
77. Ibid., 9 November 1832.
78. DHC, D/ANG/B5/76, 29 September 1854.
79. See DHC, D/ANG/B5/48, 27 April 1835. The history of the school is told within this letter by the Reverend Grant.
80. DHC, D/ANG/B5/63, 6 March 1845.
81. DHC, D/ANG/B5/48, 27 April 1835.
82. Ibid.
83. Ibid., 26 July 1835.
84. DHC, D/ANG/B5/63, Letter from the Reverend Robert Grant, 6 March 1845. John Custard was not popular among the tenants and survived in post because he had the backing of the Reverend Grant. The tenants in fact believed that Custard had been responsible in 1836 for the wilful destruction through arson of burning down two lifehold houses in the area.
85. DHC, D/ANG/B5/61, 2 August 1844.
86. R. Sellman (1981) 'The Country School' in G. E. Mingay (ed.), *The Victorian Countryside, Vol. II* (London: Routledge & Kegan Paul), p. 543.
87. DHC, D/ANG/B5/61, 8 August 1844.
88. DHC, D/ANG/B5/59, 11 April 1842.
89. DHC, D/ANG/B5/37, 10 November 1826.
90. DHC, D/ANG/B5/46, 22 January 1834.
91. Ibid., 4 February 1834.
92. See, for example, Horn, *Education in Rural England 1800–1914*, and Sellman, 'The Country School', pp. 542–553.
93. Thompson, 'Landowners and the Rural Community', p. 458.
94. Ibid., pp. 458–459.

CHAPTER 7

Conclusion

Overview

Estate studies are not new, many historians including Gordon Mingay, F. M. L. Thompson, John Beckett, David Spring, Joan Thirsk, Eric Jones, Rab Houston, Bethany Afton, Michael Turner and Susanna Wade Martins have all explored the way in which they worked to some degree.[1] The study of the landed estate continues to concentrate on the country house and its consumption with little or no reference to the wider rural landscape made up of tenant farmers, the agricultural labourer and from the mid-nineteenth century onwards increasingly industrial ventures, particularly coal mining. Historians have thus placed less emphasis on where the money was made and instead explored how it was spent which has created a narrow viewpoint of estate life. This study has sought to begin to redress the balance and to explore the landed estate in a broader financial sense. By using a detailed and extensive archive such as that of the Marquis of Anglesey and the Castleman family, it has been possible to survey the financial history of the estate in such a way as to provide a different viewpoint. It argues throughout that the powerhouse and fiscal health of the estate rested in the financial decisions made around the working, social and political affiliations with the tenant farmers and others of the local population. When surveyed as a cohesive whole, the estate moves from being simply groups of people linked through a variety of diverse relationships to one where financial links can be made across all processes of estate

C. Beardmore, *Financing the Landed Estate*, Palgrave Studies in the History of Finance, https://doi.org/10.1007/978-3-030-14552-1_7

management. The fortunes of the labouring poor were reliant on a fiscally buoyant tenantry, but they in turn were dependent on the support and aid of the landowner particularly in the volatile financial climate after the end of the Napoleonic Wars. As seen in Chap. 6, even managing the poor rate was a burden shared by the estate, and moves were often taken to employ the poor at the estate's expense. Even the simplest of customary rights had a price, and William Castleman was often called upon to decide whether the cost of continuing such expectations was feasible. Essentially every action no matter how large or small undertaken by the estate was reinforced and buttressed by some form of financial decision.

In the past little attempt has been made to examine the choices which an estate was either forced or choose to make. In general, the historiography is outdated, and although there are notable exceptions such as Susanna Wade Martins' work at Holkham; David Hainsworth's book on estate stewards in the eighteenth century; Carol Beardmore, Steven King and Geoff Monks' edited volume on the land agent in Britain; and the recent edited volume by Lowri Ann Rees, Ciarán Reilly and Ann Tindley, the rest make little reference to in-depth case studies. Unsurprisingly Eric Jones, in his latest volume, *Landed Estates and Rural Inequality in English History*, argues that histories of the long term are 'open to the charge of over-generalisation', but some research is essential to shift out what is in reality continuity and change against the transient or exceptional.[2] The beginnings of a new and meticulous archival approach to the wider landed estate are beginning to fill this gap. To appreciate and decipher the local from the regional or national, a wide range of single estate studies or those which concentrate on meticulous archival sources is essential, and the work begun in the *Land Agent in Britain: Past, Present and Future* continues in this volume with a more intimate investigation into the financial machinations of the landed estate.[3] It reveals an estate landscape which is highly individualistic and diverse because the relationship between landowner and land agent was based on personality and specific expectations. The nature of the tenantry varied according to economic circumstances created by agricultural prices and the rise of industrialisation. Without an in-depth understanding of the details of estate finances, administration, working practices, social relationships and political practices, it is impossible to identify that which is constant against the fleeting or extraordinary. For the vast majority of estates, there is no particularised history beyond those who lived in the house; still less is known about the men or women who fill the rent and account books of the land agent. It has been assumed in the past that the rural community was traditionally rigid, constructed of the patrimonial tripartite relationship of landowners, tenants and labourers. As seen throughout the chapters of this book, while these associations existed it came down to money, tenants expected certain rights, farm buildings in a good state of repair, the provision of their customary privileges in the form of audit dinners, hunts on court leet days, rent abatements, allowances for drainage, timber allowances, to be canvassed at election times, a sharing of the burden of the poor and other concessions.

There was a common belief amongst contemporary writers that in order to manage the complexity of a large estate, a landowner should ideally be in residence with absenteeism being akin to financial disaster. Absenteeism became increasingly common as politics; the London season and new leisure activities took up ever more time. The status and personality of a local agent needed to be such as to promote his employer's attitudes and requests while at the same time being able to maintain control of the local population. While an absent landowner may have been bad news for some estates, there is a growing consensus that some of the best-run estates were those where the landowner was absent. There was no reason to neglect land; in fact the opposite was true, but in days when transport was difficult, and land was held in widely dispersed counties, visiting regularly was not practical. Many like the Marquis of Anglesey found a local land agent within whom he could place his trust and while not letting him have total free reign assumed that the basics of day-to-day management would be undertaken smoothly and efficiently. As seen throughout each chapter in this volume, it was only when the extraordinary occurred that the Castlemans would revert to Anglesey. In the last ten years of the time frame covered here, the future of the estate hung in the balance and from 1844 onwards the estate was basically on the market. This made running the estate more difficult as the loyalty of the tenants began to shift, and they sought to assure that they would not lose out. Nowhere is this clearer than in the weakening of political deference as seen in Chap. 5. As Anglesey wished to sell his land in the south as a going concern, fully let and with the tenantry in good heart, this meant that it could not be left unfarmed or untenanted. Protecting revenue was important, and continuity was maintained after William Castleman's death by the employment of his sons who had long worked for the estate and understood the way in which it functioned. This was an important factor in the maintenance of stability at a time when overall the situation was becoming more unsettled as sale documents were drawn up and buyers sought. This chapter will explore each of the five main themes which run throughout this volume and argue that ultimately, they are all interlinked and underpinned by the same fiscal decision-making. This chapter will explore estate finances and administration, the working and social relationships which incorporated customary rights and expectations, the political landscape of a small political borough and the estate's input into the social control of the lower echelons of the rural community.

Estate Finances and Administration

Land agents were much more than a simple managers, collector of rents or compiler of accounts and simply put who ran the estate mattered, and any who did not perform could wreak havoc as seen with Cox in Chap. 1. The perfect agent according to Eric Richards was 'self-effacing' enough to accept and allow all public credit to be directed at the landowner while simultaneously creating respect between the landowner and rural community.[4] The Castlemans were typical of the men who ran landed estates. William Castleman was the son of a tenant farmer with a background firmly based in agriculture, and on his death, he was followed by his own sons. As a country attorney and established land agent, he brought to the role an extensive knowledge of the workings of the rural community and the administrative practices required to underpin its management. Four key themes emerge from an analysis of the administration of this estate and include the extent to which an estate was prepared to manoeuvre to ensure profitability, an understanding of the rental market which ensured land remained let and rental income secure, the importance of the accounts in estimating the health of the estate and the significance of securing mortgages in a period of growing aristocratic indebtedness.

Firstly, land management relied on more than just a good manager who ran the estate, and the way in which he interacted with the landowner and the relationships fostered within the rural community mattered. Local networks were important and ensured that when others in the vicinity reacted to falling prices and economic downturns, Anglesey's estate remained competitive. This could be achieved through reduced rents, the accrual of rental arrears, allowed abatements, altered audit days and the employment of surplus labourers to reduce the burden on the poor rate. In this sense the risks of farming in a period of fiscal uncertainty were shared. These practices helped to keep the tenants in place and on their farms, rather than quitting and moving to another estate which offered greater benefits. As part of the wider understanding of the rural community, this study brings to the forefront the agency of the tenantry as they negotiated with the estate new rental agreements, rent abatements and the employment of their labourers in economic downturns. Together this creates a narrative which links together the fiscal choices made as the estate sought to navigate the destinies of the tenant farmers as they fought agricultural depression, large rental arrears, failed crops, disasters caused by flooding and disease amongst the livestock. The tenantry were the spine of the estate, and their productivity and prosperity were intertwined with estate viability.

Secondly, to survive an estate had to maximise estate income, and the most obvious way to achieve this was to ensure that empty properties were let, and good tenants offered the right incentives to stay. Long leases benefitted either the landowner or the tenant farmer but rarely both at the same time. Farms rented when prices were buoyant found tenants struggling to keep up with rental payments when the economic climate shifted. On the other hand, landowners who found they had been forced to accept a lower-than-average rent could find themselves deprived of income as land prices improved. In the past long lifeleaseholds had been reliant on the considerable wealth of landowners to create a climate whereby farmers had the freedom and time to make the most of their farms. Landlords were expected to make a profit but not to be so greedy that they deprived farmers of the capital necessary to invest in better livestock, improvements, equipment and seeds. In an attempt to level the playing field, many landowners turned towards rack renting. Under this system rent was calculated annually and could go up or down according to the current level of prices, but importantly neither party benefitted to the detriment of the other. Contemporary writers decried both short-term leases and rack renting, but modern historians such as Gordon Mingay have argued that in fact change did not mean instability. This was particularly true of tenants who exhibited long-term and ongoing political loyalty. This suggests that even the way in which land was rented tied in with a variety of processes and was not a single standalone matter. In the historiography, there seems to be an acceptance that changes in tenure were introduced to cope with the surrounding financial land market and were widespread across the countryside. The Anglesey estate reveals that the leasing of farms was multi-faceted with agents and landowners disagreeing over systems used. William Castleman was a great believer that the lease gave the estate security and easy recourse to the law should rental arrears go beyond what was deemed recoverable and was often at direct odds with his employer. As Castleman was the man who found the tenants and organised the grounds on which farms and premises were let, he usually won the day. This did not, as seen in Chap. 2, necessarily endear Anglesey to the system, but he realised that it was better to accept his land agent's advice than create a rift. As a result, the estate issued a variety of leases across the spectrum, the fines paid when adding lives to life-leaseholds contributed vital funds to the coffers and farms were generally let on an eight-year term. There is little understanding of whether this estate was usual or not; it has been assumed that landowners rented according to the changing economic climate when in reality there were a whole range of factors that needed to be taken into account. As more single detailed estate studies are undertaken, it will be possible sometime in the future to revise the idea that rack renting became the norm.

Thirdly, as absenteeism became more common, the need to become more accountable resulted in an expansion of the bureaucracy surrounding estate management. Even a relatively small estate could see upwards of £10,000 per annum pass through the land agent's hands. The opportunities for fraud were endless. As seen with Cox in the Introduction, a lack of comprehensive record-keeping could leave the estate in a position whereby no one had any idea of the monies received or the debts outstanding. This was obviously not a good practice and in the long term affected a myriad of processes and particularly repairs, improvements and the payment of tradesmen. Although the accounts used here are problematic when trying to establish rental trends or the amounts paid for arable, meadow or pastureland, it does not mean that they should be ignored. Overall, they provide a sense of estate indebtedness and how this changed or not over time. For the family historian, they would be a useful source for the changing demographics created by agricultural depression.

Finally, the archive allows an insight into the question of Marquis of Anglesey's rising indebtedness and the amount of interest paid out on an annual basis. Historians such as F. M. L. Thompson argue that the monies raised by the aristocracy were rarely used to improve the income-producing capacity, and while this may be the case, they certainly helped to keep Anglesey solvent. His financial situation was exacerbated by his son, and as seen in Chap. 2, the two men together owed at least £556,000 with an annual interest call of £23,352. William Castleman personally lent the Marquis his own spare capital and used his networks amongst other local gentry and aristocracy to raise mortgages. The historiography on aristocratic indebtedness is relatively sparse, and even less is known about the role played by the land agent in raising mortgages and loans. The idea that having the right man at the helm is emphasised here, as without a degree of financial acumen, an understanding of who might be persuaded to lend would have been impossible as would the accumulation of a considerable comprehension of the way in which the financial market worked. Without the expertise of his land agent in this field, Anglesey may well have been forced to sell off much more of his southern acreage in 1825. At the same time as he was suffering his own pecuniary difficulties, the tenants were running up large rental deficits, and Castleman was the force that balanced the books and ensured the estate remained in good heart. A skilled administrator needed to forge good links with the tenantry as it was this group that formed the financial glue that bonded all aspects of the agrarian community. Neither of the latter two ideas are inherent in the current literature, and yet the landed estate is the sum of a range of diverse and varied relationships which interlink to create a functioning whole.

Working and Social Relationships

Working and social relationships on an estate were governed by a complicated set of rights and duties for all parties. An estate was not merely a space where money was exchanged for land but was instead a community made up of a diverse group of people. There was a common set of interests which bound and formed the landowner–tenant relationship. Until recently the generally held consensus amongst historians has been that this affiliation was reflected in the dual sharing of the costs and risks of farming. More recently Eric Jones has argued that the landed elite perpetually renewed itself, not least through its access to political power, which it then used to protect both assets and income.[5] In other words there were no shared risks and the tenant farmers stood all the costs. Jones claimed in his recent book *Landed Estates and Rural Inequality in English History* that his aim was to counter 'the bland nature of so much literature on parks, estates and great houses – the roses which disguise the rural dunghill on which they were erected'.[6] This study does not attempt to see the estate as a rural idyll but instead argues from a study of working and social relationships within this detailed archive it is impossible to argue for anything other than shared risk. That said, the fragility of these relationships is however always an issue. Four key ideas arise from a study of these relationships, the idea that the shared risks are evidenced in the large rental arrears which were allowed to accrue and repairs and investments, while the delicate balance of the rural community can be witnessed in the problems which were created by the removal of perceived customary rights and the problems of absolute poverty which led to Swing. Hardly an indication of looking at an estate through rose-tinted glasses.

Firstly, the large rental arrears which appear in Chap. 3 evidence the lengths which Anglesey went to support his tenants during economic downturns. The working relationship between landowner and tenant farmer went far beyond the simple paying of the rent on time. As seen throughout this volume and particularly in Chap. 3, the tenants expected the landlord to act as a banker allowing them to run up enormous rental arrears. The problems caused by low agricultural prices were ongoing, and the most serious recession of the post-war period occurred in 1821–1823. On this occasion even long-standing tenants were not immune. Harris, for example, who had followed his father, failed owing the estate a significant sum of money. Although he lost his farm, the estate found him a smaller property with a number of associated lime kilns, and while they took a security to prevent losses, there was still an apparent concern for this man and his family. Within the historiography, there is little sense of the empathy of the estate to its tenants or the responsibilities it showed to those in distress.

There is no doubt that in sharing the risks, the estate could be the loser particularly when tenants absconded. Two of the highest profile farmers who attempted to remove the stock for their own benefit rather than paying their debts were Dawe and Barrett. Aware that this pair were in dire straits, Castleman set a man to watch the couple and when they appeared to drive off the first of their cattle, he distrained on the farm. He was, however, too late and they had in fact removed the entire stock. The estate resorted to legal measures, and the pair was consequently imprisoned in the hope that this would prevent others from following suit. The list compiled of Bishops farm goods when Castleman thought to distrain provides a detailed idea of the value of stored and standing crops, the livestock and the implements used to work the land. It is possible to ascertain from this the amount of capital needed to set up and to stock a farm. It is hardly surprising that tenants tried to find a way out without losing everything invested.

Secondly, there was an innate sense that a tenant expected their investment to be protected through the maintenance and improvement of the soil and the farm buildings they rented. Essentially this was a relationship where money mattered, and there was an expectation that a certain amount of the profits should be reinvested. A tenant expected the estate to provide on entry a farm that was in a good state or repair and for there to be a sharing of the costs of improvements. The estate vouchers contain numerous examples of this shared relationship at work, with allowances made for drainage, sums spent on buildings damaged by bad weather, monies lent for threshing machines and abatements for planting quickset hedges. Historians have stated that a landowner needed to appear wealthy, but this was not enough; in order to successfully manoeuvre across the landowner–tenant divide, he had to be prepared to physically prove his worth by capital investment. The fiscal decision-making was usually left to the land agent on absentee estates, and thus men such as William Castleman needed to exhibit an entrepreneurial spirit that would stand up to the scrutiny of the rural community.

Thirdly, social relationships were often an extension of the existing working associations and were often exhibited through an equally important range of well-established customary rights. Audit dinners and election-day suppers regularly appear throughout the archive. When customary rights were removed such as hunting on court leet days at Hanley, the situation could quickly develop into a riot and anonymous letters sent complaining about the behaviour of the agent. Several other examples appear in Chap. 4 wherein the estate and its population came into conflict. Timber was valuable, and the estate set out to reap the profit it offered. Tenants and agricultural labours, however, had very set ideas on who owned the rights to some of the timber on the estate, and if this differed from Anglesey, then the situation could quickly develop into a riot. The day-to-day management of the estate aimed to maximise profitability, and if this brought a degree of conflict, then it needed to be dealt with swiftly. Unlike working relationships, those that revolved around customary rights were more complex because many of these were unwritten and had been forged as part of memory over a long period of time. Castleman, however, would remove these events from the calendar if they were too troublesome or the expense did not bring sufficient reward in terms of social behaviour or control.

Finally, the Swing Riots of 1830 are evidence of what might happen when grinding poverty was no longer tenable. There is no reason why these riots erupted in 1830 rather than any other. In fact, Castleman suggested that unemployment was no higher than was usually expected in the early winter. That said, once they had gained traction, their spread south and westwards was rapid. In recent years these riots have attracted considerable research, but the individuality of local tensions and the way in which different people in authority handled the rioters means that there is little cohesiveness amongst the different groups of protestors. Certainly, at Hanley the disenfranchisement of Cranborne Chase and the loss of their common grazing rights had an impact on the amount of damage caused and the number of rioters who took part in the disturbance. At Stalbridge Castleman's quick thinking action in persuading the local farmers to join the special constables probably lessened the threat and saved the estate having to compensate the farmers in this locality. In fact, the threshing machine which stood in Stalbridge Park escaped unharmed. Together these two areas demonstrate that even within a short distance and within one estate, local tensions were emphasised and played out in different ways. While no group can be examined in isolation, the daily management and where to expend funds for the maximum benefit to the estate can be seen here. At the end those labourers who were deemed the worthiest at Stalbridge and then at Bradford Abbas were rewarded with new and well-built cottages with decent-sized gardens, providing an outward symbol that good moralistic behaviour was repaid. Although these buildings cost approximately £1000 to build, Castleman believed this would pay great dividends in terms of social control in the future. Tied up with tenancy agreements were voting rights and access to the franchise, and thus the tenants who fell within this category needed to be handled in a subtler manner.

The Political Landscape

Holding the patronage of a political borough was without doubt expensive and not for the faint-hearted. Through the granting of political privileges, the landowning elite endowed their tenants with rights which allowed them to take part in the political decision-making process. It was technically possible for those who held the franchise in small boroughs to unite and to challenge those who held patronage. Politics were not taken lightly, and finding the right person to take up a farm lease, business premise or house with attached entitlement to the electorate meant seeking someone who could be relied on for political loyalty. Eric Jones argues that it was the political pressures exerted by large landowners which allowed them to protect their interest. Maintaining patronage, however, was not necessarily that simple, and as seen in Chap. 5, even seemingly safe closed boroughs such as Milborne Port could be threatened by borough-mongers like Lord Darlington. When this happened, the incumbent patron had no choice but to attempt to meet financially the challenges posed. At Milborne Port this resulted in a housing race which Castleman's correspondence suggests cost the pair more than £55,000. Eventually the Marquis of Anglesey was able to maintain his control as Castleman negotiated an exchange of property with Winchester College. The situation had hung in the balance for a while, but by watching carefully the opposition and ensuring that any tenants who could not be relied on were evicted eventually, Anglesey was able to remove the threat.

On top of fending off Lord Darlington, attention had to be given to the electorate themselves. The political system whereby every member of the electorate within a constituency/borough had as many votes as men returned to parliament meant that no election victory could be taken as a given. The ideal situation was to carry out the canvas and find that there was no significant opposition and therefore that it was unnecessary to hold a poll; it was only in these circumstances that victory was sure and the threat of a challenge to the result through petitions to parliament removed. Ultimately this kept costs down, but as seen in Chap. 5, keeping the electorate onside was a constant process. Voters expected to be indulged and feted; they knew the value of their vote and were not averse to a little persuasion from the landowner in terms of treats and dinner. Loyalty was bought not just through the entitlements that came with being a tenant or through traditional rights but through a range of extras which were centred specifically on the political nature of the borough. All in all, everything that surrounded the election process had a cost, and the role of Castleman as election agent was to attempt to mitigate any spending that was unnecessary. At the same time, he had to make sure that he was not left out of pocket, by compiling the election accounts and then persuading Anglesey to sign these off. On top of the usual expenses, Castleman charged extra for his time beyond that of his normal salary for any electoral work. Milborne Port was troublesome and time-consuming, but Anglesey determined to hold it at all costs. As part of the Great Reform Act, Milborne Port lost its franchise and Anglesey the political patronage and status to which it was connected. Consequently, the decision was made to sell this section of the estate in 1837. Immediately this wrought a number of savings but more importantly allowed the Castlemans to turn their attention back to their more conventional role of managing a large rural estate.

Unlike most other areas of the estate, the two-vote system ensured that political influence even in the smallest of boroughs was at the mercy of the foibles and idiosyncrasies of the local electorate. Rural relationships could be fragile and open to local tensions which could result in riots or outbreaks of violence. This behaviour was the opposite of that which the estate sought to foster in the borough. Smoothing out any abrasiveness was essential, and this had a pecuniary cost, whether in terms of finding ways to navigate local tensions, taking William Castleman away from his more general duties or in terms of finding ways to foster loyalty. All of these were on top of the expense of holding elections, paying for legal advice when an election result was challenged and meeting the demands of the contest fostered by Lord Darlington. While historians have concentrated on ideas such as deference and patronage which are essential aspects of prereform politics, the financial aspects of managing a borough have in general been overlooked. While it was relatively easy to exert some form of social control over those who rented land or were entitled to voting access, it was much harder with those in the estate who did not fall into this category and other means had to be found.

Social Control

The underlying idea remains that social control in nineteenth-century England was brought about through the use of a range of legal systems alongside an assortment of interactions with a multiplicity of social institutions particularly the church, charity and increasingly education. The fortunes of the poor within an estate were reliant on a buoyant economy which enabled the tenants to pay their rent and to have enough left to employ and pay their labourers. In the mercurial financial climate post-1815, as soon as poor prices or problems with livestock began to bite, the labourers were the first to be laid off. This meant that the estate often found themselves taking up the role of employer, standing the cost of putting the unemployed to work building roads, clearing ditches or working in the stone quarries. With those who were reliant on the estate for a living such as the tenant farmers, maintaining social control was relatively simple. For the rest, while trickier to negotiate, the cost was relatively small when considered against the wider disbursements of the estate. That said, the Castlemans and in particular William were not prepared to simply spend money at a whim—he expected even here to see a return on the sums expended. Overall the estate invested in three main areas, the church, small charitable donations and education. Each of these resulted in a visible contribution to the rural community. Enlarging and restoring churches was a two-way process and ensured that the clergy remained onside and willing to aid in the establishment of and the doling out of payments made by the estate for coal, food, shoes and clothes. At Milborne Port the ongoing saga was partly to keep Mrs. Owen onside. In many respects the snippets of gossip she was able to impart probably saved the estate more money than they contributed towards the enlargement of the church itself. It would have been easy for Castleman to have granted at least partial funding to every scheme that was submitted; however, he was not prepared to waste even small amounts of cash without there being some form of result.

Land agents were the eyes and ears for their employer within the rural community, and their unique position meant that they saw a wide and diverse range of social conditions. Castleman was frequently approached by the local clergy and as such became the mediator of charity, patronage and other forms of assistance. It was not unknown as seen in Chap. 6 to stop payment when it no longer seemed to be having an effect. Occasionally as with the case of the school at Hanley, the agent-in-chief might step in and prevent Castleman from refusing to meet the estate's annual commitment. In this instance while the locality was riotous and unruly, the school was seen as a calming influence, and unless it could be proven that the school was teaching the children immoral behaviour, it remained a force for good in the eyes of Anglesey. After the Swing Riots, keeping a watching brief on poverty became even more important. The estate sought to share the burden of relief with the tenants by making extra contributions towards charitable funds.

The majority of charitable monies were spent on various educational establishments. It was here that the Castlemans, Anglesey, local clergy and the agent-in-chief felt that the extra financial commitment would have the most impact. The visionary ideas of Bourne did not work not because he fell foul of the rules laid down by the vestry. If this had not be so, it is possible the scheme would have produced excellent farmers in the future, who had been taught all the skills of maintaining the soil in good health and enabled them to have gained a new form of resilience. It is possible this would have prevented them having recourse to poor relief when there were small dips in the economy. Although the estate allowed Bourne to use the house at Stalbridge Park rent free and any spare land to grow flax, it still maintained a substantial element of control. Thus, when Bourne's position became untenable, it was easy to evict him, and the land returned to the estate with relatively few problems. Schools backed by the morals and sermons of the clergy were a means of positively enforcing behaviour which the estate deemed acceptable. There is a gap in the historiography which explores the landed estates' input into the development of education. Although this estate did not establish any schools in its own name, without its support many of the schools may not have survived or coped with the number of children who attended. Overall it expended money in this area in the hope that the lessons learned by those who attended would impact upon their parents and eventually create a new generation who would be moral, hardworking, sober and industrious. If the desired effect was achieved, this would be money well spent.

While an estate was the sum of a wide range of working, social and political relationships, the narrative thread which links them together are economic and fiscal processes. Every decision taken by the estate or its agents had a financial cost, and this is seen as much in the accumulation of rental arrears as in the educational provision of its children. While some of the sums spent were extremely small, for example, the £5 or £10 spent annually to support schools or the £3 or £5 for coals in a given parish compared to the £15,000 expended on houses during the attempt on wresting patronage of Milborne Port, each was a carefully considered decision designed to have a specific impact or result. This volume has explored the estate in its broadest context and is neither a history from above or below but instead has used the correspondence of the local agent to examine the ways in which an estate was financially managed. The stormy and fragile economic climate of the post-Napoleonic period required an able man who could think quickly and make sound financial decisions. Knowing which tenants could be relied on to pay off arrears or understanding those who had the skills and expertise to see out the difficult fiscal periods was essential. Employing a man such as William Castleman who had a good local knowledge and knew where stock might be sold off and monies hidden could help to lessen some of the risks. For the estate his networks and relationships with other landowners ensured that it remained on top; if one or more landowners delayed an audit, then he was able to persuade Anglesey to do the same. Good, reliable tenants who might otherwise have left were therefore retained, and the estate remained relatively stable until it was sold in 1854. The mortgages raised by Castleman, his dogged determination to chase for outstanding rent and the payments made to keep watch on suspect tenants were perhaps the main reason that despite his enormous debts the family held on to this southern estate for so long.

Landed estates were the largest businesses of the nineteenth century—managing such an entity was not something to be taken lightly. With an absentee landowner, the financial health and the daily pecuniary decisions taken were generally made by the Castlemans. William Castleman's attention to detail was noted on his death by Thomas Beer, and it is the detail of his correspondence, estate vouchers and accounts which have allowed this financial study of the landed estate. This meticulous archive reveals the extent to which fiscal decisions underpinned the entire procedural life of those who lived and worked within the rural community. For William Castleman and his sons who followed, this was a complex and intricate business which needed careful attention and an understanding of the effects that each decision would have from winning an election, to letting a farm, supporting tenant farmers or trying to improve the morals and behaviour of the next generation. With a renewed interest in the outer estate and especially with the role played by the land agent in its financial health, this volume will form part of a new and wider understanding of how landed estates worked and functioned.

Notes

1. See, for example, G. E. Mingay (ed.) (1981) *The Victorian Countryside Vols. 1 & 2* (London: Routledge & Kegan Paul), F. M. L. Thompson (1971) *English Landed Society in the Nineteenth Century* (London: Routledge & Kegan Paul), D. Spring (1963) *The English Landed Estate in the Nineteenth Century* (Baltimore: John Hopkins Press), R. A. Houston (2014) *Peasant Petitions: Social Relations and Economic Life on Landed Estates, 1600–1850* (Basingstoke: Palgrave Macmillan) and E. L. Jones (2018) *Landed Estates and Rural Inequality in English History: From the Mid-Seventeenth Century to the Present* (London: Palgrave Macmillan) and M. E. Turner, J. V. Beckett and B. Afton (1997) *Agricultural Rent in England, 1690–1914* (Cambridge: Cambridge University Press).
2. Jones, *Landed Estates and Rural Inequality in English History.*
3. C. Beardmore, S. King and G. Monks, (eds) (2016) *The Land Agent in Britain: Past, Present and Future* (Newcastle: Cambridge Scholars).
4. E. Richards (1981) 'The Land Agent' G. E. Mingay (ed.), *The Victorian Countryside Vol. II* (London: Routledge & Kegan Paul).
5. Jones, *Landed Estates and Rural Inequality in English History*, p. 6.
6. Ibid., p. ix.

Bibliography

Manuscript: Dorset History Centre

Steward's Notebook

D/ANG/B/6/2.

Accounts

D/ANG/B4/1/23.
D/ANG/B/4/1/28.
D/ANG/B4/1/32.
D/ANG/B4/1/34.
D/ANG/B4/1/36.
D/ANG/B4/1/38.
D/ANG/B4/1/40.
D/ANG/B4/1/42.
D/ANG/B4/1/44.
D/ANG/B4/1/46.
D/ANG/B4/1/48.
D/ANG/B/4/1/50.
D/ANG/B/4/1/52.

C. Beardmore, *Financing the Landed Estate*, Palgrave Studies in the History of Finance, https://doi.org/10.1007/978-3-030-14552-1

D/ANG/B4/1/54.
D/ANG/B/4/1/55.
D/ANG/B4/1/56.
D/ANG/B4/1/82.

ESTATE VOUCHERS

D/ANG/B4/4/37.
D/ANG/B4/4/45.
D/ANG/B4/4/47.
D/ANG/B4//4/48.
D/ANG/B4/4/49.
D/ANG/B4/4/54.
D/ANG/B4/4/67.

CORRESPONDENCE

D/ANG/B5/14.
D/ANG/B5/15.
D/ANG/B5/16.
D/ANG/B5/17.
D/ANG/B5/20.
D/ANG/B5/21.
D/ANG/B5/22.
D/ANG/B5/23.
D/ANG/B5/25.
D/ANG/B5/26.
D/ANG/B5/31.
D/ANG/B5/32.
D/ANG/B5/33.
D/ANG/B5/34.
D/ANG/B5/36.
D/ANG/B5/37.
D/ANG/B5/38.
D/ANG/B5/39.
D/ANG/B5/40.
D/ANG/B5/41.
D/ANG/B5/42.
D/ANG/B5/44.
D/ANG/B5/45.
D/ANG/B5/46.

D/ANG/B5/48.
D/ANG/B5/50.
D/ANG/B5/51.
D/ANG/B4/53.
D/ANG/B4/54.
D/ANG/B5/56.
D/ANG/B5/58.
D/ANG/B5/59.
D/ANG/B5/60.
D/ANG/B5/61.
D/ANG/B5/63.
D/ANG/B5/66.
D/ANG/B4/67.
D/ANG/B5/68.
D/ANG/B4/69.
D/ANG/B5/75.
D/ANG/B5/76.

Printed Primary Sources

A Digest of Parochial Returns Made to Select Committees Appointed to Inquire into the Education of the Poor: Session 1818 Vol I.

Brown, R. E. (1869) *The Book of the Landed Estate* (Edinburgh and London: William Blackwood and Sons).

Caird, J. (1852) *English Agriculture in 1850–1851* (London: Longman, Brown, Green and Longmans).

Charnock, J. H. (1843) *Suggestions for the More General Extension of Land Draining* (London: Longman, Brown, Green and Longman).

Corbett, U. and Daniell, E. R. (1821) *Reports of Cases of Controverted Elections in the Sixth Parliament of the United Kingdom* (London: J. &W. T. Clarke).

Dean, G. A (1851) *The Land Steward* (London: Atchley & Co).

Gisborne, T. (1794) *An Enquiry into the Duties of Men in the Higher and Middle Classes of Society in Great Britain* (London: B. and J. White).

Hansard, T. C. (1812) *The Parliamentary Debates From the Year 1803 To The Present Time, Vol XIV* (London).

Laurence, E. (1743) *The Duty and Office of a Land Steward* (London: J. and P. Knapton, T. Longman, H. Linto and J. and H. Pemberton).

Lawrence, J. (1806) *The Modern Land Steward* (London: H. D. Symonds, T. Ostell, J. and J. Richardson).

Lockhart Morton, J. (1858) *The Resources of Estates: Being a Treatise on The Agricultural Improvement and General Management of Landed Property* (London: Longman, Brown, Green, Longmans and Roberts).

Loudon, J. C. (1826) *An Encyclopaedia of Agriculture* (London: Longman Orme, Brown, Green and Longmans).

Marshall, W. (1804) *On the Landed Property of England: An Elementary Treatise* (London: G. and W. Nicol and J. Robinson; R. Faulder; Longman and Rees; and Davies; and J. Hatchard).

Marshall, W. (1806) *On the Management of Landed Estates: A General Work for the Use of Professional Men* (London: Longman, Hurst, Rees and Orme).

Miller, P. (1835) *The Gardener's Dictionary, Vol. I* (London: G. Henderson).

Mordant, J. (1761) *The Complete Steward or The Duty of a Steward to his Lord* (London: W. Sandby).

Okedon, D. O P. (1830) *A Letter to the Members in Parliament for Dorsetshire on the Subject of Poor Relief and Labourers' Wages, 2nd edition* (Blandford: John Shipp).

Osborne, S. G. (1838) *Hints To The Charitable Being Practical Observations On The Proper Regulation of Private Charity* (London: T. and W. Boone, J. Hatchard and Son, J. Nisbet and Son, Roake and Varty).

Perry, G. W. (1846) *The Peasantry of England: An Appeal to the Nobility, Clergy and Gentry, On Behalf of the Working Classes* (London: C. Gilpin).

Stevenson, W. (1812) *General View of the Agriculture of Dorset* (London).

Bath Chronicle and Weekly Gazette, 16 April, 1829.

Bristol Mercury, 20 May 1809.

Leicester Chronicle, Saturday, 22 November 1822.

Public Ledger and Daily Advertiser, 16 July 1822.

Salisbury and Winchester Journal, 13 August 1804.

The Dorset County Chronicle and Somersetshire Gazette, 22 July 1830.

The Farmer's Magazine, Vol. 19 (1861).

The Morning Chronicle, 14 January 1831.

The Morning Chronicle, 20 September 1837.

The Morning Post, 31 May 1809.

The Sherborne Mercury, 5 July 1818.

The Sherborne Mercury, 6 April 1829.

The Sherborne Mercury, 6 December 1830.

The State of the Country: Sir Robert Peel's Speech in the House of Commons, Feb.17, 1843 (London: W. E. Painter, Church and State Gazette Office).

Secondary Sources

Adams, L. P. (1965) *Agricultural Depression and Farm Relief in England 1813–1852* (London: Frank Cass & Co. Ltd).

R. C. Allen (1998) 'Landlords and Economic Development in England, 1450–1800' in Nûnez, C. E. *Aristocracy, Patrimonial Management Strategies and Economic Development, 1450–1800* (Seville: University of Seville).

Anglesey, Marquis (1961) *One Leg: The Life and Letters of Henry William Paget K.G. 1768–1854* (London: Jonathan Cape).

Archer, J. E. (2000) *Social Unrest and Popular Protest in England 1780–1940* (Cambridge: Cambridge University Press).

Baxter, W. T. (Spring, 1980) 'The Account Charge and Discharge', *The Accounting Historians Journal*, 7:1, pp. 69–71.

Beardmore, C. A. (2015) 'Landowner, Tenant and Agent on the Marquis of Anglesey's Dorset and Somerset Estate, 1814–1844, *Rural History* 26:2, pp. 181–199.

Beardmore, C. A. (April, 2016) 'The Rural Estate through the Eyes of the Land Agent: A Community in Microcosm c1812–1854', *Family and Community History*, 19:1, pp. 17–33.

Beardmore, C., King, S. and Monks, G., (eds) (2016) *The Land Agent in Britain: Past, Present and Future* (Newcastle: Cambridge Scholars).

Beardmore, C. A. (2016) 'William Castleman and Sons: Agents to the Marquis of Anglesey 1814–1854' in C. A. Beardmore, S. A. King and G. L. Monks, *The Land Agent in Britain: Past, Present and Future* (Newcastle: Cambridge Scholars), pp. 87–106.

Beastall, T. W. (1981) 'Landlords and Tenants', in G. E. Mingay (ed.), *The Victorian Countryside Vol. II* (London: Routledge & Kegan Paul), pp. 428–438.

Beckett, J. V. (1983) 'Absentee Landownership in the Later Seventeenth and Early Eighteenth Centuries: The Case of Cumbria' *Northern History*, 19:1, pp. 87–107.

Beckett, J. V. (1989) 'Landownership and Estate Management' in J. Thirsk (ed.), *The Agrarian History of England and Wales 1750–1850* (Cambridge: Cambridge University Press), pp. 545–640.

Bowley, A. L. (December, 1898) 'The Statistics of Wages in the United Kingdom During the Last Hundred Years'. (part 1), *Journal of the Royal Historical Society*, 61:4, pp. 702–722.

Brooks, C. (1995) 'Building the Rural Church: Money, Power and the Country Parish', in C. Brooks & A. Saint, *The Victorian Church: Architecture and Society* (Manchester: Manchester University Press).

Burchardt, J. (2002) *Paradise Lost: Rural Idyll and Social Change in England Since 1800* (London and New York: L.B. Tauris).

Burnette, J. (2013) 'The Seasonality of English Agricultural Employment: Evidence from Farm Accounts, 1740–1850' in R. W. Hoyle, (ed.), *The Farmer in England 1650–1980* (Farnham: Ashgate), accessed online 12 September 2018.

Cannadine, D. (1994) *Aspects of Aristocracy: Grandeur and Decline in Modern Britain* (New Haven & London: Yale University Press).

Chambers, J. D. and Mingay, G. E. (1982) *The Agricultural Revolution, 1750–1880* (London: B. T. Batsford Ltd.).

Clay, C. (1981) 'Lifeleasehold in the Western Counties of England 1650–1750', *The Agricultural History Review*, 29:2, pp. 83–96.

Cook, C. (2005) *The Routledge Companion to Britain in the Nineteenth Century, 1815–1914* (London; New York: Routledge).

Cragoe, M. (1996) *An Anglican Aristocracy: The Moral Economy of the Landed Estate in Carmenthshire, 1832–1895* (Oxford: Clarendon Press).

Curtis, C. E. (1901) *Estate Management: A Practical Handbook for Agents and Pupils* (London: Horace Cox).

Daunton, M. J. (1995) *Progress and Poverty: An Economic and Social History of Britain 1700–1850* (Oxford: Oxford University Press).

Digby, A. (1981) 'The Rural Poor', in G. E. Mingay (ed.), *The Victorian Countryside, Vol. II* (London: Routledge & Kegan Paul), pp. 591–602.

Digby, A. and Searby, P. (1981) *Children, School and Society in Nineteenth-Century England* (London & Basingstoke: The Macmillan Press).

Doe, V. (2018) *Improving Agriculture in Nineteenth Century Rutland: The Life and Achievements of Richard Westbrook (1797–1861), Steward of the Exton Estate* (Oakham: Rutland Local History Society).

Donajgrodzki, A. O. (ed), (1977) *Social Control in Nineteenth Century Britain* (London: Croom Helm).

Dyck, I. (1992) *William Cobbett and Rural Popular Culture* (Cambridge: Cambridge University Press).

Edwards, J. R. (December, 2011) 'Accounting on English Landed Estates During the Agricultural Revolution – A Textbook Perspective', *Accounting Historians Journal*, 38:2, pp. 1–45.

Ernle, Lord (1919) *English Farming Past and Present*, 2nd ed. (London: Longmans Green & Co).

Fisher, J. R. (1981) 'The Limits of Deference: Agricultural Communities in a Mid-Nineteenth Century Election Campaign', *Journal of British Studies*, 21:1, pp. 90–105.

Gash, N. (1979) *Aristocracy and People: Britain 1851–1865* (London: Edward Arnold).

Gash, N. (1963) *Politics in the Age of Peel: A Study in the Technique of Parliamentary Representation* (London: Longmans Green).

Griffin, C. (2014) *Protest, Politics and Work in Rural England, 1700–1850* (Basingstoke: Palgrave Macmillan).

Griffin, C. J. (2012) *The Rural War: Captain Swing and the Politics of Protest* (Manchester: Manchester University Press).

Griffin, C. (2008) 'Protest Practice and (tree) Cultures of Conflict: Understanding the Spaces of 'Tree Maiming' in Eighteenth- and Early Nineteenth-Century England', *Transactions of the Institute of British Geographers*, 33:1, pp. 91–108.

Grove Barns, D. (2006) *A History of English Corn Laws From 1660–1846* (Abingdon: Routledge).

Hainsworth, D. (1992) *Stewards, Lords and People: The Estate Steward and His World in Later Stuart England* (Cambridge: Cambridge University Press).

Hammond, J. L. and Hammond, B. (1912) *The Village Labourer 1760–1832* (London: Longman, Green, and Co.).

Hobsbawm, E. and Rudé, G. (1960) *Captain Swing* (London: Phoenix Press).

Horn, P. (1978) *Education in Rural England 1800–1914* (Dublin: Gill and Macmillan).

Horn, P. (1980) *The Rural World 1750–1850: Social Change in the English Countryside* (London: Hutchinson).

Houston, R. A. (2014) *Peasant Petitions: Social Relations and Economic Life on Landed Estates, 1600–1850* (Basingstoke: Palgrave Macmillan).

Howkins, A. (1992) 'The English Farm Labourer in the Nineteenth Century: Farm, Family and Community' in B. Short, *The English Rural Community: Image and Analysis* (Cambridge: Cambridge University Press), pp. 85–105.

Hoyle, R. W. (2016) 'Introduction: Recovering the Farmer' in R. W. Hoyle, (ed.), *The Farmer in England 1650–1980* (Farnham: Ashgate).

Hoyle, R. W., (ed.) (2013) *The Farmer in England 1650–1980* (Farnham: Ashgate).

Hurren, E. T. (2016) 'The Making of the Modern Land Agent in Victorian Times', C. Beardmore, S. King and G. Monks, *The Land Agent in Britain: Past, Present and Future* (Newcastle: Cambridge Scholars), pp. 169–192.

Jenkins, T. (2009) 'Milborne Port' in Fisher, D. R. (ed.), *The History of Parliament: The House of Commons 1820–1832* accessed via www.historyofparliamentonline.org

Jones, E. L. (2018) *Landed Estates and Rural Inequality in English History: From the Mid-Seventeenth Century to the Present* (London: Springer).

Jones, E. L (1968) *The Development of English Agriculture, 1815–1873*, Studies in Economic History (London: Macmillan).

Jones, E. L. and Woolf, S. J. (eds) *Agrarian Change and Economic Development: The Historical Problem* (Abingdon: Routledge).

Jones, I. (1993) *The Stalbridge Inheritance 1780–1854* (Dorchester: Friary Press).

Jones, P. (2009) 'Finding Captain Swing: Protest, Parish Relations, and the State of the Public Mind in 1830', *International Review of Social History* 54:3, pp. 429–458.

Jones, P. (2007) 'Swing, Speenhamland and Rural Social Relations: 'The Moral Economy' of the English Crowd in the Nineteenth Century' *Social History*, 32:2, pp. 271–290.

Kent, D. (1997) *Popular Radicalism and the Swing Riots in Central Hampshire* (Winchester: Hampshire Papers Series).

Kerridge, E. (1967) *The Agricultural Revolution* (Abingdon: Routledge).

Kerridge, K. (1969) 'The Agricultural Revolution Reconsidered', *Agricultural History*, 43:4, pp. 463–476.

King, S. (2019) *Writing the Lives of the English Poor, 1750s–1830s* (Montreal & Kingston: McGill-Queen's University Press).
McCann, P. (1977), (ed), *Popular Education and Socialization in the Nineteenth Century* (London: Methuen & Co).
McDonagh, B. (2018) *Elite Women and the Agricultural Landscape, 1700–1830* (Abingdon: Routledge).
McKay, S. G. (1986) *Milborne Port in Somerset* (Milborne Port: Remous Ltd).
Mills, D. R. (1973) *English Rural Communities: The Impact of a Specialised Economy* (London: Macmillan).
Mills, D. (1980) *Lord and Peasant in Nineteenth-Century Britain* (London: Croom Helm).
Mingay, G. E. (1963) *English Landed Society in the Eighteenth Century* (London: Routledge).
Mingay, M. E. (1977) *Rural Life in Victorian England* (London: Heinemann).
Mingay, G. E. (1989) *The Rural Idyll* (London: Routledge).
Mingay, M. E., (ed.) (1981) *The Victorian Countryside Vols I and II* (London: Routledge and Kegan Paul, Ltd.).
Monks, G. (2016) 'The Duke of Portland and his Agent; The Education Act of 1870' *Family and Community History,* 19:2, pp. 95–105.
Monks, G. (2018) 'William Gould, Land Agent and the Rural Community in Nottinghamshire and Derbyshire, *Family and Community History,* 19:2, pp. 67–81.
Moore, D. C. (1976) *The Politics of Deference: A Study of the Mid-Nineteenth Century English Political System* (Hassocks: Harvester Press).
Napier, C. J. (1991) 'Aristocratic Accounting: The Bute Estate in Glamorgan 1814–1880', *Accounting and Business Research,* 21:82, pp. 163–174.
Navickas, K. (2011) 'Captain Swing in the North: The Carlisle Riots of 1830 *History Workshop Journal,* 71, pp. 5–28.
Noke, C. W. (1981) 'Accounting for Bailiffship in Thirteenth Century England', *Accounting and Business Research* 12:2, pp. 137–151.
O'Gorman, F. (May, 1992) 'Campaign Rituals and Ceremonies: The Social Meaning of Elections in England 1780–1860' *Past & Present,* 135, pp. 79–115.
O'Gorman, F. (Jan. 1986) 'The Unreformed Electorate of Hanoverian England: The Mid-Eighteenth Century to the Reform Act of 1832', *Social History,* 11:1, pp. 33–52.
O'Gorman, F. (1989) *Voters, Patrons, and Parties: The Unreformed Electoral System of Hanoverian England 1734–1832* (Oxford: Clarendon Press).
Oldroyd, D. (2007) *Estates, Enterprise and Investment at the Dawn of the Industrial Revolution: Estate Management and Accounting in the North-East of England, c.1700–1780* (Aldershot; Ashgate).
Overton, M. (1996) *Agricultural Revolution in England: The Transformation of the Agrarian Economy 1500–1850* (Cambridge: Cambridge University Press).

Parker, R. A. C. (1975) *Coke of Norfolk: A Financial and Agricultural Study 1707–1842* (Oxford: Oxford University Press).

Patriquin, L. (2007) *Agrarian Capitalism and Poor Relief in England, 1500–1860: Rethinking the Origins of the Welfare State* (Basingstoke: Palgrave Macmillan).

Phillips, A. D. M. (1989) *The Underdraining of Farmland in England During the Nineteenth Century* (Cambridge: Cambridge University Press).

Phillips, J. A. (1982) *Electoral Behaviour in Unreformed England: Plumpers, Splitters and Straights* (Princeton, New Jersey: Princeton University Press).

Phillips, J. A. (1980) 'Popular Politics in Unreformed England', *The Journal of Modern History*, 54:4, pp. 599–625.

Phillips, J. A. (1979) 'The Structure of Electoral Politics in Unreformed England', *Journal of British Studies*. 19:1, pp. 76–100.

Phillips, J. A. and Wetherell, C. (Dec. 1991) 'The Great Reform Bill of 1832 and the Rise of Partisanship', *The Journal of Modern History*, pp. 621–646.

Porter, J. H. (1989) 'The Development of Rural Society: Social Institutions' in J. Thirsk (ed). *The Agrarian History of England and Wales 1750–1850, Vol. VI* (Cambridge: Cambridge University Press), pp. 866–912.

Randall, A. (2009) 'Captain Swing: A Retrospect' *International Review of Social History*, 54:3, pp. 419–427.

Reay, B. (1996) *Microhistories: Demography, Society and Culture in Rural England, 1800–1930* (Cambridge: Cambridge University Press).

Rees, L. A., Reilly, C. and Tindley, A. (eds) (2018) *The Land Agent 1700–1920* (Edinburgh: Edinburgh University Press).

Reed, M. and Wells, R. (1990) *Class, Conflict and Protest in the English Countryside, 1700–1880* (London: Cass).

Richards, E. (1981) 'The Land Agent' G. E. Mingay (ed.), *The Victorian Countryside Vol. II* (London: Routledge & Kegan Paul), pp. 439–456.

Roebuck, P. (1973) 'Absentee Landownership in the Late Seventeenth and early Eighteenth Centuries: A Neglected Factor in English Agrarian History', *The Agricultural History Review*, 21:1, pp. 1–17.

Roberts, D. (1979) *Paternalism in Early Victorian Britain* (London: Croom Helm).

Salmon. P. (2003) 'Electoral Reform and the Political Modernization of England, 1832–1841', *Parliaments, Estates and Representation*, 23:1, pp. 49–67.

Sellman, R. (1981) 'The Country School' in G. E. Mingay (ed.), *The Victorian Countryside, Vol. II* (London: Routledge & Kegan Paul), pp. 542–565.

Shakesheff, T. (2003) *Rural Conflict, Crime and Protest: Herefordshire, 1800 to 1860* (Woodbridge: Boydell Press).

Short, B. (ed) *The English Rural Community: Image and Analysis* (Cambridge: Cambridge University Press).

Shrimpton, C. (1977) *The Landed Society and the Farming Community of Essex in the Late Eighteenth and Early Nineteenth Centuries* (New York: Arno Press).

Smith, E. A. (1969) 'The Election Agent in English Politics, 1734–1832' *The English Historical Review*, 84:330, pp. 12–35.

Snell, K. D. M. (1985) *Annals of the Labouring Poor: Social Change and Agrarian England 1660–1900* (Cambridge: Cambridge University Press).

Snell, K. D. M. (August 1999) 'The Sunday School Movement in England and Wales: Child Labour, Denominational Control and Working Class Culture', *Past and Present*, pp. 122–168.

Sokoll, T. (2001), Essex Pauper Letters 1731–1837 (Oxford: Oxford University Press).

Spring, D. (1963) *The English Landed Estate in the Nineteenth Century* Baltimore: John Hopkins Press).

D. Stead (2003) 'The Mobility of English Tenant Farmers, c. 1750–1850 *Agricultural History Review* 51:2, pp. 173–189.

Stobart, J. (2016) *The Country House: Material Culture and Consumption*, (Swindon: Historic England).

Stobart, J. (2017) *Travel and the British Country House: Cultures, Critiques and Consumption in the Long Eighteenth Century* (Manchester, Michigan: Manchester University Press).

Stobart, J. and Rothery, M. (2016) *Consumption and the Country House* (Oxford: Oxford University Press).

Stratton, J. M. (1969) *Agricultural Records* (London: John Baker).

Tames, R. (1972) *Economy and Society in Nineteenth Century Britain* (Abingdon: Routledge).

Thirsk, J. (ed.) (1989) *The Agrarian History of England and Wales 1750–1850* (Cambridge: Cambridge University Press).

Tholfsen, T. R. (Spring 1980) 'Moral Education in the Victorian Sunday School', *History of Education Quarterly*, 20:1, pp. 77–99.

Thompson, E. P. (1963) *The Making of the English Working Class* (Harmondsworth: Penguin).

Thomson, E. P. (1971) 'The Moral Economy of the English Crowd in the Eighteenth Century', *Past and Present*, 50, pp. 76–136.

Thompson, E. P. (1975) *Whigs and Hunters: The Origins of the Black Act* (London: Allen Lane).

Thompson, F. M. L. (1971) *English Landed Society in the Nineteenth Century* (London: Routledge & Kegan Paul).

Thompson, F. M. L. (1981) 'Landowners and the Rural Community' in G. E. Mingay, *The Victorian Countryside Vol II* (London: Routledge and Kegan Paul), pp. 457–474.

Thompson, F. M. L. (May, 1981) 'Social Control in Victorian England' *Economic History Review*, 32, pp. 189–208.

Tomkins, A. and King, S. (2003) *Poor in England: An Economy of Makeshifts* (Manchester: Manchester University Press).

Turner, M.E., Beckett, J. V. and Afton, B. (1997) *Agricultural Rent in England, 1690–1914* (Cambridge: Cambridge University Press).

Wade Martins, S. (1980) *A Great Estate at Work: The Holkham Estate and its Inhabitants in the Nineteenth Century* (Cambridge: Cambridge University Press).

Wade Martins, S. (2009) *Coke of Norfolk 1754–1842* (Woodbridge: The Boydell Press).

Walsh, J. & Taylor, S. (1993) 'The Church and Anglicanism' in J. Walsh, C. Haydon and S. Taylor (eds) *The Church of England c.1689–c.1833* (Cambridge: Cambridge University Press), pp. 1–66.

Webster, S. (2007) 'Estate Improvement and the Professionalisation of Land Agents on the Egremont Estates in Sussex and Yorkshire, 1770–1835, *Rural History,* 18:1, pp. 47–69.

Wells, R. (1988) 'Tolpuddle in the Context of the English Agrarian Labour History, 1780–1859 in J. Rule, (ed), *British Trade Unionism 1750–1850: The Formative Years* (Harlow: Longman), pp. 98–142.

Williams, S. (2005) 'Poor Relief, Labourers' Households and Living Standards in Rural England c. 1770–1834: A Bedfordshire Case Study', *Economic History Review*, 58:3, pp. 485–519.

Williams, S. (2011) *Poverty, Gender and the Life-Cycle Under the English Poor Law, 1760–1834* (Woodbridge: Boydell and Brewer).

Wood, F. & Wood, K. (1992) *A Lancashire Gentlemen: The Letters and Journals of Richard Hodgkinson 1763–1847* (Stroud: Alan Sutton Publishing Ltd).

Wordie, J. (1982) *Estate Management in Eighteenth Century England: The Building of the Leveson-Gower Fortune* (Woodbridge: Boydell and Brewer).

Worthington Smith, R. (June, 1969) 'Political Organisation and Canvassing: Yorkshire Elections before the Reform Bill', *The American Historical Review*, 74:5, pp. 1538–1560.

https://www.historyofparliamentonline.org/volume/1790-1820/constituencies/milborne-port accessed 23 September 2018.

http://www.oxforddnb.com.ezproxy3.lib.le.ac.uk/view/article/21112?docPos=3 accessed 6 June 2018.

http://www.oxforddnb.com.ezproxy3.lib.le.ac.uk/view/article/21110/21111?back=,21110,21110 accessed 15 June 2018.

Unpublished Thesis

Bawn, K. P. (1984) *Social Protest, Popular Disturbances and Public Order in Dorset, 1790–1838* unpublished thesis, University of Reading.

Index[1]

[1] Note: Page numbers followed by 'n' refer to notes.

C. Beardmore, *Financing the Landed Estate*, Palgrave Studies in the History of Finance, https://doi.org/10.1007/978-3-030-14552-1

Kolibri 360 GmbH
Ferdinand-Jühlke-Straße 7
99095 Erfurt, Deutschland
produktsicherheit@kolibri360.de